STRICTLY
GHETTO
PROPERTY

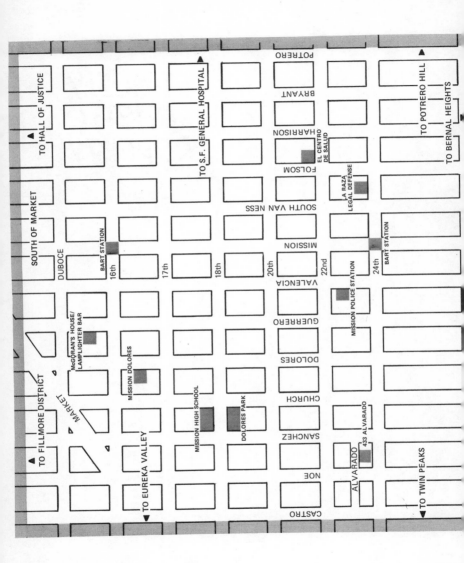

FREE LOS SIETE

STRICTLY GHETTO PROPERTY

The Story of Los Siete de la Raza

MARJORIE HEINS

Ramparts Press
Berkeley, California

KF
224
L64
H4

Son los siete de la Raza
En sus vidas hay un cuento
De la historia de la Raza
Y de todos que se aman

De la gente vienen
Y a la gente regresan

There will be no dead martyrs in this revolution

Donna

Contents

Preface   *11*

1. Hidalgo's Statue   *17*
2. Strictly Ghetto Property   *33*
3. We Wanted to Start the Revolution Then and There   *49*
4. The Man   *65*
5. The Weird Experience   *87*
6. Whitey's Building   *107*
7. Beginning to Get It Together   *123*
8. Mayday   *141*
9. Serving the People Doesn't Mean Being a Waitress   *159*
10. In the Halls of Justice   *181*
11. The Community Must Take Control   *191*
12. Mind If I Call You Piggy?   *209*
13. Nobody Walk Every Day the Same   *229*
14. Power to the People, Streeter   *253*
15. All-American Boy   *269*
16. The Prosecution Doesn't Understand   *291*
17. To Fight Another Day   *313*
    Photo Credits   *326*

R

Preface

A little after 10:20 A.M. on May 1, 1969, a police officer was shot to death in San Francisco's latin *barrio*, the Mission district. Newspapers said that the dead cop and his partner had been attacked by members of a "burglary ring" they had staked out; police were seeking an undetermined number of "latin hippie-types" as suspects. After a week of what the papers called "the largest manhunt in the history of Northern California," six young Latin Americans were arrested for the murder.

About a month later I got involved in a short-lived underground newspaper called *Dock of the Bay*. Somebody on the staff mentioned that a new and probably newsworthy radical organization called *Los Siete de la Raza* had been formed in the Mission district. So on a hot June day I went to a small storefront in the heart of the Mission and spoke to a young man named Ralph Ruiz who was in charge of press relations for the organization.

Los Siete de la Raza, Ralph told me, meant "the seven of the race," or of the Latin American people, and it referred to the seven suspects in the recent cop-killing, six of whom had been arrested. The new organization had been formed by friends of the seven, to help in their legal defense.

I asked Ralph what the six now under arrest were like. He said they were all "bad brothers," a compliment in ghetto or barrio language, meaning they were tough. But, he added, they weren't hoodlums, as the papers had said: several of them had been involved in recruiting other young latinos for a special "Readiness

Program" at a local college. All six were politically radical.

Ralph told me the media had already condemned the six with sensationalist headlines and strict adherence to the police version of the incident. In fact, he said, the two cops involved were a notorious plainclothes team in the Mission—"One played the good guy and the other played the motherfucker." It was the "good guy" who had been killed. Ralph said the six were considered heroes in the barrio for having stood up to these two "pigs."

My next stop was the office of the *San Francisco Chronicle,* the larger of the city's two dailies, where I bought copies of all the back issues containing articles about the incident. After studying these articles I understood what Ralph meant: the *Chronicle* had taken its stories from police announcements and the stories all played on racial stereotypes, leaving little room for doubt that all six latinos charged with murder were guilty.

From the articles and from my talk with Ralph I wrote my first story on Los Siete for *Dock of the Bay.* I began to follow the pre-trial hearings in the case, and to get to know other people in the Los Siete organization. One of them, Donna James, had attended San Francisco State College, been active in the recent strike there, and finally quit school to work with Los Siete full-time. Like Ralph, Donna had known several of the "brothers," as the six who were arrested came to be called. When, almost a year after the incident, Ramparts Press suggested I write a book on Los Siete, Donna agreed to give me help and advice.

The need for such a book was obvious. The police hoped to convict all six in jail and with the help of the dead policeman's widow had begun a vigorous pro–capital punishment campaign. Mayor Joseph Alioto, conscious of the law-and-order reaction which followed the college strikes of 1968 and '69, had called the suspects "punks" and offered a $5,000 reward for information leading to the capture of each. Responding to these pressures, the city's mass media steered clear of any in-depth reportage about the lives of the six young men, the conditions in the Mission district which produced their confrontation with the two cops, or the political consciousness which led to the formation of the Los Siete defense organization. Only once did a liberal TV network film a story favorable to Los Siete, and it was not aired. Outside of the barrio and the underground press, then, Los Siete's story was never told.

The story is worth telling for several reasons. First, the lives of the six defendants demonstrate an important aspect of recent barrio or ghetto experience—the promise of upward mobility through the mid-sixties' poverty programs and through expanded admission to colleges, and the political radicalization that came with these new, but limited, opportunities. Second, the six had experienced the oppression familiar to most brown people in the United States—particularly, destructive schooling and brutal treatment from the police and the courts. In chapter 4 I have tried to show that one of the institutional reasons for this oppression is the business community's need for a safe, white San Francisco—a need which ignores most minority people in the city and in fact considers them expendable and obsolete. Third, the nineteen-week trial of Los Siete was a documented condemnation of sloppy, corrupt police investigation—what amounted to an attempted railroad. Relating the events of the trial will, I hope, heighten public awareness of the injustices experienced by thousands of prisoners who are not fortunate enough to have a community group like the Los Siete organization working in their defense. The tactics used by the district attorney and the police during the trial suggest why many radical organizations, including Los Siete, consider all poor or nonwhite people in jail "political prisoners."

Finally, the most important function of this book is to give white America some insight into the response of many young Latin Americans to their experiences in this country. College strikes and barrio uprisings are just two indications of the rebellious mood among brown people, a mood which is shared by many blacks, Asians and young whites. These are not a few "hard-core, self-styled militants," as the media often describe them. Their anger is widespread and justified, and their feelings of solidarity with revolutionary movements in Asia, Africa, and Latin America have roots in common indignities suffered at the hands of what Los Siete would call "this racist, capitalist system."

My friendship with members of the Los Siete organization and my identification as an underground press reporter meant I could not gain the confidence of the police department, or of the family and friends of Joseph Brodnik, the policeman who had been killed*. This story is the story of Los Siete, not of Brodnik or the police, though they figure prominently in it.

Parts of the book consist of transcribed tape-recorded interviews with six of the young men known as Los Siete: Tony Martinez, Mario Martinez, Nelson Rodriguez, José Rios, Danilo "Bebe" Melendez, and Gary "Pinky" Lescallett. (I did these interviews while the six were in jail; consequently I never interviewed Gio Lopez, the seventh suspect, who was not caught.) Except for minor syntactical changes, these are the words of the young men. The quotes express their observations and opinions, which aren't necessarily my own.

The quotes in the trial chapters have all been checked against the transcript for accuracy, but I have often removed extraneous words in the interests of readability. In addition, I have sometimes moved testimony out of the order in which it was given during the trial; this again was for readability, and nowhere has the meaning been changed.

I would like to thank Donna James for permission to quote one stanza from her poem about Los Siete; Roberto Vargas for permission to quote one stanza from his poem, "They Blamed It on Reds," and the San Francisco Mime Troupe for permission to reprint their "Los Siete Cranky."

For their support and cooperation, I would like to thank Mr. and Mrs. Rodolfo Martinez, Donna James, Oscar Rios, Reynaldo Aparicio, Ralph Ruiz, Audelith Morales, Aaron Manganiello, José Delgado, Al Martinet, Maria Elena Ramirez, Tony Herrera, and Los Siete themselves—Tony Martinez, Mario Martinez, Nelson Rodriguez, José Rios, Bebe Melendez, and Gary Lescallett.

---

* With one exception: Brodnik's niece, Colleen Crosby.

1. Hidalgo's Statue

Dolores Park, across the street from Mission High School, is a convenient place for latin teen-agers to cut classes and smoke dope. In the center of the park is a statue of Miguel Hidalgo, the parish priest who began the struggle for Mexican independence in 1810. A respectable figure nowadays, Hidalgo wanted the Indians he led in rebellion to own land and share in the wealth of their country. Hidalgo failed, and when Mexico finally won independence it was without economic upheaval.

According to the inscription, Hidalgo's statue was presented to the city of San Francisco in 1962 by its "Mexican colony." Presumably it is meant to be a symbol of certain myths—that latin immigrants share the Anglo "democratic" ideals; that they will be assimilated and "make it" in the promised land. But, standing as it does in Dolores Park, looking eastward to the Mission district, the statue seems to express Hidalgo's unfinished revolution.

The old Mission of St. Francis, or Mission Dolores, two blocks north of Dolores Park, was founded in 1776 by Father Francisco Palou, a Spanish missionary who wanted to Christianize the "savages." But the Indian tribes died off more quickly than they adapted to the white man's civilization, which for them meant slavery and new diseases.

When Mexico won independence in 1821, San Francisco, like most of the present American Southwest, became part of the Mexican nation. But in the war of 1846–48 Mexico lost a third of her territory, including San Francisco, to Manifest Destiny. San

Francisco, then called Yerba Buena, was a small village near the Bay, connected to the old mission by a dirt path. There were about four hundred inhabitants, mostly Anglo traders, Spanish officers, mestizos, Indians, and Pacific islanders.

By 1850, two years after California became part of the United States, San Francisco's population had grown to twenty-five thousand, and ten years later it was eighty thousand. Most of the new residents were white men attracted by the Gold Rush, and these quickly outnumbered the Spanish-speaking population. But the Gold Rush also brought Mexicans from the province of Sonora, and South Americans mainly from Chile and Peru.

The Treaty of Guadalupe-Hidalgo, which ended the 1846–48 war, guaranteed Mexicans living in the ceded territory full political rights and a bilingual society. But the treaty was immediately ignored, and La Raza* became a despised minority. *Californios* (the Spanish-speaking population which had governed California before the war) were cheated out of their land. Inordinate numbers of Mexicans were whipped, banished, or hanged. San Francisco's *Daily Alta Californian* wrote in 1854, "It was almost a byword in our midst that none but Mexicans could be convicted of a capital offense."

Although the Spanish-speaking remained a part of San Francisco's population, their numbers didn't increase rapidly until after World War II. During and after the war, large numbers of black people came to northern cities for defense-related jobs. In San Francisco, the black influx was followed by a large immigration of latinos, mostly from Central America. In 1952 there were only about sixteen thousand Latin Americans in San Francisco. By 1970 the number had grown to about one hundred thousand,† most of them concentrated in or near the Mission district.

* "La Raza" has many connotations. Basically it means "the Latin American people," descendants of Spaniards, Indians, and, in some areas, blacks.

† Estimates of the latin population of San Francisco vary from a low of 62,500, given by the California Department of Human Resources, to a high of 120,000, given by a local organization called the Mission Coalition. This is between eight and seventeen percent of the city total. The state figure un-

This immigration of latinos made the Mission district unique. In most southwestern barrios the Raza population is predominantly chicano—Mexican-American—and it is at least a few decades old. In the Mission the traditional Raza problems of language, culture, and racial discrimination are augmented by the problems of new arrivals—adjusting to the society, finding work, maintaining old country values. At the same time, the latinos who came in the 1950s and '60s were not so different from the *Californios*, Sonorans and *Chilenos* before them, or from the Mexican farmworkers who had been doing much of the farm labor in California's rich agricultural valleys since the early part of the century. Their language was the same, their culture was very similar, and most of the Anglo population, especially the working-class people who inhabited the Mission district, did not make fine distinctions.

Many white residents of the Mission had come in the late nineteenth and early twentieth centuries from Ireland, Italy, and Eastern Europe. As their status and incomes rose, many of them moved out of the Mission and the neighboring South of Market area, and into suburbs or wealthier parts of town. Many of those who remain today can't afford to move out. Others have jobs which make it convenient to remain—like police officer Joseph Brodnik, the man Los Siete were accused of murdering—or have property or a business in the Mission. Many of the Mission whites view the newer arrivals as threats to their status and jobs, and the western Mission is a traditional stronghold of right-wing candidates in local elections.

The eastern Mission is still working-class, but now it is mostly nonwhite. In addition to the Spanish-speaking there are many Samoans, Filipinos and blacks. Only a relatively small area centering around eastern Twenty-fourth Street is predominantly Raza, with many latin-owned businesses—bakeries which make tortillas, Central American restaurants, and "Mexicatessens."

---

doubtedly missed many illegal immigrants. A *San Francisco Chronicle* survey found approximately 90,000 Spanish-surnamed people in the city in February 1969. But many latinos, especially those from the Caribbean, do not have Spanish surnames.

Although there are no statistics to prove it, Central Americans clearly form the majority of the Raza population in the Mission. Nicaraguans and Salvadorians are probably the most numerous nationalities. There are also South Americans (especially Peruvians), Cubans, and Mexicans in the district. Some of the Mexicans come from farmworker families; a few can trace their lineage back to the eighteenth century. In any case, their earlier arrival gave the Mexicans a political edge in the Mission, and they have tended to dominate what official voice La Raza has in city affairs.

The Mission District, unlike much of San Francisco, is broad, flat, and sunny. Most of its houses are two or three stories high, painted in pastel colors which reflect light and give the streets an air of serenity not found in the barrios of eastern cities, with their tall, dark tenements. Inside, though, are the usual rats, cockroaches, ants, broken faucets, leaking roofs, cracked walls, stopped-up toilets and lack of central heating. Mission Street itself, the district's main shopping street, is three blocks east of the old Mission Dolores. Alongside its small shops and open-air markets are discount department stores and cheap food stands like "Señor Taco" and "Doggie Diner." Flashy clothing stores, realtors, loan sharks, gaudy jewelry and furniture showrooms also abound. Kay Jewelry bluntly proclaims "IT'S OKAY TO OWE KAY."

To the west of the Mission district are Noe and Eureka valleys, quieter and whiter than the Mission, with some splendid, well-kept houses. Old notion shops scrape along beside the newer discount stores. The valleys have a high concentration of white working-class residents. Joseph Brodnik, the cop who was killed, and his partner Paul McGoran considered this area their turf; Brodnik lived in Eureka Valley, and it was on Alvarado Street in Noe Valley that he and McGoran stopped seventeen-year-old José Rios and several of his friends on May 1, 1969. The ensuing incident resulted in Brodnik's death.

West of the Noe and Eureka valleys are the Twin Peaks which tower above the city and divide the Mission from the more affluent communities beyond. In the late sixties, large areas of Twin Peaks were already blanketed with expensive view apartments inhabited largely by white-collar workers who spent their days downtown—and were thus open to the threat of daytime burglary. Officers Brodnik and McGoran distinguished themselves as the nemesis of daylight burglars in the Twin Peaks region.

II

The Rios, Martinez, and Rodriguez families—the families of four of Los Siete—all came from El Salvador in the early 1960s, the time of the large latin influx. Rodolfo Martinez Sr. grew up in a *campesino* family of thirteen children and went to work in the fields at the age of nine for thirty-five or forty centavos a day. He left home and worked on coffee plantations all over the country. When he was fifteen he got a job in a government project, carrying cement. When he was sixteen he went to San Salvador, the capital, and became an apprentice in a body and fender shop.

He met his wife in San Salvador. "She was about nineteen; he was twenty-one," says Rodolfo Antonio "Tony" Martinez, the slim, curly-haired eldest son, and one of the young men who became known as Los Siete. "Her family was real strict. When my mother was eighteen she had never been out of her village. But one of her sisters had split from home. She had managed to get to San Salvador. So my mother finally convinced my grandfather to let her go. And she went there, working in this restaurant my aunt used to own. And this was where she met my father."

Tony, like his younger brother Mario, another of Los Siete, speaks of El Salvador's stricter moral values with a sense of loss. A distinguishing characteristic of the Martinez family is their firm adherence to these values.

"We lived in a barrio in San Salvador," Tony remembers. "It was pretty bad. They had a whole lot of killings all the time. We lived in an apartment with one big room and a kitchen, and a loft upstairs. The loft was divided into two rooms with curtains. In one room slept the kids, and in the other, my mother and father.

"El Salvador is a beautiful country. In the summer we used to go out to the country, where my mother's family lives. We used to look forward to the summers. In the countryside the people are more simple. The houses are adobe, painted white."

Nelson Rodriguez, a cousin of the Martinez family and another of Los Siete, also remembers El Salvador in a sentimental way. His grandfather had a ranch: "He used to own several hundred head of cattle. Now he's too old; he sold them all. Once when I was younger I ripped off about twenty head and went fifty-fifty with one of the hands. We got seventeen hundred pesos and split it. I spent my half in a week's time at a fiesta. I was staying in a hotel; a friend told me there was a far-out whorehouse in town. I didn't want to go there 'cause I looked so young and the whorehouse would be hassled by the pigs, especially at fiesta time. So I had him send one of the whores to me. That money went fast." It was only one of many off-color adventures that Nelson delights in describing. At five feet ten, he is taller than both Martinez brothers and classically handsome.

"I had run away from home that time," Nelson continues. "When I got back I got spanked. My grandfather was mad at first, but then he found it kind of amusing. I'm really his favorite grandson. Every time school let out I would just go to my grandparents' house in the country. I used to spend all my time there."

A recession in the 1950s intensified the poverty of most Salvadorians and many of those with ambition thought of moving north. In 1958, three years before Rodolfo Martinez or José Rodriguez, Nelson's father, came to San Francisco, the average hourly worker's wage in San Salvador was less than twenty-five cents. The average family income throughout the country was about two hundred dollars a year. Meanwhile, movies, billboards, newspapers and schools described the United States as the land of boundless opportunity.

A growing radical mood in El Salvador, partly inspired by the Cuban Revolution, led to street demonstrations in 1960. A right-wing coup followed, resulting in severe political repression. "My father and his brother were involved in politics when they were students," Nelson Rodriguez says. "I remember there was a coup in San Salvador. We were downtown when it happened. All of a sudden there were explosions and everything. We just left town.

Later I found out two of my uncles were in jail and had been tortured."

The rightist coup marked the beginning of a large influx of U.S. capital. Industrialization centered in San Salvador, and more *campesinos* were drawn to the city. With the increased capital came new forms of counterinsurgency—the average army officer received more in military equipment than most of his countrymen got as a yearly wage. Central America became a training and staging area for attacks against Cuba. Increased repression, increased economic exploitation, increased pro–U.S. propaganda, were some of the stimuli for emigration.*

Another important factor—decisive for the Martinez family—was education. Rodolfo Martinez wanted to send his children to college. The ambition rubbed off on Tony and Mario. "At the end of every school year I would get first prize and my brother would get second prize," Tony remembers. "Or else he'd get first and I'd get second. One year I got third prize: I remember I went home and cried."

"I think the schooling's pretty good there," Tony says. "From the first grade through high school they do a hell of a good job. When I came to this country, once I learned English and could comprehend what was going on in class, I found there was nothing to learn. I had already learned it. So I went through sixth, seventh, eighth, and ninth grades without learning nothing—especially in math and history, because all that math and history had already been given to me.

"But the colleges—it's not that big a country, first of all, and they don't have that much money. So if you want to go to college, it would be better to go outside the country."

Mario—his full name is José Mario Martinez—is heavier than his older brother Tony, with a broad face and almost Indian features. "In our countries," he says, "if you're educated in the U.S., it has a lot of weight—the all-powerful American thing. You see a lot of doctors there—it says their names, doctor, educated in the United States. And everybody goes to them."

* A San Francisco Human Rights Commission researcher, James Stirling, found the same reasons in a 1964 study of Nicaraguans in San Francisco.

In 1961 Rodolfo Martinez Sr. came to San Francisco. "All I thought about was work, work, work," he remembers. "Getting enough money together." Seven months later he had enough to send for his family. He continued to be a prodigious worker—"the best body and fender man in the Mission," according to his children. But he resented the fact that his salary was four dollars an hour, while the shop charged twelve dollars for his work. He wanted to open his own shop but couldn't save enough to buy the expensive equipment. Ten years later, on the job, a piece of metal flew into his eye, ruining it for precision body work.

The Martinez family's first apartment was half a block from Mission Street. "It's supposed to be real good here," Mario says. "People would tell me how in the streets you see dollar bills laying around and people are so rich they don't even pay attention to them. I thought we were coming to a castle. I mean a big mansion like the Hollywood stars have. I thought there would be a swimming pool, horseback riding in the yard. It surprised me, because when we came here we came to this little apartment in the Mission, and it was no mansion. I was looking all over for the chandeliers, but I couldn't find any."

Each of the young immigrants had his own private vision. Nelson Rodriguez expected to see "a lot of cowboys riding on white horses."

III

Many of the latin immigrants were skilled and upwardly aspiring city workers. Others were professionals or semi-professionals—Nelson's father had been to college—but unlike the European workers who populated the Mission before them, the latinos faced racial discrimination in jobs and housing,* profound cultural dif-

* A San Francisco Human Rights Commission telephone survey in 1969 found that of fifty landlords interviewed, eighteen said they would definitely or probably not rent to blacks. This often meant latinos also. In 1971 the U.S. Secretary of Labor announced racial hiring quotas in five San Francisco union locals because their proportions of minority members were so low.

ferences, and anti-latin prejudices which had developed among the Anglo population during one hundred years of California history.

Also, the economic situation was very different. By the mid-sixties, San Francisco was no longer a booming industrial town. Industry had been leaving the city for cheaper, more spacious quarters elsewhere in the Bay Area. San Francisco lost nine thousand manufacturing jobs—fourteen percent of its total—between 1953 and 1966.* Replacing them were thousands of new white-collar positions for which most latin immigrants weren't considered qualified.

In a short time the Mission district acquired many of the characteristics of a ghetto. In 1968 its average income level was $5,280 a year, in contrast with a $6,717 city average (the average income for Spanish-surnamed residents of the Mission was only $4,290).† According to the 1960 U.S. census, twenty percent of the Mission's residents had incomes under $3,000. In the late sixties the Mission qualified as one of the city's five "war on poverty" target areas—the other four being the densely populated Chinatown ghetto, the rundown South of Market and Potrero districts, and two black ghettoes, the Fillmore/Western Addition and Bayview/Hunter's Point.

By the late sixties the housing situation in the Mission had become particularly grim, with a vacancy rate of almost zero for

* According to the City Planning Department's report on "San Francisco Industrial Trends," October 1968. Lack of space and high rents in the city were the main reasons manufacturers gave for leaving; other reasons included high city taxes, high wages, parking problems, labor unions, insurance, building codes, availability of skilled labor and the "character of the labor force."

† San Francisco City Demonstration Agency, "First Action Year: Comprehensive Development Plan," Mission amendment, 1971–72, released in April 1971. Figures are projections to 1968 from 1960 census data and describe the Inner, or eastern, Mission which in 1970 and '71 was the subject of a Model Cities planning survey. The Mission as defined by the city's Economic Opportunity Council is a larger area which includes Bernal Heights, Noe Valley, and part of Twin Peaks.

low-income units and with over five thousand names on public housing waiting lists. In addition to the continual flow of new immigrants, for whom the Mission is a traditional "port of entry," young longhairs were moving into the sunny district because it was one of the most appealing in San Francisco, and the Haight-Ashbury was getting run-down. Blacks displaced by massive urban renewal in the Western Addition were also moving in, making the housing squeeze even more acute. And even by 1960, according to the census 16 percent of the housing units in the Mission were substandard and 9.3 percent were overcrowded.

The Department of Labor found in 1966 that thirteen percent of the residents of the Mission and Fillmore areas were under-employed; twelve percent were unemployed and not seeking work because they didn't think they could find any; and seven percent were full-time employees earning less than $60 a week. The 1960 census gave the unemployment rate for Inner Mission men as 9.5 percent; a 1965 study found 15 percent. Like all unemployment figures, these are highly flexible in the upward direction, as they don't include illegal immigrants, those who aren't seeking work, or anyone else not standing on the unemployment line. In one of the few studies *not* done on the basis of how many people are collecting unemployment benefits, the Department of Labor in 1966 found a thirty-six percent unemployment rate for young people in the Mission and Fillmore. One report commented: "Increasing dropout rates indicate that the actual youth unemployment rate is much higher."

But whatever the true unemployment rate in the Mission, it is easy to see that jobs are very scarce, especially for Spanish-speaking immigrants. Major Joseph Alioto's application for a Model Cities Planning Grant in 1968 asserted that the Mission had the highest unemployment rate in the city, while its under-employment rate was about double the city average.

Mission High School reflected the dismal situation. With thirty-six percent of its student body Spanish-speaking, and sixty-eight percent Third World (black, latin, Asian, Filipino, Samoan and other nonwhites), Mission High had the lowest average family income of any school in the city. The average daily absence rate

26

was twenty-five percent. In 1966, Mission High sent only five percent of its graduates on to four-year college, as compared to fifty percent for the city's most affluent—and mostly white—public high school.* In the Mission district as a whole, the dropout rate in 1969–70 was twenty-nine percent for males and twenty percent for females. As for the Mission's adult population, in 1966 between forty and sixty percent had less than nine years of education.

IV

"When school came around every year, I didn't have any enthusiasm," Mario Martinez says of his elementary and junior high school years. "Back in my country, when school was coming we used to get prepared. You buy all your new books and you fold up the covers real nice.

"When I first got here they put me back in the fifth grade. I would just sit there. This guy who spoke Spanish and English would sometimes interpret for me, but the rest of the time I would just sit, try to listen. The only thing I could do was when it was time to draw—I always drew something about my country. I passed that grade, but I don't know why they passed me."

His older brother Tony's strongest impressions were of racism at school. "A lot of times the teachers won't even talk to you," he says. "They looked at us and thought, 'Well, this guy probably don't even understand what I'm saying.' Plus they call you names. I remember the first time I was called a Mexican was in Marshall

* "A Study of After-Graduation Plans," San Francisco Board of Education. June 1966 was the last date for which complete figures of this kind were available; after that the Board of Education continued to survey high school graduates on their plans but didn't compile the figures—possibly because the differences between poor and rich schools were too glaring. Although statistics for later years are incomplete, it appears that the proportion of Mission High graduates going on to four-year colleges increased until 1969 and then began to decline again—a reflection of budget cuts in the Economic Opportunity Program, which provides financial aid to poor and minority students.

elementary school. I remember this teacher real well; she was a drunk. You could smell it a mile away. I remember I was coming down the steps in front of the school. You wasn't supposed to walk there or something. At that time I didn't understand English. It wasn't till later I found out she had called me a fucking greaser. I remembered by the sound.

"In junior high the Dean of Boys was pretty nasty. He was always making racist remarks. Not only to the brown kids but to the black kids, calling them motherfucking niggers and shit. All the time—it would be a continuous thing. They couldn't refer to you—you never had a name. When they call Mary in the classroom, it's Mary, and John is John; but when they call us it's 'You, the Mexican kid.' Calling us farmworkers and *braceros* and peons and all this. After a while you just don't want to hear it."

Mario adds, "In junior high this one guy, if you were late to class he would call you down and hit you with a paddle. Once I was late and so he called me down. He told me to bend over, and he hit me with a paddle. I didn't know what he was going to do. He just hit me. And I got real mad. I didn't come to school for about two weeks. All I could think was, nobody has a right to hit me, only my parents. And this stranger, even though he does belong to this big school. he don't have no right hitting me.

"Even after I learned English, I still had problems. Like with the kids. There was a lot of little *pochos*—guys whose family was born in our country, but they were born here. They don't speak Spanish. Even if they know Spanish, they won't speak it to you. Like I would ask someone in Spanish to tell me something and he would say, 'I don't speak Spanish,' and I knew he did. It got me upset, because I thought, these guys, they're ashamed of our culture, ashamed of our people. So I didn't get along with them at all. 'Cause you've got to be proud of what you are.

"Our culture has never left us," Mario says. "With my parents, when I speak to them in English, you just call somebody 'you': in Spanish you have a formal thing—you say 'Usted.' That's the way I treat my parents: 'Usted.' If I wanted to say 'you,' I'd just say 'tu.' But that's a kind of friendly thing. There's no respect there. I rebelled against a lot of things, but not my culture or my parents, 'cause I don't see much to rebel against there."

"I used to go to school in the morning," Mario says. "And my friends would ask me, 'Are you going to class?' And we would just split. It was a better experience. I learned more on the streets than in school, just being with people I could relate to."

The Martinez brothers were quickly turned off to school—with its pressures to speak English and abandon their culture and its run-ins with racist teachers or administrators. Like most young latins they began to spend their time on the streets—going to dances, frequenting pool halls, tasting wine and grass.

"I would hang around with guys a lot older than myself," Tony remembers. "Hanging around with bigger guys helped me not get hung up on drugs. I seen all these guys, first smoking a lot of grass, then using a lot of hard stuff. Chicanos and latinos don't usually go for the psychedelic drugs, you know. Don't dig the synthetic kick. So they use a lot of hard drugs. But the thing about hard drugs is—people you know, they might have a job, and then they get hooked. Then they have to steal. Pretty soon they're going to jail. You see them become all skinny and weak and they're dying and they're OD'ed and stuff. So this is why I never touch the stuff. And in our case our family is tight-knit. So we always had somebody behind us. We had time to think about these things, because we wouldn't have the many problems our friends would have. All my partners on the street, they have to hassle to find a job or a room where to stay—go steal so they can pay a week in a hotel. Hassles we wouldn't have to go through."

The Martinez family moved to Daly City, just south of San Francisco, and Tony and Mario went to Jefferson High School. Some of their old partners from the Mission district were also going to Jefferson—among them three more of the seven who were eventually to become Los Siete: Nelson Rodriguez, José Rios, and Gary Lescallett. Reynaldo Aparicio, another friend whose family came from El Salvador, remembers: "At Jefferson we weren't only friends but *paisanos*, coming from the same country, having the same principles. The school was predominantly white; we stuck together. As a group we had a fight against the white cats; then about six months later we had a fight against the blacks. In all these instances we were together as brothers. We played on the soccer team for the PAL—the Pigs Athletic League—and we got to be champions because we were all aggressive and we would always rely on each other, have confidence in each other.

"In school most of us were not doing as good as we should have. We cut school a lot. We were young cats on the street to have a good time and we didn't do homework. But the majority of us were very intelligent and could manage to go back to school and take the exams and pass them."

Another friend later wrote a description of these years—1965 to 1968: "Tony and Mario went through what most of us have gone through: they were 'stylin' hard,' 'being bad,' 'dressing bad.' It was much more important to wear out-of-sight clothes than to do well in school. School was just a prison. The students there were divided against each other. White kids didn't like brown and black kids. About the only thing Mario and Tony learned at school was racism against black people.

"The brothers had a car and would go 'lowriding' in the Mission. Or they'd stand out in front of the Doggie Diner on Mission and Eighteenth, feeling mellow. But latin brothers standing on the street are a target for the cops, so they had to pretend they were waiting for a bus. The cop car would come around the block again and tell them to get moving or else."

"The first time we got busted was for trespassing," Mario remembers. "A girlfriend had invited us to her house. Somebody called the pigs and they chased us to a back yard; they handcuffed us. My mother had to go get us out. She felt really bad.

"Then, when I was sixteen, I got busted with some friends [among them José Rios, another of Los Siete] for a strong-arm robbery. We went to Juvenile Hall. I stayed there three days. We went to court and they cleared us on it. They had no evidence. That was the first time they took my picture. I felt really bad then. You feel degraded. They treat you like a dog."

"Walking in the Mission," says José Rios, "you're just a victim. You're walking down the street. The pigs say, 'There's a target.

Let's get him.' And you're not doing anything wrong. You complain to them, 'What have I done? Why am I being stopped?'

"They say, 'You're being questioned.' Excuses, they give excuses to harass you. For a little while I would try to resist, and then get all clobbered up. After so much you realize it wasn't worth it to resist. Go along with them, get out sooner."

Another young latino, Francisco Flores, who used to hang around with Los Siete and later became part of the committee to defend them, points out a crowd of teenagers cutting classes:

"You see those hundred people out there in Dolores Park? They are latinos. Why are they in the park? Because they have been smoking grass. And why have they been smoking grass? Because the school don't teach them nothing that is relevant to them, that they can say, 'This is my own.' "

2. Strictly Ghetto Property

I

Danilo "Bebe" Melendez, another of the young men known as Los Siete, grew up on the street; his personality and imagination are products of street culture. "I may leave the Mission once in a while," Bebe says, "but I always come back. I can't get away from it. I'm addicted to it. It wakes me up."

For a young man like Bebe, the Mission had many attractions. It was familiar, the only place in the city where he, as a latino, could feel at home. In the streets, despite the day-to-day violence, he felt a certain brotherhood—what attorney Charles Garry later described as a "cementing of solidarity among people who have been discriminated against." In addition there was the street culture, which mixed the experience of La Raza with the values of the North American underworld. As an example of this kind of mixture, Bebe recites one of his favorite poems, "Mexicali Rose," written by a convict named Moon Miller:

I was driving south with my partner, Cocaine Smitty,
We was on our way to pick up some whores from Mexico
   City,
We were big-time pimps from the San Francisco scene,
And I must admit that we was dressed pretty clean;
I had a raw silk suit that was powder blue,
My alligator shoes were the same color too,

Had a Stetson hat with a hundred dollar tag,
My alligator wallet was filled with slag. . .

I said to Rose, "Let me be your pimp—
There'll be no rings on your fingers, no fancy clothes,
You'll be kicking mud like the rest of them whores,
And if there should be a night when you don't come aright,
I'll kick you out in the street like an ordinary slut,
But if you should come aright, our life will be out of sight,
We'll be on easy street, with plenty of wine, reefers, money
    and meat . . ."

Smitty yelled out, "If I can't have Rose for my own,
I'll slice both you motherfuckers and drive on home . . ."
I took Rose's body back to the city,
And in a cigar box the remains of Smitty;
I gave her a funeral, didn't spare no cash,
Bought her an emerald green gown with a golden sash,
I copped a Hope diamond, some Cinderella shoes,
Hired Lou Rawls to sing the señorita blues . . .

"I'm strictly ghetto property," Bebe Melendez says. "When I was growing up I had one ambition. I wanted to be Alexander Mundy, that professional thief dude. It was the easiest way to make money. I'm my own boss. But you know the name of the game is cop and blow: if the Man catches you, you got to accept that you're going to do a little bit of time."

Bebe was two years old, the second of two children, when his family came to San Francisco from San Pedro Sula, Honduras, in 1952. His father had been a *zapatero*, a shoe- and saddle-maker, in Honduras, but eventually gave up this trade for car-painting. The family's first apartment was in the mostly black Fillmore district, but they had to move often: five more children were born.

Bebe took to the streets early. "I started cutting in elementary school. I would go home for lunch and instead of going back to school I would go to the park with my friends. I started smoking grass when I was eleven or twelve. You go to the park and the Man kicks you out of the park. If you ain't got no more park, then you hit the streets. There is nowhere else to go."

The fact that Bebe came to San Francisco early, and was thus more acculturated than the Martinez brothers, did not make him tamer. For Bebe wasn't acculturated to white middle-class America but to ghetto America, the values expressed in "Mexicali Rose." He became involved in the gang scene which dominated Mission Street life in the fifties and early sixties. As a young street brother of twelve or thirteen he would be a member of a "son" club which would imitate the styles and activities of the older "father" clubs.

"When I was in the Little Saints," he remembers, "we used to go to James Lick Junior High School [in Noe Valley] and start kicking ass. One day in school we had an assembly. My cousin Louie Romero had just come to school. So some Caucasian dude called him a greaser. Now Louie, he's pretty small but he's pretty bad. He just kicked his ass.

"The Caucasians, they wanted everybody to know, so the next day after school we was walking home and there was this pack of white boys just waiting for us, waiting for Louie. We got halfway down the street and they started pulling out sticks and bats. They just opened fire on us. They brought their zip guns and all kinds of stuff. They cut me on my arm. I still got the scar.

"We used to have this club, the Frisco Monarchs," Bebe goes on. "All them Caucasians just hated us. We would get into a fight every other week, and they would call us greasers and wetbacks. During them days we still wore khakis and Stacey Adams shoes and we were big high-haired dudes. Punk comes up to me and tells me I'm a spic, I'll bust him in his lip.

"I was president of one club up by Daly City, the Little Marquis. We drank wine together. We had drugs—we was popping reds and yellows and smoking grass. But there wasn't drugs like today. Last fight I had was in the Constellations. We all got to fighting against the Royal Chessmen. The Constellations didn't have jackets. The only clubs that had jackets that I was in were the Frisco Monarchs, the Young Counts and the Little Saints.

"But they break up. The leadership goes. The Man's always

taking the leadership. There was no more gangs by '67—well, there was, but you're not aware of them 'cause it's not your bag anymore. I just got sick and tired of getting hit over the head. Got tired of fighting. It's a drag. It ain't what's happening, really.

"During then we didn't have a brown movement like there is now [1970]. If there was a brown movement, I'm sure we would have all been involved. During them days we were just fighting other gangs, that's all."

II

"I knew José Rios from the Mission," Bebe says. "He used to go to the dances I went to. Once in a while we'd pull out our bottle and take a nip. And smoke a joint or something like that—then go on our way."

José Rios, the fifth of seven children and the youngest of Los Siete (he was only seventeen at the time they were arrested for murder), came to the Mission with his family in 1961. His mother, who came first, had been a nurse in El Salvador, but found she couldn't qualify in the U.S. unless she learned English and took additional training. There wasn't time for that since she had to earn money to send for the rest of the family. She became a hospital laundress.*

José's father held down two low-paying jobs, working fourteen to sixteen hours a day. The whole family picked fruit on weekends to bring in an extra fifteen or twenty dollars. José always cooperated in these family efforts, and later held dishwashing and janitorial jobs. But he was disgusted by the menial work and the degrading schools, and soon began to seek out street life. He and

---

* The San Francisco City Demonstration Agency (which oversees Model Cities programs in the city) describes this experience in the "Comprehensive Development Plan" for the Mission (April 1971). The plan notes that "Restrictive licensing . . . mandatory internships" and requirements for "further schooling" make it almost impossible for professionals and technicians from Central and South America to use their skills in this country, and that this is a major cause of poverty and unemployment in the Mission.

his older brother Oscar and their friends Reynaldo Aparicio and Nelson Rodriguez began to hang around together; their families were all members of the same Mormon church group.

José rebelled first against the family's religion. "The Mormons are racists," he says. "They don't let black people take the regular ceremonies. A cousin of mine married a Puerto Rican and he's real dark, and in the church they would only let him go to a certain point and then no further. That really started putting question marks in my mind. I just stopped going to church. I left the church before Oscar. He and Reynaldo continued to go. I think they kept going because our parents were hassling us and they just didn't want to give our parents a lot of trouble.

"Oscar and myself, we're a lot different. I guess you could say I'm the wild one. I used to get together with Nelson [Rodriguez] at the pool hall and we'd have our nightly trips and afterwards wind up back at the pool hall. I got to learn a lot about that game.

"I had a car, too, that had belonged to Oscar, a '62 Chevy. Oscar was working at the airport after he graduated from high school. He used to take his car out there and one day it was ripped off. They found it a week later all stripped down. It still had the engine but the transmission was a little fucked up. He told me, 'You fix it.' I didn't really know much about cars but I started fixing it up. I fooled around with the electronics, put in six speakers. It was really a trip, driving down the freeway, especially when you're loaded.

"I got loaded a lot, experienced just about everything. And you know what? I never had a bummer. My older brothers used to tell me, 'Don't do this. If you do, I'll kick your ass.' After so much I started rebelling against them. I didn't want to be told nothing. I wanted to experience it all myself. I got a couple of ass lickings from all of them. Then after so much they just left me alone.

"A couple of years later I started realizing my brothers weren't squares. They were pretty hip to what I was doing. My older brothers were pretty wild. One of them was a teenager when all the gangs were running around fighting. He got busted a couple of times, carrying a machete."

José was good friends with Gary "Pinky" Lescallett, the sixth of Los Siete. "It used to be a thing of everybody in suits," Pinky says of the street scene, "and there were some cold-blooded ties, man. Me and José used to run around together and like we used to look crazy, all dressed up, wearing white, and white on white. He'd be wearing white and I'd be wearing black. Next day he'd be wearing lavender but lavender's too loud for me. It was a righteous cold-blooded scene. It was fancy, but you could tell it was ghetto. I would walk into jail a lot of times and people would say, 'You're from the Mission, huh?' I says, 'How could you tell, man?' He says, 'There's something about you dudes.' "

Pinky's nickname refers to his long, crooked right pinky, broken many times in fights and accidents of ghetto life. He is tall and broad, by far the tallest of Los Siete. Unlike the others, Pinky was born in this country and is only half latin, his mother being from Nicaragua, his father from Ohio. But being half "white" didn't make much difference, as Pinky explains:

"They look at your hair, your eyes, and your skin's a little dark, and they say 'spic.' Whew! You tell them, 'I'm half white and half Spanish, man.' It's a heavy trip. I feel sorry for the purple dude—righteous! If there was one purple dude he'd be in a world of trouble. 'Cause everybody'd be down on him.

"When I was little," Pinky remembers, "I used to be a righteous 'A' student. Come home and study. When I got older I got to see the teachers as they really are, to see their racist ideas towards you. Shit, there may be a few good teachers in there, but I have never seen a teacher in the pool hall. I have never met a teacher that lived on my block. So how can they teach someone? They don't give a damn about us; they never have.

"Then as I grown up I found what the street was about. It's going places, seeing different things, having fun. You go to the pool hall, you see these old Spanish cats. They tell me, 'You been coming around quite a bit.' I says, 'Yeah.' They say, 'I been coming here for thirty-five years.' Man! Can't you find nothing else to do? They says, 'Ain't nothing. Pool hall is what's happening.'

"Now that I look at it, it really wasn't nothing. It was just the fad, the idea, man; you want to be like everybody else.

"When you look at the Mission, when you righteously go up from Eighteenth all the way to Twenty-fifth, you see Kay Jewelers, Grayson's, that Granat Brothers place [all jewelers]—they got nerve! When you go by, you can see them setting diamonds. I think: now what's that doing there? I don't got no diamond rings. When you get finished paying on the installment plan, which is maybe four or five years, you want to buy something else, you know? 'Cause the Joneses got it.

"In my house, I never had no allowance. And I started buying my own clothes at the age of thirteen. Yet I didn't work. I don't like to say I stole anything, 'cause all I understood was I was taking 'cause I had a need. I had other brothers and sisters as far as I was concerned that came before me. I always wanted them to have more than I had. It's like the Man puts a gun in your hand and *says* go rob. 'Cause he isn't properly training you to do anything. And when you're little, you don't be thinking about the future. You're just thinking NOW. Damn ten years from now. I'll worry about that when it comes.

"They say the strong survive and the weak die. Well, it may be like that, like the Man says, but it isn't always like that. I have met cats in the streets, and they say, 'Give me a dollar.' Man, I knew them, and I gave them the dollar that I had took from somebody else—to give to them."

Pinky soon got into trouble with the police. For a time his family lived in the Westlake section of Daly City, a suburb along the coast famous for its rows of pastel-colored tract housing. "Westlake's a heavy place," Pinky says. "I was the only Spanish cat. Boy, I got accused of everything! From breaking into schools to rolling cars down hills. And I don't do those things, man—it ain't my trip, breaking into schools. I don't even *like* schools. 'Cause that's where they give you indoctrination, right there.

"They used to stop me at night and ask my name. I would tell them. They'd say, 'Roll up your sleeves.' I don't know what they mean. I roll 'em up; I'm looking at them too. And the Man says, 'I'm gonna give you a ride home.' So they take me all the way to my house, flash the light up my stairs. I tell my father to get up and tell the police to split because they're staying there all night. They had nothing else to do but mess with somebody, you know?

"I got in trouble, went to Juvenile Hall. After I got out, we moved back to the Mission. I got sent to St. Vincent's School for Boys. It's like a boarding school—they just keep you. Stayed there two years, graduated from junior high. Went to Jefferson High in Daly City—that's where I saw Mario and Tony [Martinez].

"I only stayed in school two weeks. I got tired of it. I can take only so much. People get down on me and I can't take it. Stepping on your heels, kicking you—I don't go for that. I got in some fights with white kids, but nothing I would brag about. It got to the point where I thought they were gonna lynch me. Man, *I know*. So I went and told them; I said I want to go. Over to Mission [High School]. Really, I didn't want to go to school, period. I wanted to drop out. I figured if they give me a transfer I got a little time in between, before they find out. So I just don't go to school.

"I got arrested in Pacifica; they accused me of burglary. What had happened is this other cat had burglarized the house and come to my house after he did it. So I let him in, said, 'What you got?'

"He said, 'I got some money. I want to count it.'

"And I says, 'Where'd you get it?'

"He says, 'Oh, from this girl's house. You want some money?'

"I says, 'Sure!' So we count it, and he's got $2,000. He gave me $75.

"The police come one day and tell me I'm under arrest. So I say, 'Okay, let's go.' They ask me questions, saying I'm a punk. They brought me down to this office to interrogate me. They always got the bad dude and the nice guy. Well, the nice guy comes in, but I'm getting bad with him, so he gets mad; we start cussing at each other and I'm calling him all kinds of names. He has this big folder there and when he turns around and splits I read all these statements. One of the statements is by this cat, saying I did everything *he* did. I thought, Oh, goodness!

"They wanted me to say I did it, but I kept saying I didn't. So I went to Juvenile Hall. I stayed there for a little while before they got ready to send me away. Then *he* came in. And I said, Oh my goodness, we're gonna fight. I told the lady counselor there: 'Hey, you better lock him up, 'cause I get mad and I don't know what I might do.' But she didn't lock him in his room.

"And he lied to me. He says, 'Man, I heard you got busted. I didn't tell nothing.' So I hit him. We fight. Then we both go to our rooms and stay locked in.

"They shoot me to YA [Youth Authority Prison]. I'm fifteen—I don't even know what jail is. YA's a pretty bad place. I mean, I've been in Juvenile Hall, you know, but it didn't mean nothing. They just give you probation and let you go. But this was a serious thing they had put on me: burglary. Usually it's just a curfew or petty theft or something like that, or not going to school. But burglary was a heavy crime. Whew! I didn't even know what burglary was.

"So I got there: they give me ninety day observation. Which is, they test your attitude—they set you up to see if you get mad, mess with you so you get mad, say something bad, so they can shoot you somewhere. That's how it works.

"This psychiatrist gives me books. Like, here's a picture. It's got a dude with a gun and a dude on the ground. And he says, 'Which one is you?' Man, no one wants to be the one on the ground! Don't want to be the one with the gun either. Man, I couldn't answer those questions. Whew! It's a trick they do.

"In YA it's righteously divide and conquer. The black brothers are sitting here, the white boys are sitting there, the brown dudes here, and the Chinese dudes, they're all over the place. The black boys are called CBP—Cool Black People. The white dudes are called the straights—no one talks to them. And then La Raza. It's a cold trick, man. It's a game, and the Man advocates it all the time.

"I got in quite a few fights. I stuck with La Raza. I had to, 'cause as soon as I walked in, they said, 'Ese' [a slang greeting among Chicanos] so I had to go, whether I liked it or not. I knew that much.

"I was in one riot. And I was with La Raza. I never stopped to realize this until not too long ago, really. But when you think about it, it's a bad scene. These dudes are ready to kill each other. I seen companies fight each other just because they're in that company and if you don't fight, you're no good, you know? Then the Man comes in. He don't say, Halt; he just comes in and *whoosh! whoosh!* I got punched in the head a couple of times with billyclubs. I split; I crawled away. Then they got to launching them gas things. I don't know if it's the same gas they use at Berkeley, but if it is, it's some cold gas. The place gets to looking like smog all over.

"I get in a lot of fights. If you say the wrong thing to anybody, you're in a fight. I ended up staying there a year and a half. Whew! It's hard to get out of them places.

"I finally got out and went home. They don't have no program to adjust you back; they just shoot you straight out. Some dudes come out okay, because they can take it. But for a person that doesn't know anything and hasn't been around, a year is a long time to be away from the streets. You still think you're in the steel and concrete jungle.

"I stayed out a year and got into trouble again. They gave me parole, but I got in trouble again and they shot me to Preston. I got out after seven months. Then I got in trouble again. The parole officer was saying, 'Preston or Tracy?'* And I was saying, 'Camp.'

"He says, 'Have you worked?' I ain't too good on work; I don't know what work is, really. But I did have one job for $1.99 an hour gardening in Golden Gate Park. I said that's the only work I had. He said, 'What makes you think you can make it?' I had a few calluses from carrying flower cans. I said, 'I got these calluses.' And the dude says, 'Okay, we'll get you into camp.'

"The board member didn't like me; he says, 'I know you're gonna run away in a week's time.'

"And I says, 'Can I make a liar out of you?'

"He says, 'I hope you do.'

"So we drove through all these hills. You didn't even want to

* Preston School of Industry, a Youth Authority facility; Deuel Vocational Institute at Tracy, California.

run, 'cause you couldn't find your way out. I met some people there I knew, but I was the youngest cat there—seventeen.

"Now, camp is a good place. It didn't make any difference what color you are. No racism at all; if there was, then I was blind. It was a nice place, because everybody was working hard to maintain a righteous morale within the company.

"They give you one of these righteous steel helmets, and big combat boots. Hey, you're righteously out there logging it! The boots come up high in case rattlesnakes bite you. And see, when you go to fight them forest fires, limbs fall out of the trees. That's why they give you a helmet, in case the branch would fall and hit you in the head.

"They righteously take care of you. They feed you good. They give you steaks at night. In the morning you get eggs. If you want six or seven eggs, they give it to you, with pancakes.

"I wasn't very strong. I wasn't used to work like that: I never did any. They put me with this Spanish cat and he told me he was gonna work me hard the first day. We'd be down on the ground sawing and I'd say, 'Break! Break!' It got to the point where my arms were stiff. I couldn't move. And everybody's talking: Ah, new boy got hurt. After a week, it ain't nothing. And they give you a new boy, so you do your thing back to him.

"Then I came down with a sickness I don't understand how I got. It was hepatitis. I only know one kind of hepatitis and that's from that thing you do in your arm. And I *know* I don't do that: I'd never done that. And I says, Oh my goodness, how am I gonna explain this?

"The next day they take me to a hospital. They take these blood tests. 'You're sick, man,' they says. Yeah, I'm sick. So what am I gonna do? They shoot me to Perkins [Northern California Reception Center at Perkins] and they keep me in the room for two months—laying in the bed. I went crazy in the room. The Man kept telling me, 'You're a hype, you're a hype.' And I don't know what a hype is, you know?

"After two months they let me out of the room. They shot me back to the board, the same man. He said, 'I see you're back from camp; what for, running away?'

"I says, 'No, man, I wasn't running away.'

"He says, 'How good you doing?'

"I said, 'You got my record there.' I had been there for two months. And it said: 'This boy would be an asset if he got to settle down to the work.'

"So the man said, 'That's better than nothing. At least you didn't run away.'

"I said, 'Well, does that make you a liar?'

"He said, 'Liar? Oh!' And he laughs.

"My liver was still infected, so they told me to rest. One day the Man calls me down and tells me I got to talk to these kids 'cause they're on the verge of getting in trouble. So me, a black cat and a white dude all go up to this room and there are all little kids, nine, ten, eleven years old. We were supposed to make the place sound *bad*. Like, don't come here, or you're really gonna get it.

"Well, this black brother was rapping to them about black dignity, black community. And I listened to him. It made sense to me, you know? We told our different sides of the story and then we got in a conversation between black and brown people. He says, 'I don't see no difference; it's just a trick the Man has made to make us go at each other's throats.' He says, 'Me, I've always known brown people. I'm even getting to the point where I don't think white people's as bad as they say.' This dude is from Oakland. And he tells me a little bit about the Panther party. Oh man, I don't want to hear about them! 'Cause at the time, they seemed like a cold-blooded gang. People in jail, some of them looked at it as a gang, not a political thing really, until the Panthers started coming out more.

"I never ran away. It entered my mind, but I'd say to myself, if I run now, I got to pay the consequences later. Where you gonna go? 'Cause if you run away and get committed to YA, it's one year straight, plus the time you had to serve.

"I knew by now how to feist the Man; I know what he wants to see in me. I'm gonna have to keep going good, and I'm gonna be just like he wants me to be. Then he says, 'You're doing good, you're gonna get out and be a good citizen in society. You're gonna be one of them high-class citizens, you know. Go get your

Cadillac.' You say, Yeah, yeah, yeah, sure. You know, everybody in jail is talking about big cars, houses and things. That's fine if you want it, you know. But the game the Man plays is that he always makes you think you're better than everybody else.

"That black brother and me, we was talking to the Man for different things. There had never been a Christmas furlough in Perkins the whole time anybody been there. So we organized Christmas furloughs for dudes that won't run. Like, they made me the first one. The Man explains to me, 'You're the first boy getting this. And with your record, I don't know how you did it. If you blow it, don't get caught, you understand?'—he's trying to force me to run.

"I got in this car with this dude. He drives me to the bus station; he says, 'Get out.' I got out of his car and shut the door, told him Merry Christmas and all that. I went into the bus station and bought me some big sunglasses. When they called the bus, I got on.

"It seemed like a long ride. Every time you go, it's a fast one, but on the way back, it's looong. I had gone this road so much that I could almost tell what was ahead.

"We finally got to the Bay Bridge and I yelled, 'Yippee!' real loud. The old lady next to me said, 'What's wrong, kid?'

"I said, 'Lady, you wouldn't understand.'

"First thing I did was call my parole officer and say, 'Hey, is there any way you can arrange for me to be released while I'm out here? 'Cause I was due to be back anyway.' I even went to see him. And I did get released. I got a phone call from Sacramento, and the Man says, 'What are you doing at home? Why ain't you out looking for a job?'

"I says, 'I'm on my way now. What you stopping me for?'

"And he says, 'You're released. How do you feel?'

" 'I don't know, man, I done went this trip a hundred times,' I tell him.

"He says, 'You ain't got no feelings.' Man, it ain't nothing no more, you know?

"I was eighteen now [1968]. I walked down Mission Street, and it had *changed*, you know? I didn't see no dudes in slacks no more. Blue jeans. There's a lot of things going around. The Brown Berets* coming on. The so-called new rock music, which I didn't dig at first. Taking acid, I usually don't mess with that stuff. I did drop acid, though; it was an accident. Boy, what a trip! I righteously freaked out, man. I seen diamonds falling from the sky, horses running up and down mountains ... whew! I can't even remember half the things that happened. Gone for three days. It ended up the police showed up, kicked down the door and I got in a fight with them; they maced me and I stayed in the hospital for a week.

"I don't like that stuff. It makes me do things I don't need to do. There's a lot of people within La Raza that taste it, and they're gone. Some people say you smoke weed, you're gonna end up shooting heroin. Well, I don't believe that. But I seen three or four friends that almost OD'ed. And I know for a fact that you can't talk nice to a hype. You know he's lying to you. I get so mad, I grab the dudes. 'Man, why you doping, man? You're killing yourself!' If a dude's no good and he's killing himself, I'll even tell him don't do it. But especially when the dude's a good friend of yours, you been through years with the cat—you don't want to see him go like that. It's a heavy trip, man.

"And it's righteously in the Mission, too. I seen a lot of hypes; they say, 'I'm naked, man, 'cause I ain't got my rig.' I don't see how they feel naked; they didn't come with it, really. I seen a twelve-year-old boy shoot up. And he asked me if I wanted to do it! These white-collared people, they sit in their office and talk about Stopping Drugs. They ain't gonna be able to stop drugs. But I believe if people got their ideology together and righteously told the people where it was at, and they righteously led them, well then we could start acting against those things. But how can we do anything if we don't control our own communities? Someone like me that's been in the Mission knows where drugs is coming from, how it gets in. People in the community can stop it."

* One of the early brown movement groups. See page 51.

3. We Wanted to Start the Revolution Then and There

Some of the changes Pinky noticed when he got out of jail had to do with rising political consciousness among La Raza people. A brown movement was beginning, which would replace feelings of hopelessness and inferiority among La Raza with pride and determination to change the conditions of their lives. This movement got its start in 1965 with the struggle of chicano farmworkers in California's San Joaquin Valley. Cesar Chavez, Dolores Huerta and other organizers had founded the National Farm Workers Association (later the United Farmworkers Organizing Committee) in Delano, California, and in October 1965 joined with a largely Filipino union to strike against Delano grape growers for higher wages and union recognition. The growers refused to recognize the union and pretended there was no strike. They sprayed pesticides near the strikers, got injunctions against bullhorns and rallies, and imported scabs from skid rows, depressed rural areas, and Mexico. The workers turned to boycotting Delano's second largest grape grower, the Schenley Corporation.

The strike and boycott captured the imaginations of chicanos and other sympathetic people across the country. In San Francisco protesters succeeded in stopping grape shipments when longshoremen refused to cross their picket line. The farmworkers' symbol, a stylized eagle derived from an Aztec migration myth,* appeared on buttons and, as graffiti, on the walls of Mission High.

In March 1966 the farmworkers held a pilgrimage through three hundred miles of California's San Joaquin Valley, from Delano to Sacramento. They marched behind an image of the Virgin of Guadalupe, Mexico's patron saint, the same saint whose image was carried by Miguel Hidalgo and the Indians of his parish when they began the war for Mexican independence in 1810.

"We are conscious of the historical significance of our pilgrimage," the NFWA (National Farm Workers Association) wrote in its Plan of Delano.

> It is clearly evident that our paths travel through a valley well known to all Mexican farmworkers ... because along this very same road, in this very same valley, the Mexican race has sacrificed itself for the last hundred years. . . .
>
> We are sons of the Mexican Revolution, a revolution of the poor seeking bread and justice. . . . Across the San Joaquin Valley, across California, across the entire Southwest of the United States, wherever there are Mexican people, wherever there are farmworkers, our movement is spreading like flames across a dry plain.

When the farmworkers arrived in Sacramento they learned that Schenley had finally agreed to come to the bargaining table. Eventually all the wine growers accepted the union. A few years later the huge table-grape-growing corporations began to give in. The struggle spread to other parts of the country, and to other crops.

Among those who marched to Sacramento was a young chi

---

* According to Luis Valdez, a picket captain in the early days of the Delano strike and later the founder of *El Teatro Campesino*: "Nezahualcoyotl, great Indian leader, advised his primitive *chichimecas*, forerunners of the Aztecs, to begin a march to the south. In that march, he promised, the children would age and the old would die; but their grandchildren would come to a great lake. In that lake they would find an eagle devouring serpent, and on that spot they would begin to build a great nation."

cano from south Texas, Aaron Manganiello. Manganiello was already a veteran of civil rights sit-ins, jazz tours with John Handy's Freedom Band, and Berkeley's Vietnam Day Committee. He would eventually have a strong influence on three of Los Siete—Mario and Tony Martinez and Nelson Rodriguez—and on the political direction of the organization that grew up around their case. (Manganiello was one of the first to emphasize the need for brown radicals to study Marxist literature.) With the growth of the farmworkers' struggle, Manganiello, like many other politically minded brown people, saw the need for some kind of organized movement in the urban barrios.

The Brown Berets were one response to this need. Founded by David Sanchez, who was once elected Los Angeles's "outstanding high school student," the Berets combined paramilitary-type training with a desire to establish cultural and political self-determination for La Raza in the Southwest, the area which the chicano movement calls *Aztlán*.* In March 1968 the Berets led a massive walkout of chicano high school students in Los Angeles. They were demanding courses in their cultural history, teachers who lived in their communities, bilingual instruction, an end to corporal punishment, and an end to students' doing janitorial work. The walkout spread the name of the Brown Berets across the Southwest, and many young chicanos began, unofficially, to call themselves Berets.

Aaron Manganiello and a friend, Manuel Gomez, convinced the Los Angeles Berets to let them set up an official Northern California branch in Oakland. Chapters soon spread to barrios in dozens of cities throughout the country. The chapters varied in their political outlook. Many were strongly "cultural nationalist," believing that Raza cultural unity was the best basis for organizing; others disagreed, feeling that this perspective was too narrow and could become damaging if an attachment to cultural traditions were to stand in the way of change.

* An Indian word meaning "lands to the north"—originally, north of the present site of Mexico City. Often used nowadays to mean the southwestern United States.

Cultural nationalism had a tremendous appeal for young chicanos and latinos. Cultural symbols used in the mid-sixties by the grape strikers in Delano quickly popularized the rich artistic and mythical heritage of Mexico and Central America. Raza *teatros* produced some of the best and most inventive political theater in the country. Like many black people, whose political awakening began with the "black is beautiful" slogan, the chicanos and latinos began to organize themselves largely around common cultural and racial interests.

But as the Raza movement grew and began to analyze conditions in the United States, some of its leaders came to believe that cultural nationalism was only a phase—perhaps a necessary phase—and that in the long run, class interests would be more important than racial or cultural ones, and that poor brown people would be better off allying with poor blacks and whites than with their own middle class. Aaron Manganiello believed this and eventually had to leave the Brown Berets for this reason.

In the meantime the Berets had attracted some of the most politically aware brown youth in San Francisco, including students like Donna James and Roger Alvarado, who would later be involved in forming the Los Siete defense organization. South of San Francisco, in the Palo Alto area, Ralph Ruiz and Nelson Rodriguez became Berets. Donna James remembers the San Francisco group sponsored dances and once attempted a cleanup of Mission Street.

The Berets concentrated their organizing on cultural themes. Bebe Melendez remembers: "Once they held a Brown Beret festival in Dolores Park, back in '68. I heard the poem 'I am Joaquin.'* They used Mission High School as a theater. The brothers got a projector, and the film had pictures of Mayan and Incan ruins and scenes of Mexico, Guatemala, Honduras. They played the guitar with the congas. It really sounded *bad!* I walked out of that auditorium with tears in my eyes. It was beautiful."

* By Rodolfo "Corky" Gonzales, a leading chicano organizer in Denver. This poem was made into a movie which was shown at the Brown Beret festival.

Gary "Pinky" Lescallett also related to the Berets, at least to the extent that he carried a brown beret in his back pocket. For Pinky it was the first time that any group had articulated many of his own feelings—the desire to share what he had with his people, even if he had stolen it from someone else; the need for a positive cultural identity, an outlet for his feelings of violence against "the system."

But by late 1968 most of the San Francisco Berets had scattered; many became involved in college strikes. In other cities, the Brown Berets continue to be one of the most popular and diverse Raza movement groups.

Donna James remembers she had hardly been aware of the existence of a brown movement before the middle of 1968 (shortly before the Brown Berets came into the Mission). She was attending San Francisco State College that May when a friend asked if she'd like to join the Bay Area contingent to the Poor People's Campaign in Washington. She went along, not knowing what to expect. There, she and the other brown people from the Bay Area met young Puerto Ricans from New York, as well as radical chicanos from Denver and northern New Mexico. They spent many hours together exchanging information. On the way home Donna stopped in New Mexico with some of the people she had met, among them Reies Lopez Tijerina.

Tijerina was an important symbol for the new brown movement. On June 5, 1967, he and several other chicanos, members of an organization called the *Alianza* (the Alliance of Free City-States), had staged a "raid" on the county courthouse in the poor rural New Mexico town of Tierra Amarilla. They wanted to make a citizen's arrest of the local district attorney. He wasn't there, but the action—in which there was much shooting and some policemen were held captive—focused worldwide attention on the struggle of rural chicanos to regain land that had been taken from them through a hundred years of legal chicanery and outright theft. Although northern New Mexico differed greatly from urban barrios like the Mission district, young latins could relate to Tijerina, as to Villa and Zapata before him, as a fighter for La Raza.*

Young latinos in the Mission had other, lesser known, heroes. One was the Nicaraguan Augusto Cesar Sandino, who developed many methods of modern guerrilla warfare while fighting the U.S. Marine occupation of Nicaragua during the 1920s. Another, popular throughout California, was the Mexican Joaquin Murieta, a legendary rebel of Gold Rush days who, as the story goes, vowed revenge on all Anglos after a gang of them hanged his brother, raped and killed his wife, and drove him from his mining claim. But, according to many young latinos and at least one California historian, Murieta "had higher aims than mere pillage and revenge. His continuous conflict with military and civil authorities, and with the armed populace, would in any other country than America have been dignified with the term revolution."†

In the middle and late sixties, political awareness developed through the independent brown movement: young people started joining organizations like the Brown Berets or, on college campuses, "Brown Heritage" clubs and "Third World Liberation Fronts." At the same time, another (not always distinct) vehicle for political education developed in the federally funded poverty programs—counseling and job-training programs in the ghetto, "Upward Bound" programs to motivate low-income kids to go to college, Economic Opportunity programs to support them when they got there. In the Mission district the largest and most important of these programs was the "Mission Rebels in Action." Although the Rebels organization had basically reformist goals— more jobs, better education, recreation facilities for ghetto youth—it often had radical rhetoric. It was in the Rebels that Bebe Melendez got his first political education.

* In 1969, two years after the courthouse raid, Tijerina was jailed on charges arising from the raid and subsequent confrontations with the police. In July 1971 he was freed on bail, pending appeal of an assault conviction. (*See* Nabokov, Peter, *Tijerina and the Courthouse Raid.* Berkeley: Ramparts Press, 1971—Ed.)

† Hubert Howe Bancroft, quoted in *The Barbary Coast*, by Herbert Ashbury (New York: Capricorn, 1968).

II

Bebe, like Pinky, had discovered early that street life led to trouble.

"The Man took us off to the Juvenile Hall," Bebe says, remembering one of his early busts. "He was saying, 'We're gonna throw the book at you; we're gonna throw the book at your mother, punk!' I felt pretty bad 'cause I had just gotten out of Juvenile. Hall the week before. I thought they were gonna send me away for good. That visiting day my parents said, 'How would you like to go to Honduras?' At first I didn't want to go, 'cause I dug Frisco, you know? I dug running around the streets. I liked being with my partners, smoking, that culture. But my parents manipulated me into going. [The same thing happened to José Rios once in Juvenile Hall. He took a trip to El Salvador rather than go to jail.]

"When I got back I got busted for car theft and went to Log Cabin. I was fifteen. Cabin's a camp; they tell you it's not a jail—they don't have no walls. But shit, they still tell you when to go to bed and when to smoke and when to get up and when to brush your teeth.

"We would go half a day to school and half a day to work. They don't teach you nothing. You go to English classes, they give you crossword puzzles to work out. Science classes ain't nothing but a bunch of movies. All we seen was baseball movies in science class. The teachers were nothing but athletic freaks.

"After Cabin I had one job, landscaping, for $1.35 an hour. I was just waiting, 'cause I couldn't get back into school that month. A bunch of us went to this Neighborhood Youth Corps and they gave us $1.35 an hour to dig holes. They tell you to dig a ditch and that ditch will become a reservoir someday and all you got paid for it was $1.35. They tell us, 'That's all you're good for.'

"So me and this brother, we would go up on the hill and just watch everybody else work, and smoke our grass. We'd go down and tell them we did this and that, and they'd pay us. After a month was up, I went back to school.

"But I quit around two months later, because I told the Man to go to hell. He demanded an apology from me for coming late to school. I told him, 'Why should I apologize to you?'

"He says, 'Because I'm the Dean of Boys.'

"I says, 'So what? I'm one of the boys that employs you.' So the Man tells me not to come back to school.

"I tried to get a job—not $1.35 an hour digging holes, though. I was thinking about a job at the airport where they train you, first as a janitor, then as a mechanic. I took mechanics at Cabin and I kind of dug it. So I tried to get into this program. They said no, I couldn't qualify. Every place I went, I never got the jobs. You just get disillusioned after so many turn-downs, you know? I knew why I wasn't getting them. It's just that the Man doesn't dig your color. I don't see what color has to do with a job when it's the brains and the hands that work. But the Man has these colors in his eyes and he thinks only his is the best. Well, he's crazy. He calls us wetbacks, greasers—that's okay. La Raza is beautiful!

"I got busted for drugs. They took me down to Potrero Hill Station, and they was saying, 'What's your name?'

"I said, 'You know everything—you tell me.'

"Man says, 'Look, if I book you as John Doe, I'm gonna kick your ass.'

"I said, 'You know what? If you take off that badge, I'll fight you.' So he takes off his badge, but he comes in with six other pigs! So they did me in at Potrero Hill Station.*

"Then they start bringing in these bags they had. These bags look kind of familiar; I know what they are. So he says, 'Hey, doper.' I don't answer that, you know. 'Look, John Doe, you been pushing pretty heavily.'

" 'Not so much as you push.'

"He tells me, 'Why don't you come clean? You cop out to this and we'll forget about everything else.'

" 'I ain't copping to nothing, man. You'll have to prove it.'

"So he goes, 'Aw well, we'll just put it down on the record.' Then he reaches in my pocket and like I ain't got nothing in my pocket, but he pulls out a lid. He says, 'We got you now.'

* Pinky Lescallett describes similar police beatings in station houses. Removal of the badge seemed to be part of the ritual.

56

"At court they told me YA [Youth Authority]. Goddamn! So two weeks later I went to Perkins. I was busted with a lot of people I was doing business with. It was a pattern—we all got busted. Somebody was snitching on us. But we couldn't find out who it was. We was all in the joint trying to figure out who. They shot me to Preston for a four- to twelve-month institutional referral. I was just convicted of possession. They couldn't prove I sold anything.

"It's terrible to be kicking. Even though I wasn't really *on,* righteously. But I would get the urge. When I went to YA they had to give me some downers. Shot me to Preston, put me in this drug addict program. That don't do any good. They tell you the same old thing. You get up and talk. It don't work.

"In Preston I was in kitchen—culinary arts! It's called Preston School of Industry. You're supposed to go there and learn a trade. Hell, anybody can mop floors or clean a table off. They just don't teach you nothing. It's a waste of the people's money.

"After I got out of Preston, I got into the carpenter's program at the Mission Rebels. Carpentry half a day and school the rest."

III

The Mission Rebels began, according to local legend, in November 1965 when a black reverend named Jesse James was approached by some brothers asking for money to buy wine. James said, "You don't need wine, man; you need something else," and set up a rap session at a nearby church. Less than a year later the sessions had grown into a non-profit corporation, Mission Rebels in Action. A year after that the Rebels got their first anti-poverty funds.

They instituted a job-training program called Operation Opportunity, sponsored cultural events, and became a place for street youth to hang out—in a barrio with very few recreation facilities. Their ideology combined the cultural pride which was so current among black and brown youth with a desire to be recognized both inside and outside the community as spokesmen and leaders. They chose as their motto, "Please, we would rather do it ourselves—all we ask is the opportunity."

Despite their emphasis on "making it," the Rebels were a vehicle for spreading radical consciousness. "We had one righteous teacher in the carpenter's program named Sonia Sanchez,"* Bebe remembers. "A black sister in the Panthers married to a Puerto Rican brother. She taught us math and everything, but she was *interesting*. She started giving us political education. She really got to us. We wanted to start the revolution then and there.

"She started off reading us some black and brown poetry. Then she would get down on capitalism and imperialism, why we were still in the ghetto. See, a lot of brothers in the Mission were aware, but yet we really couldn't express ourselves. We knew the Man as a dog or pig. We didn't know him in terms of exploiter or oppressor.

"I was digging the education we were getting. I asked her for some books. She gave me *Che Speaks,* some other works of Che, *Black Boy,* and some other literature. I took them home and read them all. After that you wouldn't see me without a book of Che in my back pocket.

"Sonia had to split: the Man was coming down hard on her. When she split I stopped going to classes. I just came to pick up my check [$80 every two weeks for being a work counselor].

"One day," Bebe says, "we was supposed to hold a meeting in one of the classes, and they got to talking about revolution. They asked for somebody to talk. I told them, 'Man, you gotta know who the enemy is—we can't just be popping caps at everybody.'

"There was one black brother saying, 'Well, why do we have to have an enemy?'

"I say, 'Why do we have to live in this ghetto?'

"He says, 'Because we dig it.'

"I says, 'No, it's not 'cause we dig it. It's because the Man makes us live here. Because he don't want us to get out of these ghettoes. And the only way we're gonna get out is when we start

* Sonia Sanchez had been the center of a controversy at S.F. State's experimental college when administrators objected to giving credit for her poetry course. They eventually conceded, but the dispute was a portent of things to come at State.

58

practicing unity and self-defense. . . . We should work inside the community to gain political knowledge. Political education is one of the steps toward revolution. And when you start practicing self-defense, there's your second step. And when the masses start thinking in one term, of one road, then let's go get it. Let's get what belongs to us.' "

How much of Bebe's political education was talk and how much was commitment remained to be seen. Eventually, though, the radicals (like Bebe) and the reformists in the federally financed programs, both in the ghettoes and on the campuses, would have to clash; and it was inevitably the radicals who left, or were kicked out, and returned to the independent brown movement.

Another federally financed program, Upward Bound, brought tough kids from ghetto schools to San Francisco State for the summers. "The idea was to give us the motivation to go on in school," says José Delgado, one of the Mission High students who got into Upward Bound in 1967, and who two years later became part of the Los Siete organization. "But the program backfired on them the very first summer. The dorms were a wreck, with a couple of TVs broken. We didn't relate to the teachers, who were mostly white liberals. They would bring us to talk to these classes for secondary school teachers. We had to tell them what we thought was wrong with the schools. This was supposed to make us believe they cared what we thought, to give us motivation."

Although many of the kids in the Upward Bound program didn't respond to these attempts to motivate them, they did develop political ties among themselves. José Delgado remembers that one of their major subjects of discussion—as in Youth Authority prisons around this time—was the young Black Panther Party. Discussion soon led to activism. Back at Mission High the next year, Delgado and a few other students began to challenge their civics teacher's version of history. In the hallways they pasted up antiwar posters which said, "NO VIETNAMESE EVER CALLED ME NIGGER."

Like Upward Bound, the Mission Rebels had programs which

sometimes backfired. One of their first activities in the promotion of private enterprise among ghetto youth, a candy sales operation handled by a New York contractor, grossed $1,000–$2,000 a month but came under State Labor Commission scrutiny as a possible violation of child labor laws. (It also became known that promoters in other California cities were sending kids out to pose as Rebels salesmen, selling candy at inflated prices in the purported interests of helping the ghetto poor.)

Meanwhile, in their first four years of existence the Rebels collected almost $800,000 in federal funds, in addition to individual, church, and business donations, candy sales, and receipts from a janitorial business. In one year they received almost $400,000 from the government.

These federal funds were often based on a system of matching grants. Edlo Powell, the young black man who replaced Jesse James as president, had to spend a good deal of time fund-raising among wealthy liberals, as did other ranking Rebels. As a staff member once described it, there were three levers to pull when fund-raising: white guilt, the specter of the alternative (presumably riots—perhaps even revolution), and person-to-person contact. Rebels officers became necessarily glib, and, though they probably wouldn't admit it, a little contemptuous of their constituents. One day a sign appeared on the door of the Rebels' office: "This office is for secretary and staff. It is not to be used as a hangout."

Sometimes Rebels officers seemed to ignore the membership. During the summer of 1969, one officer was cited by a *San Francisco Chronicle* music columnist as a "Third World" type who endorsed an upcoming "Wild West" rock festival which had been attacked by many radical artists and musicians as a "ripoff."

"Half the Mission Rebels didn't even know what the Wild West Show was," a secretary in the Rebels office later said, "and certain people didn't feel it was right for [the officer in question] to represent the Mission Rebels the way he did." But the Rebels officer responded that he was *the* spokesman for the Mission Rebels.

The real problem with the Rebels, as with any federally funded group, was the limit imposed on its activities by the government—and in the Rebels' case, by an adult board of directors which mediated between government and ghetto. For example, Operation Motivation was an educational program in which ghetto kids were supposed to be hired as junior high and high school counselors on the assumption that they could best communicate with their peers. In planning Motivation, the board of directors advised the Rebels to reduce their request from sixty counselor salaries to twenty-five. One director explained, "Sixty would be out of the question in this day and age . . . with this political climate."

Twenty counselors were finally approved. Although this meant an expenditure of about $100,000 in salaries alone for the year's operation, twenty counselors would have little effect on the vast majority of the city's junior high and high school students. Said one Rebels staffer philosophically: "Crumbs is all this community ever gets."

The alternatives for those involved were either to accept the crumbs, thereby achieving a measure of personal status and social mobility, or to become disillusioned with the limited and divisive nature of federal programs. Bebe Melendez, who was probably just not smooth or ambitious enough to "make it" in the Rebels hierarchy, took the latter course.

"When they were putting together Operation Motivation," Bebe relates, "counseling jobs were supposed to go to people from seventeen to twenty-one. But the jobs were given to people from twenty-one on up. We were the ones who promoted this program. We were the ones who should say who gets the jobs. But the staff was running it.

"So at this meeting I jumped up and started calling them a bunch of motherfuckers. 'Look, man,' I said, 'you tell me this and then you turn around and do something else. You can stick it up your ass, man, 'cause if you tell me I have the power over something, I'm gonna use that power to benefit the rest of the people.'

"They said, 'Sure, sure, you have the power. We just want to make sure the power's not abused in any way. 'Cause we have the right to fire any staff.'

"So I says, *'You're fired.'*

"He got mad and said, 'You can't tell me that.'

" 'What do you mean? You just told me I can.'

"He said, 'You're just one individual. What do the rest of the people say?'

"They said, 'You're fired.' They had to close down the meeting. We felt the people that had the jobs weren't equal to us. Some of them owned houses and had nice apartments, while the rest of us didn't have nothing. So we wrote a petition, and mostly all the people in the Rebels signed it, saying, 'These are the people we want to be fired.' After that petition got through the board of directors we found our voice didn't mean nothing. So next day I told Powell, 'Take my job, I don't need it.'

"What the Rebels were trying to do—and I didn't realize it then—was trying to make Tio Tacos and Uncle Toms out of all the brothers down there, and I was falling into that bag. I was thinking I want to be director of that motherfucker.

"When I was with Sonia [Sanchez] I was starting this Spanish culture program. But that went down the drain 'cause Edlo Powell was talking about separating the group.* I got disillusioned. The Rebels turned out to be hypocrites."

* Powell and Jesse James were both black, as was much of the membership.

4. The Man

I

In the same years when political awareness was beginning to change the lives of young people in the Mission, plans were being made to transform the district and the entire city. In 1967 a prominent corporation lawyer named Joseph Alioto, a Democrat, was elected mayor of San Francisco, and an accelerated drive to redevelop and reorient the city began. Although the average resident didn't know it, the Mission district would be a major target of redevelopment. What the average resident *did* know was that the street-level representatives of the power structure—the police—were becoming increasingly hostile, behaving more like an occupying army than like protectors of citizens' rights. Joseph Brodnik and Paul McGoran, veteran cops in the Mission, were good examples.

"There used to be a time, Friday nights," Bebe Melendez remembers, "when everybody would be going to a dance. And we had a favorite spot to hang out, the Doggie Diner on Eighteenth and Mission. Everybody would meet there around 7:30, 8:00, see who comes by, who's going to the dance. Well, one particular night when I first met Brodnik and McGoran I had been going to Salon Mejico, to a dance, and I had a little fifth of wine with me. I was going to feel good, same thing everybody does. . . .

"Next thing I knew a white pickup drove up and McGoran called out, 'Hey, punk, come here.'

"I started looking around. I told him, 'There ain't no punk here.'

"He said, 'I'm talking to *you.*' I asked him what he wanted. He just told me, come here, and he grabbed my wine and threw the bottle away, and I started walking away, and he spun me around and hit me with his fist. I still got a scar [where McGoran drove Bebe's teeth through his lip].

"Then they threw me in the back of the truck and they dumped my wine and drove me all the way up to Twenty-third past Castro [in Noe Valley]. Then McGoran told me, 'Get out.'

"So I get out and say, 'Now what?'

"They say, 'Walk back.' I walked back but I was mad. I went to that dance mad.

"The second time, same thing. I was going to a dance; they had a paddy wagon and was just busting a lot of people. I got smart with one of those pigs, and I got my ass whipped. They drove us all the way up and made us walk back to the Mission."

Brodnik and McGoran were well known in the district, not only among young latinos. Like much of the Irish Catholic brass in the police department, Brodnik and McGoran grew up in the Mission and attended Mission High School during the patriotic wartime years. McGoran's police career began in 1952, after stints in the Navy, then as a milkman, and later as an Army MP. Brodnik was a Mission High athletic star and in 1946 led his alma mater to the first all-city basketball championship in her then fifty-year history. After graduation he married his high school sweetheart, Jessie Crosby, and went into the furniture business. He joined the police force in September 1956. His wife later explained, "He had a lot of friends in the department. It seemed like a good life." They settled in Eureka Valley, west of the Mission, and had three children. McGoran, who lived in Pacifica, along the coast south of San Francisco, had four.

Brodnik and McGoran became a team in March 1966. Called Mission Eleven, they were the only plainclothesmen officially attached to Mission Station. Their specific assignment was daylight burglaries, but their day-to-day work was more varied. Brodnik and McGoran were zealous cops. Once in a Twenty-fourth Street steam room they arrested a prominent Methodist minister because, they claimed, he had made advances to them.

Brodnik and McGoran were known by many of the local residents and small businessmen in the Mission and Noe Valley. People would sometimes point them out admiringly as they drove past in their familiar white truck. Perhaps this was because many white people in the Mission and Noe Valley had come to consider the police their political representatives—in an increasingly nonwhite city. The Irish, for instance, had had seven representatives on the eleven-man Board of Supervisors in 1960; in 1970 they had none. With many working-class Irish residents (as well as Italians, Germans and East Europeans), Noe Valley was a stronghold of local conservatism.

Brodnik's local reputation got a boost in October of 1967 when he cleverly caught a would-be burglar in the act. "Policeman Joe Brodnik has a photographic memory," the *San Francisco Examiner* reported. "Off duty, he was shopping in a supermarket ... when he recognized another shopper using the phone. He had arrested him for burglary years ago. When the fellow walked out, Brodnik followed. A few blocks away the ex-con tried in vain to jimmy the doors of three homes, obviously those he had phoned to make sure no one was there. When he got into the fourth home, Brodnik made his pinch, and went back to his shopping."

That same year Brodnik and McGoran developed the idea of leafleting Twin Peaks on the perils of daytime burglary. In their first effort they distributed a thousand leaflets asking residents to phone police "if you see a suspicious auto or person in your neighborhood." Police said burglaries in the area were soon reduced from eight or ten a day to one or two. The technique was widely praised and imitated by departments across the country.

"He was without any bigotry," a clerk at Mission Station said later of Brodnik. "He spent hours doing everything possible to help young people involved in crime." But young people in the Mission remember a two-foot rubber hose Brodnik carried with him to use on uncooperative suspects. Ralph Ruiz, a founder of the Los Siete organization and a close friend of Nelson Rodriguez and the Martinez brothers, called Brodnik's good-guy approach "just a pig trick. [He] played the good guy and [McGoran] played the motherfucker." Police sometimes call this a "Mutt and Jeff" routine.

As McGoran described this technique at the trial: "I would play the part of the bad guy to an extent . . . that I didn't want to give anybody a break. And Joe would always say, 'Let's give him a break,' and we'd talk it over in front of them. If they wanted to give us information to lead us on to other and greater arrests, other criminals, and they would be willing to talk, we'd give them a break and release them."

McGoran used to say that someday he was "going to take Brodnik and teach him how to be a policeman"; that Brodnik was "a minister and handled people with kid gloves too much." Brodnik responded that McGoran "had a violent temper" and was "too much with his gun."

II

The good guy-bad guy routine was not just an act. It represented in microcosm a conflict between progressive and reactionary methods of maintaining the status quo which permeated the whole San Francisco Police Department. In the early sixties, pressures from liberal civic leaders had led to the formation of the police Community Relations Unit (CRU) to smooth dealings with minorities. Police Chief Thomas Cahill, a barrel-chested, thick-brogued Irishman, also a Mission High alumnus, was reluctant to form the unit but was finally convinced after a near-riot situation in which a black crowd disarmed a cop who was chasing a teenager, gave the teenager the gun and said, "Go ahead and kill him." The CRU, according to Cahill, would "teach minorities respect for law and order."

A tough twenty-two-year veteran, Dante Andreotti, was named head of the new unit. But Andreotti, and other policemen assigned to the CRU, experienced a strange transformation: they began to see the world from the ghetto point of view. "I had no ideas, no background, no experience," Andreotti said later. "I learned about community relations from the people in the street, and I am glad for what they taught me."* Community Relations Unit officers job-hunted for convicts so they could get paroled, and for kids with arrest records. They appeared in court on behalf of their constituents.

But fellow cops began to think the CRU was a threat and was working against the department. They called the CRU the "Commie Relations Unit" or rolled down the windows of their patrol cars and yelled "nigger lover" when CRU officers drove by. "Our war was with the police department," Andreotti later said. "We were never successful in getting the message down to the foot soldier: that community relations is the most important job."

Police Chief Cahill's position was "ambiguous," according to Andreotti. He refused to add more blacks to the CRU's staff of fourteen (four of them black). "[Chief Cahill] thought one of them had been planted by the Muslims." After a five-day riot in the black Hunter's Point ghetto, Cahill said, according to Andreotti, "I'll know how to handle this situation next time. After all I did for those people. I was the only police chief in America without a riot. They spoiled my record."

"I told him, 'You ought to be damn glad you had a good Police-Community Relations program going.' "

Andreotti quit in 1967—"out of despair," he said.

Opposition to the CRU from Cahill down to the foot soldier was the product of a generalized reaction within the department. Far from being free of politics, the San Francisco Police Department was overrun with politics. The most dominant trend among members of the two-thousand-man department was right-wing sentiment dosed with racism. Reporters have observed pictures of the Ku Klux Klan Grand Wizard with captions like "Our Hero" in station houses, as well as John Birch Society literature. In June 1971 the San Francisco Crime Committee report on the police observed "controversial political materials . . . ultra-conservative in

---

* Alvin A. Rosenfeld, "The Friendly Fuzz," *The Nation* (April 21, 1969), and Mary Ellen Leary, "San Francisco: The Trouble with Troubleshooting," *Atlantic Monthly* (March 1969).

tone" in station houses. "I did not see any liberal political material," one investigator said.

"Some of the policemen in San Francisco are clear and distinct racists, the type who would be prime Nazi material," one CRU officer said. "There are a number of men in the department that I would immediately fire. There are others I would put in jail because I know what they have done and that is where they belong."

In 1967, the same year Andreotti quit, the elite Tactical Unit was formed as a more repressive response to rebellion in the ghettoes and on college campuses. A month before his election in November 1967, Mayor Alioto had proposed the creation of a "highly trained Mobile Tactical Force that would move into areas of high crime." The new Tactical Unit was specially trained in wrestling, karate, judo, baton use and house-to-house combat, and was specifically intended for riot situations. One sergeant in the unit said his officers must be "outstanding physical specimens . . . we don't want little guys."*

The Tactical Unit—or Tac Squad, as it came to be known—inflicted a record of injuries in its short career which would take many pages to enumerate. In January 1968 the squad attacked peace demonstrators at the Fairmont Hotel on Nob Hill, sweeping the street and cornering some demonstrators in a blind alley. In July, two drunk off-duty Tac Squadders went on a rampage on the southern part of Mission Street, in the Excelsior district, and beat up at least seven youngsters. The two officers had just been relieved from a security detail guarding then–Vice President Hubert Humphrey. Police Chief Cahill admitted to the *San Francisco Chronicle* that "they had been drinking; there is no question about it." The Tac Squad climaxed its career in late 1968 and early 1969 at the San Francisco State College strike, where students, reporters and bystanders were bloodied in unprovoked attacks.

* Kay Boyle, *The Long Walk at San Francisco State* (New York: Grove, 1970).

The young victims of the Excelsior beatings and their parents complained to the Police Commission. Subsequent commission hearings were jammed with citizens who had similar horror stories. They demanded abolition of the Tac Squad. Mayor Alioto responded, "Even the Lord in selecting twelve disciples only got eleven good ones." The Police Commission merely ordered a rotation of Tac Squad members. Six months later the two officers, who had feared dismissal from the force, got only light suspensions. One had been convicted of assault in criminal court and both had been found guilty of assault by the Police Commission. The *Chronicle* reported, "The officers admitted lying in statements to a police investigating team."

Despite more protests of brutality, Cahill and Alioto continued to praise the Tac Squad, citing their excellent record of arrests, over half of them for felonies. In 1971 the San Francisco Crime Committee recommended abolition of the unit, but was met with bitter criticism from the new police chief, Alfred Nelder.

. In 1968 and 1969 many other scandals involving on- and off-duty policemen came to public attention. A young officer, Michael O'Brien, killed a black man after muttering, according to one witness, "I want to kill a nigger so goddamn bad I can taste it." The police at first arrested four blacks for assault but at the insistence of the CRU, and in the face of overwhelming evidence that the blacks were not at fault, charged O'Brien with murder. The grand jury indictment reduced the charge to manslaughter. O'Brien was acquitted in a politically explosive trial. (The presiding superior court judge, Joseph Karesh, was later to play a strange role in the case of Los Siete.) Two others blacks were killed by police in 1969—one a young joyrider in Hunter's Point, the other a man shot on a busy street by a cop moonlighting as a security guard; a teller claimed the man had passed a bad check.

Brutality was not the only problem. In 1969 an alleged police burglary ring was discovered. The department, after a quick investigation, admitted some negligence, but didn't press criminal charges. One disaffected officer told a reporter that cops had been selling hot color TVs for $50 out of the basement of the Hall of Justice. "It was a long time before the old officers accepted me enough to steal in front of me,"* he said. Later in 1969 a cop was suspended for stealing $821 from a black carpenter he had arrested. The next year a police inspector was arrested and subsequently convicted for selling stolen credit cards.

Meanwhile, the CRU had become much less significant. CRU officers had helped citizens file so many complaints that a rule was established prohibiting them from doing more than accompanying the complainant to the proper office. Andreotti was at first replaced by men who lacked his interest in and rapport with ghetto people. In 1969 a new CRU leader, a black man, was harassed and nearly fired for a possible minor dereliction of duty. About a year later another black CRU officer was brought for disciplinary hearings because he failed to address a white superior officer with the proper respect.

In early 1969 the Police Officers Association refused to help a black policeman who had been charged with an off-duty offense (though they had hired their chief counsel to defend Officer O'Brien). The black officers, numbering fewer than a hundred, combined with a few liberal white cops, mostly from the CRU, to form a rival organization, the Officers for Justice. They complained of racism in the department and publicly criticized the San Francisco police administration as being, as one officer said, "based on seniority and cliques and filled with veterans whose police mentality was formed in the 1940s."** But the Officers for Justice remained a small organization with fewer than a hundred members in a department numbering over two thousand.

In 1969 a reporter wrote, "Black and white officers are in open conflict, notably over the handling of arrest situations. On occasion they have engaged in fistfights in the streets; in a few shocking instances guns have been drawn."†

* Robert A. Jones, "San Francisco Police: Black vs. White in the Station House," *The Nation* (October 13, 1969).

** Jones, *op cit.*

† Rosenfeld, *op. cit.*

Only a small sampling of racist or illegal police behavior ever becomes public, as defense attorneys for Los Siete were to show at their trial. The incidents themselves were not just accidents or deviations in an otherwise humane and prejudice-free department. The attitude of much of the police hierarchy toward minorities was later spelled out by Brodnik's niece Colleen Crosby: "Once I tried to ask my uncle about racism in the police department. He said it was a long discussion and he didn't want to get into it. . . . So I asked my cousin [Brodnik's daughter, also named Colleen] about it. She said there was a strong feeling among the San Francisco cops about the brown people in the Mission—that the whole purpose of their lives was to cause trouble. My cousin said they related to latinos in the street as dirty. They said they were going to bring peace to the Mission where the dirty latinos are."

III

The hostile attitude of many cops—especially old-timers of McGoran's and Brodnik's generation—didn't come out of nowhere. Partly it was a product of what the whites saw as threats to their jobs, neighborhoods, and cultural identities posed by the blacks and latinos. And it was encouraged, sometimes actively as in the formation of the Tac Squad, by the incumbent wielders of power in San Francisco—Mayor Joseph Alioto, his political allies in the districts, and the downtown businessmen who provided much of his financial backing. The Los Siete organization was eventually to realize this, and to understand that it would have to expand its attack on what it considered to be police atrocities to include an attack on the decisions about the city's future which made the atrocities possible—decisions which flowed from Mayor Alioto's drive to make San Francisco the financial and business center of the West.

San Francisco is already the "business capital of the Pacific Basin," according to the Chamber of Commerce; "decisions made on the seven prime blocks of Montgomery Street [San Francisco's banking district] affect all of California, the West, and often the nation and the world." But San Francisco also has severe economic problems, among them the ghettoes, declining industry, and a shrinking tax base. Alioto and his backers planned to solve these problems by stepping up the city's business development in hopes that office buildings would replace the vanishing industry and bring the white middle class back to the city. Ben Swig, a Nob Hill hotel owner and one of Alioto's main backers, had announced this strategy of intensive commercial development as far back as 1958: "The whole San Francisco skyline is going to change," Swig predicted. "We're going to have a great building boom, become a second New York."

After Alioto's election in 1967, the new mayor began, as he said, to "beat the bushes" for major corporations willing to build in San Francisco. By 1969 the once low, pastel-colored skyline had begun to disappear under new highrises, the tallest of them the massive Bank of America world headquarters. A pyramid-shaped Transamerica Corporation tower, to be finished in 1972, will be even taller—forty-eight stories. Twelve other skyscrapers are slated for completion before 1976—a total of six hundred new stories of construction. A huge renewal project called Yerba Buena Center is under way in the rundown South of Market area which separates downtown from the Mission district; plans include a convention hall, indoor stadium, Italian cultural center, and sites for Crocker Citizens Bank, Del Monte, and General Electric. Current planning for the waterfront east of downtown includes a four hundred fifty-room luxury hotel with more convention facilities, parking lots, luxury apartments, offices, and headquarters for major corporations. A massive "Embarcadero Center" will include three more office buildings, one of them sixty stories high.

But the new office towers will not provide jobs for many of the latinos—or blacks or Asians—who have moved to San Francisco in the last twenty-five years. Few of them have the clerical or managerial skills required by an expanding commercial center. The industrial and manufacturing jobs for which blacks and latinos came to San Francisco ten or twenty years ago have been diminishing: the city lost nine thousand manufacturing jobs between 1953 and 1966—fourteen percent of its total. Meanwhile, the minority populations have increased. Conceivably minority people could be trained to fill white-collar jobs. But, as Mayor Alioto pointed out in an application for a Model Cities planning grant for the Mission district, "The requirement that a person forego income for even a short period of time for education, training or business development is a requirement few Mission district residents can afford." From a latino's point of view, the revival of the city as the business center of the Pacific Basin offers few opportunities. From the downtown businessman's point of view, most people in the Mission are surplus population. The police sense this and know they can treat latinos with considerably less respect than the white population.

The city's planning energy and access to public funds have been absorbed in the business development drive. In the six years preceding 1969, no low-rent housing was built for families in San Francisco. The little which was built was for the elderly.* Between 1960 and 1969 there was a net decrease of more than three thousand low- and moderate-income housing units, according to the Department of City Planning. San Francisco's policymakers are not interested in housing and the poor; on the contrary, they seem to want to remove the poor from the valuable space they now occupy in the Mission and other districts near the downtown area, and to replace them with middle-class whites drawn in from the suburbs. The president of the Chamber of Commerce spelled this out at a January 1970 press conference: "There is public concern over the plight of the poor, and the rich can take care of themselves, but San Franciscans in the middle-income bracket—$12,000 to $25,000 a year—are the forgotten people." He said the Chamber was working on plans for middle-income housing "convenient to downtown.... The emphasis would be on its main purpose—attracting and holding our middle-income population." The most likely areas for such housing are the black Fillmore district, west of downtown, and the Mission to the south.

The accelerated business development poses several interrelated problems for city planners. First, land is needed close to

* "The Shame of the Cities," a report released in the fall of 1969 by the Citizens Emergency Task Force for a Workable Housing Policy.

downtown for office buildings, trade centers, and apartment houses for white-collar workers. Second, many thousands of new clerical and managerial workers must be recruited—if possible attracted back to the city from the suburbs to help restore the tax base. Third, efficient transportation must be available for those office workers who choose to remain in the suburbs. And fourth, the ghettoes must be replaced because their low-income residents provide a poor tax base and are taking up valuable land needed for new offices and apartments. In addition, being undereducated, underemployed and often rebellious, ghetto residents pose a threat to the smooth operation of a commercial center. As an executive of the Raytheon Corporation once put it:

> The American business community is sharply aware that the commercial world cannot exist without the marketplace, and the strength of the marketplace is the city. Thus, when the social and economic sickness of the American ghetto affects the commercial health of the population centers, it also gnaws away at the tissues and bones of the living cells of American industry.*

As a response to these problems, a commuter railway called Bay Area Rapid Transit (BART) was built; and massive urban renewal was begun, its main goal being to eradicate the ghettoes and bring back the white middle class.

Mission district residents first began to feel the effects of San Francisco's "Manhattanization" in the late sixties through the construction of BART.

IV

In 1962 the first BART bond issue was passed, fueled by a public relations campaign more than half financed by banks, construction companies and the Downtown Property Owners Association.

---

* Quoted in Peter Wiley and Beverly Leman, "Crisis in the Cities: The Business of Urban Reform," *Leviathan* (March 1969).

BART, they claimed, would reduce auto congestion and smog—though some experts now doubt whether BART will even keep pace with the increasing need for transportation. The bond issue committed taxpayers to a $792 million burden for a nine-county system; costs for the present, much more modest, three-county system quickly exceeded $2 billion.

The central BART station is in the heart of the financial district. Three lines run to outlying suburbs east across the Bay; the only San Francisco line runs down Mission Street and south to Daly City. As a former director of Harvard University transportation research program pointed out, "Downtown is increasingly becoming the headquarters for the more prosperous workers, and it seems that BART was especially created to serve these workers, not the poor who probably need it most, and not the masses who represent the bulk of San Francisco's and Oakland's populations. . . . People who live in the posh suburbs of Orinda and Lafayette [both in the East Bay] will be better served by BART than most San Francisco residents."*

Meanwhile, the San Francisco line is expected to change the Mission district completely. The first feasibility study for BART in 1953, financed by the three biggest banks in the city, found that property values along the route of Toronto's new rapid transit system had increased as much as tenfold.† Such an increase on the BART route would make the central Mission district far too expensive for the present latin population.

The BART line on Mission Street, now nearly completed, has already changed the barrio. In 1969, brown mothers could be seen trying to maneuver their strollers through the scaffolding of BART construction. Young latins couldn't hang out on the streets anymore, with the dust and the din of construction jarring everyone's

* Martin Wohl, as quoted in the *San Francisco Bay Guardian* (November 1, 1968).

† Danny Beagle, Al Haber, and David Wellman, "Turf Power and the Taxman: Urban Renewal, Regionalization and the Limits of Community Control," *Leviathan* (April 1969).

nerves. Furniture and clothing stores lost business; some folded. BART construction exhausted much of Mission Street's life.

This was only the beginning. In 1966 the City Planning Commission had sponsored a "Mission District Urban Design Study" which outlined BART's long-term effects. The study concentrated on the Mission Street corridor between the two BART stations at Sixteenth and Twenty-fourth Streets, and on what its authors saw as extensions of the stations going west three blocks on Sixteenth to the old Mission Dolores, and going east five blocks on Twenty-fourth to San Francisco General Hospital—a span which includes the heavily latin Inner Mission. The planners suggest that the stores spread along Mission Street be replaced by a concentration of commerce around the two stations, the corridor in between to be used for highrise housing. Sixteenth Street would become a tourist area, with an outdoor rotunda, dining facilities, promenades, displays of Mexican crafts, shops and offices, a plaza with a fountain, an "international food market," and a hotel and office tower. A pedestrian walkway leading west to the old Mission Dolores would be studded with gift shops, kiosks and outdoor cafes (the accompanying drawing suggests "taco" and "piñata" stands). Miniature vehicles would be available for tourists who didn't want to walk the three blocks. Twenty-fourth Street, at the other end of the Central Mission, would concentrate on a strong retail area, with more elevated walks and high-density housing "primarily for couples without children and for single persons"—in other words, for the new downtown labor force.*

The Urban Design Study predicted what BART and its palm-lined walkways will do to the Mission and its current latin population: "The impact of rapid transit on residential land use will be considerable, *with the Mission ultimately serving as a major moderate-income residential resource for the entire Bay Area.'* [Author's emphasis] Anticipated effects of this increase in residential development will be "greater densities, slightly higher rentals, and concentration near the stations and along the feeder

* San Francisco City Planning Commission, "Mission District Urban Design Study," February 1966.

78

arteries." Commerce will show a decline in furnishings and an increase in supermarkets. BART will be "particularly severe on marginal operations." The district will need between three hundred fifty and five hundred fifty more hotel rooms, between thirty and forty more eating and drinking establishments, and a lot more parking space. These changes, the study concludes, will "increase property values" (and hence rents), "change the character of retailing," "increase parking demand," "increase tourist accessibility," and "provide new image potentials and characteristics for the Mission."

BART will cut the Mission in two. In all likelihood, brown people will be forced first out of the two or three blocks surrounding the line, then out of the now largely latin Twenty-fourth Street area, then out of adjacent neighborhoods. There is no rent control in San Francisco, and as values rise, landlords will raise rents liberally; others will sell out to big realty companies which will tear down the two- and three-story buildings and construct box-like apartment houses for "couples without children and for single persons."*

By 1970 many such apartments had already been built right off Mission Street. Their rows of mailboxes, their plush lobbies and sparkle-dust ceilings present a strange contrast to the big rundown flats and the latin children playing in the streets.

V

"Detailed renewal planning," the Mission District Urban Design Study suggested in 1966, "should begin at once." By the time young latins in the Mission were beginning to acquire a radical outlook, the Mission Street BART line was already under construction. But redevelopment in the Mission was still to become a

---

* Police brutality also plays a role in forcing people out. When the people who control the police condone racism and brutality because they don't include a large latin population in their plans for San Francisco's future, the barrio becomes not just oppressive but physically dangerous, and its residents begin to look for less hostile places.

political battlefield, and one of the key issues on which latin radicals were to challenge both the downtown business interests and Mayor Alioto's friends in the Mission.

Urban renewal in San Francisco is very much a part of the business development program. Seed money for the first renewal project, the Golden Gateway, had been provided by the Blyth-Zellerbach Committee, a group of businessmen representing major West Coast corporations—the Bank of America, Standard Oil of California, Pacific Gas and Electric, and local giants like Levi-Strauss. Instead of providing the moderate-income housing for which it was presumably intended (and for which it received federal funds), Golden Gateway became a luxury apartment complex renting unfurnished studio apartments for $200 a month and townhouses for $700. It has fountains, immaculately landscaped lawns, and a private tennis club—all for the white-collar population. Golden Gateway also provided the site for two new skyscrapers: the Alcoa Building and the Security Pacific Bank.

Meanwhile, the mostly black and Japanese Western Addition, just west of downtown, had been slated for urban renewal as early as 1948. By the time the first renewal project in the area was finished, some six thousand families had been displaced; only *three* were later able to move back in.* In those areas where renewal has been completed there is a Japanese cultural and trade center, a lavish new cathedral, and one luxury and one moderate-income apartment complex. Low-income housing is currently being completed in the second Western Addition renewal project, but the rents are not low and poor people live there only by virtue of federal subsidies. When the subsidies go, the poor will probably go too. Meanwhile, Fillmore Street, the core of the Western Addition (as Mission Street is the core of the Mission district), has been destroyed by the redevelopment blight. In 1970 all that remained of a once-lively Fillmore Street were bars, a few record shops, and boarded-up storefronts covered with posters announcing Black Panther rallies held at least a year before.

The Redevelopment Agency's plans for the future are equally

* Beagle, Haber, and Wellman, *op. cit.*

discouraging. Though twelve thousand seven hundred urban renewal units were planned in 1970, fifty-seven percent of them (seventy-two hundred) were to be luxury housing, and only forty-three percent low- and moderate-income. Much of that forty-three percent must be reserved for old people displaced by theYerba Buena project in the South of Market area. Very little will be left for poor families, like those in the Mission district. And the few poor families which do benefit from the new housing will do so only as long as federal subsidies continue. The new units will probably not even house those displaced by urban renewal, let alone cope with current shortages.

Yet the Redevelopment Agency continues to insist that urban renewal is a generous effort to improve the living conditions of poor people. In 1970 the late Redevelopment Director M. Justin Herman wrote in a letter to the *Chronicle,* "There is a benefit in being in redevelopment. You can go to bed each night knowing you have helped people in the slums."

The process by which redevelopment entered the Mission district after Alioto's election was to provide an education in urban politics for many of the young radicals who later formed the Los Siete organization. It first became known that redevelopment was planned for the Mission in 1966. Local people, warned by the example of the Fillmore, stirred up enough trouble for the city's Board of Supervisors to kill the project by a one-vote margin; similar movements were stalling renewal elsewhere in the country. In response the federal government passed the City Demonstration Act (popularly called the Model Cities Act) of 1966, which ensured community participation in the redevelopment process. Every program funded under the Act was to provide for a Citizens Demonstration Agency which would represent the community in bargaining with City Hall and Washington. This was the situation which faced Alioto and other redevelopment backers in 1968.

The Alioto administration already had friends in the Mission. During the 1967 election campaign, Alioto had the active support of the city's largest construction union, Local 261 of the International Laborers (Alioto is an honorary member). The union plays a strategic role in San Francisco politics; it is located in the Mission and is dominated by an efficiently organized Spanish-speaking caucus, the Centro Social Obrero. The president of the Centro, and business agent for Local 261, a Mexican-American named Abel Gonzalez, wields considerable power in the unemployment-ridden district. Gonzalez had campaigned for Alioto in 1967 and was appointed to his cabinet after the election; other benefits flowed to the union, and for the first time in over sixty years a Mexican-American was appointed by the mayor to a vacant seat on the Board of Supervisors. Meanwhile, Abel Gonzalez and another Mexican-American, a Democratic politician named Herman Gallegos, began the process of smoothing redevelopment's entry into the Mission.*

Early in 1968, Alioto proposed a community control organization to meet the Model Cities Act requirement. Gallegos had already sent a relative, Ben Martinez, to Washington to study the Act, and an organization with which Gallegos was associated put up the initial funds; Gallegos chaired the founding convention in Centro Social Obrero hall.

The new organization, called the Mission Coalition Organization, or MCO, attracted more than a hundred community groups, ranging in ethnic and political makeup from the Welfare Rights Association to the Junta Hispaña de Real Estate Brokers, from the St. Kevin's Teen Club to the Mission Rebels. Although some of the member organizations existed mainly on paper, together they represented a broader base of the Mission population than any single group. The overwhelming sentiment of these organizations was against redevelopment unless it was strictly community controlled. Martinez won his presidency because he seemed the most vocal adherent of this line. "We don't want the money [for renewal]," he said, "unless we in the Mission have a

---

* Gallegos, an influential man in Mexican-American politics, belongs to the board of directors of the Ford Foundation's Southwest Council of La Raza, whose self-declared purpose is to "rise on the tide of spontaneous and autonomous efforts of the barrios to help themselves."

major voice in how it is spent." He laid down two "non-negotiable" demands: appointment by the Coalition of two-thirds of a Model Cities Neighborhood Corporation (fourteen out of twenty-one members), and veto power over all renewal plans. After a massive organizing campaign culminating in a heavily attended Board of Supervisors meeting, the demands were accepted.

But a few months later the Department of Housing and Urban Development in Washington rejected the plan as giving too much power to a community group. With much less fanfare, Alioto and MCO President Martinez renegotiated. Martinez agreed that MCO would submit twenty-three nominations for the Model Cities Neighborhood Corporation, from which Alioto would pick fourteen; Alioto would pick the other seven himself. This meant Alioto would need only four friends out of the twenty-three people recommended by MCO to control a majority of the Neighborhood Corporation. In addition, Martinez gave up the veto power. With this agreement, the Alioto administration had virtual control over redevelopment in the Mission.

Ironically it was the right-wing law-and-order faction of the Mission and Noe Valley which first saw through the Mission Coalition, calling it a "paper organization of imported foundation grant tramps."* These people, who came from the same social and political milieu as policemen like Brodnik and McGoran, had more in common with the latin population than they thought, for both groups had a stake in keeping the Mission a lower-middle-class and working-class district. And both groups faced "urban removal" if redevelopment were accomplished in such a way as to raise property values and rents.

The right-wingers realized that MCO had been created not to fight redevelopment, as some of its members thought, but to make redevelopment palatable to the Mission population. Only gradually did this become clear to sections of the latin community, for in

* Two foundations, the United Bay Area Crusade and the San Francisco Foundation, put some $85,000 into MCO member organizations in 1969; the San Francisco Foundation gave $12,500 to the Coalition itself.

those first years the right-wingers were a small splinter group and MCO was a big militant organization. Later, as the Coalition made its compromises and Centro Obrero chief Abel Gonzalez advanced to a leading role in the organization, many people in the Mission realized they would be powerless to control redevelopment; in addition they would be saddled with an organization officially accepted by City Hall as their representative, congratulating itself on the "victory" it had won. And it would be in part through the Los Siete organization's efforts that MCO would begin to be discredited in the district.

The deception involved in the creation of the Mission Coalition is paralleled in other aspects of ghetto politics. Outside money, whether from business or government but usually the latter, arrives with the announced intention of improving conditions, but in fact with powerful strings attached. Actually, whether in redevelopment or in poverty programs, this money promotes and enriches a small group of ghetto entrepreneurs while leaving the majority of the population as powerless as before. The same phenomenon was at work in the Economic Opportunity Programs on college campuses in the late sixties. The EOP money was supposed to help Third World students "make it"—but only by deactivating them politically and taking them out of the ghetto. Coming to understand this phenomenon was one of the key experiences of young black, brown and Asian American radicals in the late sixties. Bebe Melendez discovered it to an extent through the Mission Rebels. Tony and Mario Martinez discovered it while pursuing higher education—the dream which had first brought their family north.

5. The Weird Experience

I

"The only thing that kept us with the idea of going to college was the family," Tony Martinez says of his school experience. "At Jefferson [High School], none of the teachers made any efforts to find out whether we wanted to go or not. My father got a friend of his that spoke English to make sure to tell the counselor that we wanted to go college. But all through high school, they never mentioned it.

"Every time we would make out the program for the next year, they'd say, 'There's not enough classes,' or, 'The classes you want have already been taken. So we're going to put you in this class.' And it always turned out to be a wood shop class or a machine shop class or a study period where you sit around the cafeteria doing nothing."

Another of Los Siete, Nelson Rodriguez, adds: "I kept noticing my counselors always tried to stick me in the handcraft classes, not in the intellectual classes. Most of the blacks and browns are put in wood shop, machine shop, metal shop. They don't encourage you in taking solid courses. There were courses there that I didn't even know were available.

"I wasn't aware of it then. I was just passing time. The thought of going to college never crossed my mind. I just lost interest in school and kept cutting classes. My parents were afraid I was going to be drafted. So they sent me back to El Salvador for a while, and

87

I started going to school down there. They stuck me in a real low grade, ninth grade, but they taught me more than I learned at Jefferson. The history, geography and mathematics was real advanced. I never took a mathematics course while I was in high school."

What Tony and Nelson describe is their personal experience with the tracking system, a system which has its roots in California's "Master Plan for Higher Education." Written in 1960 by a panel of businessmen appointed by then-Governor Edmund G. "Pat" Brown, and approved by the legislature the same year, the Master Plan was a response to a financial crisis in California's system of higher education. The volume of college students had been steadily increasing and was expected to triple between 1960 and 1975. The state could not continue to support higher education without revising its regressive tax structure, which it was unwilling to do. The Master Plan aimed to cut costs by reducing university enrollment (i.e., by raising standards) and shifting the burden of mass education onto the two-year junior colleges, which are financed mostly by local taxes.

The Plan defined three levels of higher education: universities, state colleges, and junior colleges. The universities were to be restricted to the top twelve and a half percent of high school graduates; they had previously accepted the top third. The state colleges were then restricted to the top third—previously it had been the top seventy percent. The junior colleges were theoretically open to anyone; this provided the basis for claims that the Master Plan had broadened the scope of higher education in California and made it accessible to anybody.

Actually the junior colleges turned out to be glorified vocational schools, specializing in nursing, electronics, occupation therapy, broadcasting, and the like. Libraries and facilities are below standard college level and teacher workloads are heavier. Only five percent of the students at these two-year schools go on to four-year college; about fifty percent drop out before finishing the two years. Competition is high, as there is room for these students neither in the overcrowded four-year colleges nor in the managerial and professional job market.

The Master Plan also contained "selection and retention devices" to make competition stiffer and hence flunk out more students, especially at the junior college level. These devices, the Plan conceded, "will not guarantee that all able young Californians will go to college." Minority college enrollment dropped drastically after the Master Plan went into effect. The proportion of blacks at San Francisco State College fell from twelve percent to four percent, even though the city schools which State supposedly services were about thirty percent black.

"If a racial bias seems to be reflected in the Master Plan," says a report published by Columbia University, "a class bias is even more obvious."* According to one study, two-thirds of the state's junior college students come from families with incomes under $10,000. Half the state college students are in this income bracket; at the universities, only one-third. The state spends twice as much on a university student as on a state college student and three times as much on a state college student as on a junior college student. Yet those with incomes under $10,000 pay over half the state taxes—and at least half of these taxpayers are Third World: three and a half million chicanos and latinos, one and a half million blacks; plus Chinese, Japanese, Filipinos, and American Indians.†

Limiting four-year college enrollment depended on the use of a tracking system in the primary and secondary grades. Usually as early as elementary school, students are categorized by I.Q. as either vocationally or academically inclined. As some educators have conceded, I.Q. tests measure not intelligence but familiarity with white middle-class social and intellectual life: such I.Q. test questions as "Why is it better to pay by check than in cash?" and

* Carol Lopate, "The College Readiness Program: A Program for Third World Students at the College of San Mateo, California," the Study of Collegiate Compensatory Programs for Minority Group Youth, ERIC Information Retrieval Center on the Disadvantaged, Horace Mann–Lincoln Institute, Teachers College, Columbia University, New York.

† Peter Shapiro and Bill Barlow, "S.F. State," *Leviathan* (April 1969).

"Who wrote *Romeo and Juliet*?" are good examples.*

While it is theoretically possible for a student to change tracks, it is not likely. Once a child is put in a vocational track, he or she learns less, becomes less receptive, the teacher expects less, and the child falls further and further behind the academically trained students. As an American Federation of Teachers local recognized, "If he [the high school graduate in California] is a member of the black or brown communities, his chances of escaping his oppressed condition through the educational system are minimal. Nothing in the ghetto schools . . . or in his environment has equipped him to cope with the rigid standards erected to shut him out."**

In the case of latino children, language is an additional handicap. Like many Chinese and Filipinos—about a third of San Francisco's public school children in all—they come from homes in which English is not the spoken language. In 1970 it was discovered that normal or bright Spanish-speaking children throughout California had been trapped in classes for the mentally retarded because of their low scores on English I.Q. tests. When some of these children were retested in Spanish, their I.Q. scores improved on the average fifteen points; one score went up forty-nine points.† A federal judge in San Francisco ordered that students whose home language was not English be retested in their own language before they could be kept in mentally retarded classes. When the tests on elementary school children were completed, it was found that forty-five percent of the Spanish-speaking children in mentally retarded classes were of average intelligence or better. (But only two of these children were moved immediately into normal classes. As for the rest, the city's Assistant Superintendent for Special Services explained, "We are working . . . to seek a proper transitional program for these young

* Cited by a California Rural Legal Assistance suit in January 1970.

** "The Decline of Our State Colleges," a summary published by AFT Local 1352, AFL-CIO, January 1969. Quoted by Kay Boyle, *The Long Walk at San Francisco State* (New York: Grove, 1970).

† According to the suit filed by California Rural Legal Assistance. The children were retested by an accredited bilingual psychologist.

sters." School districts receive $550 extra per year for each child in a mentally retarded class.)

Other studies showed that Spanish-speaking children did better if they weren't required to learn English right away. If they could learn English gradually, meanwhile studying other subjects in Spanish, they would progress faster and gain confidence. (A friend of the Martinez brothers, Francisco Flores, remembers pleading unsuccessfully with his teachers, "Give it to me in Spanish. I can do it.") But not until 1969 was a program begun in which Spanish-speaking children could learn other subjects in their own language, and this in only three classes at two schools in the city.

"The boys cut classes not because they were lazy or because they had no ambitions," Mrs. Gloria Martinez later said of her two eldest sons. "They did so because they got no moral or physical help from their teachers. Tony said he wanted to be an engineer. The professor asked why did he want to do that? That was a big profession and required lots of study and especially an aptitude to do the work. If he wanted to do carpentry he could start right away earning money."

Tony: "When I got to the lower twelfth grade I told them I wanted to go to college. By this time I pretty well knew—I was getting catalogues. And they're looking at the record: 'Well, you're not prepared to go to college.'

"I told them, 'I told you a long time ago that I wanted to go to college.'

"So the counselor goes, blah blah blah, and it turned out they didn't want me to go. They kept telling me, 'You're not gonna make it.'

"So I told them, 'You know what? Just take that application and give it to me. If you don't want to send it, I will.' She saw she had a lost argument so she gave me the application and I filled it out. I took it to City College [a two-year college in San Francisco]. That's where I went first.

"It was hard at the beginning. I was going to school, taking an engineering program, and at the same time I was working every night as a busboy at the Olympic Club. Hey, you want to see racists, that's the place to go. That's a rich man's club. The second 'best' club in the whole United States. The New York Athletic Club is the 'best.' "

Mario: "Two summers I had gone to summer school because I was so behind in my grades. The last time I went to summer school I was really good. I went all summer and hardly missed twice. But you have to be getting up early when everybody else is on vacation. And five days before summer school ended, I was late and the bus left me. The next day I got there and they said, 'We dropped you.' There was only about three or four days to go, and they just told me, 'We dropped you.' So I got really upset about that, because I had really worked that summer.

"I was going to Jefferson, not doing too well in my classes, and I was eighteen already and I had gone through all the grades. Every time the year ended I got promoted to the next grade. So every year I thought, I'm not doing so badly. Then when the twelfth grade came around, I got hip to all these points you need. I found out I only had a hundred and twenty points. I was a hundred points short to graduate. So after those four years, I still had to do another year and a summer school without failing any classes.

"I didn't want to do another year and a half. I'd be nineteen and a half and still going to high school. So I just decided not to go back to school. I had asked the counselor for information about what I needed to get into college. I always had this picture of Stanford or Berkeley, going to school and finally becoming a doctor. I always had this ambition. But they used to tell me, 'You know, this is really hard; not just anybody can go to college. There's so much work involved, and you have to have straight As or Bs at least. And with your grades, you ain't never going to do nothing.'

"It *works*, in a way. You say, Fuck it; you take an attitude that's stupid, childish. But then again, you're no grown-up. That's when you most need help."

Their friend, Reynaldo Aparicio, who also attended Jefferson adds: "In high school, the guy who used to teach us soccer, hi mother was from El Salvador. But he told Mario that he was much better off going to work in a cannery or something, because he wasn't going to be able to make it in college. Mario proved to him later on that he was wrong, and that he could do well in college. Not only that, but he recruited all of us to go."

Mario: "Towards the end of the year [spring 1969], some people from the College Readiness Program at the College of San Mateo came to school and they said they had this program over there just for people of color. So I got interested. I went to San Mateo that summer. I took a biology course and an English course. I was breaking into the college thing. It was real difficult. In a way it was like getting back to my country, where they demand that you work or they expel you. You don't just go through and come out worse than before."

Mrs. Martinez: "When Mario was finally admitted to San Mateo he was so happy—we were all so happy at last. And the friends he brought home, he pulled into this program. And he got more enthusiastic and happy every day, and we celebrated. My son always talked about the same thing—that now our people have the opportunity. We are not going to stay like this, without a profession, or go to the factories like the teachers want."

Mario expressed his guardedly hopeful feelings in an essay he wrote that summer for phonics class:

Let the hope of the people be the cry of help, and let that cry be a sign for each individual to register his conscience, to see if he's doing his share for the survival of the degrading world. Let ourselves be united, and forever set aside the differences between our races, creeds or colors. Only by doing this can we overpower the unjust oppressor and make this world a better and fit place to live.

Let's free this world of injustice, prejudice and many more problems which we are now facing or will be facing if no action is taken. This has been a dream of the people of this world, and it's becoming real every time an individual understands it. This dream is not only a basic need for our present times, but more of a need for the future. For our survival, know where you as an individual stand, and do something about it. Start now or you'll never see the rewarding results. You might never see them anyway but you will know you did your part.

The College Readiness Program at the College of San Mateo was exclusively for students of color, although many whites worked there as tutors. The program's philosophy was one of social commitment, both to serve and improve the surrounding ghettoes where many of its students lived, and to study the larger political issues of the day. On the big, suburban, predominantly white San Mateo campus, the Readiness Program was necessarily close-knit (Ralph Ruiz called it a "great family"), and strong friendships developed.

"My tutor that summer [1968] was a Puerto Rican brother," Mario Martinez remembers. "He used to come to my house. I introduced him to my family. We got along real good. I only got a D in the biology class, but it was fun studying, learning all those new things. And my brother Tony, we started talking to him. Tony was calling me a communist and saying that all I learned over there at CSM [College of San Mateo] was to hate the white man. I tried to explain to him what was going on. And finally we convinced him to go up there."

Tony: "My brother and his tutor would come to the house and talk. I listened to what they'd say. They'd say something about the press, and this was my bag, so we'd start talking. Mario's tutor would suggest things and I would think about them, do research. Like about politics, the way people are excluded from the government. So I'm beginning to see more things—things I already had inside me but wasn't able to say. So I decided I wanted to go to San Mateo. The thing was so fast that I find myself—I'm not even going to school yet, but I'm helping recruit people.

"The program was totally black before, but Ralph Ruiz was going there and he was mainly influencing Bob Hoover [the Readiness Program's black co-director]. The two of them opened up the

94

whole thing for Third World students. Ralph was a leader. He was able to explain things. He was a great influence on me—the way he talked to the students, the brotherhood thing. Before, I was never that close to black kids. Relating their problems to mine. Not only theirs, but also yellow people, Indians, poor whites. This gave me a further understanding."

Ralph Ruiz, a high school dropout and ex-paratrooper, later a founder of the Los Siete organization, had been one of the first latinos to enter the Readiness Program back in 1967. "Tony was going to City College [in the summer of 1968]," Ralph remembers. "But he couldn't hack it; he was thinking of dropping out. I told him to come up to the College of San Mateo—we'd see if we could get him some financial support. I told him it wouldn't be much, and he'd have to change his style some. I told him I used to be a good dresser myself for a while, but I decided to go back to school and use the little money I could get to feed myself—and feed my brain."

With Ralph Ruiz, the Martinez brothers began to get involved in political work. They collected clothing and supplies to send to the striking grape-workers in Delano. They, along with Nelson Rodriguez, made friends with Aaron Manganiello, the Brown Beret organizer who was working for the Office of Economic Opportunity that summer. They set up an information and college recruiting center in South San Francisco. Manganiello was also a volunteer tutor in the Readiness Program, a situation which was to cause much controversy in the coming months. (Manganiello's name was already familiar in the boardroom of CSM. Three years before, when he was a music instructor there, he had tried to sell peace buttons and Robert Scheer's book *How We Got Involved in Vietnam* on campus. He was carried bodily off campus two or three times a day when he tried to do this. Manganiello explained, "It was a controversial issue, and true to CSM tradition, controversy was not allowed in the curriculum.")

During that summer session of 1968 and after it was over, Ralph, Mario and Tony tried to recruit their friends for the Readiness Program. Mario was probably the most avid recruiter: among the more than thirty students he brought in were Gio Lopez, a friend from the Mission (and the only one of Los Siete who was never arrested), and Nelson Rodriguez, who had just come back from El Salvador.

"I could see how good the education was," Mario explains, "and I wanted my friends to get hip to this. With Ralph I learned about the struggle of our people, and he got me hip to some books and literature. First we went to the library and we listened to some speeches by Malcolm X. and H. Rap Brown. I liked what they were saying. Then Ralph started telling me about some books. I read some by John Gerassi and Frantz Fanon. And I started reading some about Che. I got more interested in this than in the classes."

"I remember in those days how the influence of a younger brother began to change his older brothers," Reynaldo "Ray" Aparicio says. "Mario was about a year younger than Tony. Because Mario was obese—not really obese but heavy—we always made fun of him. He was the one with the fewest girlfriends, and he was the least well dressed. If you grow up in a low-income family, you take pride in how you dress. Especially people of color, 'cause we never had such things. Tony was always well dressed; he really had supercapitalistic ideas of dressing. And he always had a lot of girls, so he would always get down on Mario most. We would all get down on Mario.

"But after knowing Mario for a certain time, we would realize that he was a special person. Not only was he a leader, but he was a person who always put himself in the position of his brothers. And whenever we'd be with Mario we'd enjoy ourselves.

"After Tony started seeing that everyone was paying attention to Mario and not him anymore, he started realizing that just being well dressed wasn't necessarily what friendship was. So he started more or less becoming like Mario. Mario got him to go to San Mateo and Tony started getting politically aware. By the time I came back from the Army in December, Tony was much on his job. Because he was understanding all that Mario showed him." (Ray relates that after he was drafted the Army asked him to work as a CIA agent in Guatemala. "I was tempted," he says; but he refused, partly because of the influence of Mario and Nelson, who were sending him letters from home. Ray was then told he would be sent to Vietnam. When he came home for Christmas leave in 1968, his friends helped him get a medical discharge, and he registered for school at San Mateo.)

II

The two-year College of San Mateo is a landscaped suburban hilltop campus. It draws students from the mostly well-to-do communities of the peninsula south of San Francisco, and was almost all-white before 1966—it had never had more than eighty nonwhite students at any one time.

In the fall of 1965, CSM President Julio Bortolazzi, upset about the recent rioting in Watts, asked for faculty volunteers to recruit students from the nearby black neighborhood of East Palo Alto. Out of three hundred faculty people, only one volunteered: a white English teacher named Jean Wirth. She interviewed one hundred and fifty young people and got thirty-nine to agree, somewhat dubiously, to attend CSM the next summer. To qualify for admission you had to be nonwhite and poor, with a high school grade average below C, low scores on aptitude tests, and no previous plans to go to college. In addition, most recruits had police records and were unemployed. As a later study of the College Readiness Program said, "Few expected more than a summer's pay or a weird experience from the project."*

Robert Hoover, a black man who later became co-director of the Readiness Program with Jean Wirth, described recruiting:

"We go to the high schools in the spring. We talk with the counselors a little bit, but not a great deal, because they probably know less about the student than we do the first time we see him and spend one half hour with him.

"We look for the student who represents the *majority* of the minority race—the student who has a very poor high school record academically. He not only has a poor high school record, he has taken every wrong course he could possibly take. He has the 'nothing' English course, one year of general mathematics in the

* Lopate, *op. cit.*

97

ninth grade, every useless shop course (or, if a girl, cooking and sewing and all that nonsense). He has not been prepared to do anything in high school. He has kind of floated through school, and they have given him a diploma that is worthless. . . .

"We recruit these students, bring them to college, and then begin an intensive de-brainwashing . . . to convince the student that he does have a brain. Because he has been pretty well convinced through the twelve years of 'education' he has just received that he does not have a brain. In order to convince the student that he is a human being with a functioning brain, you must have a program that relates to the student, that speaks to him about his culture, his heritage, his contributions to this society, and about the possible solutions to the problems and frustrations he faces in this society."

Each day that first summer of 1966, the students went to classes in the morning, had three hours of studying in the afternoon, and three hours of tutoring after dinner. The program chartered a bus to bring them to campus, and if they missed the bus tutors picked them up personally. Through work-study grants, the students were paid for the time they spent in class; most had no other income.

Of the thirty-nine students who came to CSM that summer for a "weird experience," thirty-six finished the program, thirty-four coming back in the fall. Almost all of them showed up at registration with one or more friends. One hundred fifty black students registered in the fall of 1966.

By fall 1967, the College Readiness Program had two hundred fifty-six students receiving tutorial and counseling help, eighty-seven tutors (mostly white) and another two hundred students active but not "officially" in the program. The program recruited its first two brown students that year: Ralph Ruiz and Jackie Montoya, both high school dropouts from South San Francisco. By fall 1968, the numbers had grown to four hundred directly associated with the program, and almost three hundred indirectly. Of these, about forty-five percent were black, twelve percent brown, thirty-two percent white (almost all of them tutors) and the rest Asians, American Indians or other nonwhites.

The program depended from the start on a strong personal bond between student and tutor. As Mario says, "A lot of the tutors were white. They came out and helped tutor the minorities. But one of the things we were doing was getting as many people of color as we could to replace the white tutors. It was supposed to be from the start a program of just people of color. It was a thing to establish identity and self-pride. To get into a program like that and have a white student be tutoring you—telling you all these things—you're just back on the same road. I had a couple of white tutors but I always felt better when a brown brother was teaching me. There was a better contact thing. More mutual understanding.

"That's why we'd tell a lot of kids to really study. 'Cause if you pass a class and a new kid comes in, you can teach that kid that class. And it makes a big difference. It's getting the thing going, brother to brother. Like, the way I think now, we're all brothers. But some of us don't think that way: they don't see white people as brothers and sisters. You can't blame them."

As important in the program as the development of strong personal relationships was commitment to the community. In the summers of 1967 and 1968, co-director Hoover ran a "teen project" in East Palo Alto in which thirty CRP students tutored three hundred fifty local high school students every morning; the high school students themselves taught pre-schoolers in the afternoon.

Most students in the College Readiness Program were radical— or quickly became so. As one of the teachers involved in the program later said at the Los Siete trial, "Minority students sometimes required motivation to read things about their own people." This led naturally to discussions of conditions in the Third World as well as in the ghettoes of the United States. Students began to study Asian, African, and Latin American liberation movements against U.S. imperialism. They put up posters of Mao, Che and other revolutionary heroes on the walls of the Readiness Center. They didn't abandon their street language and culture but brought them to the campus, creating a comfortable atmosphere in which they could relax and learn.

Not only the rhetoric but also the functioning of the College Readiness Program was radical. The students chose their own staff and generally told co-directors Hoover and Wirth what to tell the administration on their behalf. Their demands for an autonomous Third World Studies Department in the fall of 1968 were only extensions of the autonomy they already had within the program. It was also radical—indeed revolutionary—to recruit large numbers of high school dropouts off the streets. The CRP believed in mass education, in direct contrast to the Master Plan, with its many "selection and retention devices." The heavy emphasis on recruitment led to a rapid expansion of the program; and this expansion was soon to make the CRP intolerable to the college authorities.

Late in 1967, Director of Research Franklin Pearce conducted a study of the program's success. He found that in the program's history only twenty-three percent of the students had dropped out of school—in contrast to a near ninety percent dropout rate for nonwhites at the College of San Mateo as a whole before the program started (the rate among whites was about fifty percent).* Of that twenty-three percent, most dropped out for financial, not academic, reasons. The report said, "It would appear that the withdrawal rate could be reduced twenty-three to seventeen percent [virtually to zero] simply by increasing the financial support for students." In two and a half years the CRP had increased minority enrollment at the college from eighty to nearly eight hundred students, and reduced the dropout rate among "risk" students from ninety to fifteen percent.

Pearce's study also revealed that college board aptitude tests were virtually worthless in predicting the academic success of Readiness Program students. Three-fourths of the CRP students had scored at or below the twenty-fifth percentile in college boards. The report noted, "The variance is so great that the reliability of scholastic aptitude tests for program students is practically nonexistent." The same went for high school grade averages.

The program's success was achieved by working cooperatively, tutoring one another, and relating education to political concerns. The Readiness Program, it seemed, had managed to end student

* Lopate, *op. cit.*, quoting from Frank Pearce, "A Study of Academic Success of College Readiness Students at the College of San Mateo."

alienation, a true fluke in the modern corporate-oriented academic system. Not only was the CRP one of the few successful college programs for Third World youth, it also had a lot to teach white education. The Readiness Program became widely recognized as "the finest program for students of color anywhere in the country," with a loyalty and morale among its members "rarely achieved in any facet of academic life. . . . Community members, trustees, administration, faculty and students, both in and outside the program, acknowledged its dramatic if frightening success."*

The CRP *was* frightening, partly because of the politics of the students and partly because of its success. Its students were not settling for the vocational and technical programs they were supposed to want. Fewer than three percent concentrated their studies in vocational areas—most had had enough of that in high school. And they didn't understand, apparently, what junior colleges were for. Director Hoover remembers being told he "wasn't putting enough students into vocational training."

"I didn't know I had a quota," he said.

"You don't, but you should still put more students into vocational training," he remembers the administrator replying.

Whatever part racism, fear, or lack of funds played in precipitating a crisis in the fall of 1968, one major consideration must have been that the CRP was negating the vocational purpose of the California junior college system.

To some people, the program was frightening for additional reasons. The Readiness Center was originally located in a bomb shelter next to the Building and Grounds office. Building and Grounds personnel had to walk through it on their way to work. The animated life of the center, its often obscene language and revolutionary posters, made some of the staff uptight. One secretary developed the habit of loudly announcing her fear of being raped as she walked past. This finally led to insulting words from

* Lopate, *op. cit.*

one CRP student. The secretary, with her boss's approval, circulated a petition demanding the CRP's removal.

The center was moved to the cafeteria, and later to the Horticulture Building on the outskirts of campus. This isolation made it harder for the whites to get to know their Third World brothers and sisters. But as Mario says, "We didn't need to go look for friends. It was the white kids who made friends with a lot of us. They did it on a kind of experimental basis. I find that in a lot of white people. It was something new in San Mateo, seeing brown and black faces. They say to themselves, 'What's this weird dude doing here?' They start conversations with you." The overwhelmingly white campus elected a black "Homecoming Queen" two years running. There was a core of hostility, however, concentrated in technical fields like electronics. The electronics headquarters was scornfully called "Whitey's Building" by the Third World students.

There was also a cultural problem: manners. Most of the middle-class students had been trained to act respectfully to administrators and faculty. The nonwhites were often less polite. Mario, who was deeply concerned with the survival of the Readiness Program, had little tolerance for bullshit. Later, when he became a leader of the program, he would walk out of meetings with the financial aids officer if he felt he wasn't getting through. Nelson and Ralph, even less cordial, would sometimes taunt the newly installed president, Robert Ewigleben, calling him "Bobby"; as race relations worsened on campus, they sometimes used stronger epithets. Ewigleben developed a strong aversion for Nelson and Ralph.

College Readiness Program students sometimes had problems with teachers. Mario's description of a Latin American history course is illuminating:

"I went to a class they had in Latin American Studies: I wanted to learn more about my people, refresh my memory from things I had learned back home. But the teacher—you just wouldn't believe the kind of guy they had teaching that class. Like, every other minute I would have to interrupt him. And he would say, '*I'm* the authority here; what I say goes.'

"Most of the kids were white. The only brown people were me, Ralph [Ruiz] and somebody else. The way he was teaching this class, it was a joke, but that joke was very harmful. This is the kind of history he was teaching: in Mexico, the churches have big clocks. That's only because the Mexicans are too cheap to buy watches. I raised my hand. I had to interrupt him, you know, run it down to him: It's not because people are too cheap to buy watches.

"He made other racist remarks. He said you can compare the burro population in Mexico to the burro or donkey population in the United States. And the relevant thing is the intelligence of the people. The burro is supposed to be a stupid animal. Like, there's so many burros in Mexico, and far less in the United States, so the people in Mexico are more stupid, and the people in the United States are real smart: that is what he was saying. And I raised my hand. I had to interrupt. And he wouldn't like me correcting him. Those were his jokes, but still, they go into people's minds. They create an image that's far away from reality. When I questioned him, he got real red, like he was going to have a heart attack. I was just telling him the truth. But he said he's traveled down there a lot, and he knew more about my people than I did.

"If you came in late one time, he made you do a report on somebody—Cortez, you know, something to do with Latin American history. And the next day you'd come—you're supposed to have three pages. And if you don't bring it, the next day it has to be four pages. Like, one time I came late and he told me I was up to thirty-two pages. He says, 'You're breaking the record.'

"I said, 'I don't care. I don't care about no record. I'm not going to do your paper. I don't go along with your rules.' He said if I didn't like it I should get out of the class. He said, 'You're not passing anyway.' I said, 'Well, I'm going, you know. Because I'm not learning what I came here to learn. I know I'm not passing this class, but it's cool because I'm not learning anything anyway.' I told him he was just lying to all these people. I didn't see how people could be so ignorant as to believe these lies and racist remarks. So I just walked out of the class and never came back."

Nelson was less academically inclined. "The classes I took in El

Salvador when I was back there in the ninth grade were harder than the ones I was taking at CSM in the first semester," he remembers. "But experience is better than books anyway. I don't relate to sitting in classes. Me and Ralph sitting on the grass, smoking dope and rapping, that was a better education than I got in any class."

6. Whitey's Building

In 1966–67, $10,000 had been budgeted for the College Readiness Program and almost $30,000 spent. By 1968–69 the expenditure had reached $104,000 and the request for 1969–70 was $180,000. Most of this money was raised by and for the program, from the federal government and private donations. Only five percent came from general college funds, which in turn came from local taxes.

In the late summer of 1968, the CRP won a $150,000 grant from the federal government, which had to be matched by local contributions. The college administration delayed in giving the go-ahead for the CRP to start fund-raising, on the grounds that an audit was being done to determine why the CRP had overspent its budget during the summer. The audit dragged on and valuable time was lost. There was also a bond issue coming up in the local election—to create two more junior colleges in San Mateo County—and the college didn't want any competing fund-raising to be done until the election was over.

The inability of the CRP to raise funds to match the federal grant created a financial crisis that was felt at once in the fall. Even those Third World students who lived at home couldn't depend on their families for books, lunches, and spending money. Part-time jobs were scarce in the San Mateo area. As work-study checks stopped coming or were drastically cut, CRP students had to begin dropping out. Aaron Manganiello recalls one story "about a girl in the program—she's twenty-six years old and a mother of three children. The college had promised her $140 a month to live on. But after two months, completely without warning, her next check was $12.75. All checks of any size were cut down so that the biggest check given out was $40."

Some whites said that the black and brown students were simply irresponsible with their money—always spending it foolishly and then having to apply for emergency grants. They said the CRP was "draining" the college, which was patently false.

Carol Lopate, author of a study of the CRP, observes, "The Protestant ethic also seems to have played an important part in the attitudes of the most conservative members of the college community towards the use of financial aid by program students. A small number of black students had expensive cars which, for those interested in finding fault, were parked conspicuously behind the CRP center."

As far as CRP students were concerned, the financial situation was only part of a larger problem that fall. "We could have ridden out another financial crisis," one black girl said. "We have before. But the communication problem is what killed us." Former president Julio Bortolazzi, despite his frequent differences with CRP policies, had always been available for discussion, and could be bargained with. The new president, Robert Ewigleben, could rarely be reached for discussion. When he did make himself available, he couldn't be pinned down on any promises.

Since President Ewigleben would not commit himself through private or informal channels, the CRP students, on October 11, 1968, made a public presentation of demands. The most important of these demands concerned an overhaul of financial aids procedures and personnel, more tutors and counselors to serve the much expanded body of CRP students (four counselors were expected to serve over seven hundred students), and an autonomous Third World Studies department. The students also wanted Aaron Manganiello and an Asian woman, Pat Sumi, to be hired as tutor-counselors (both were working as volunteers).

Presentation of the demands was accompanied by much fanfare, both on the part of the administration and the local press. A faculty senate meeting was televised. President Ewigleben said the demands were "reasonable ... None of them will be shelved. That's a promise." The head of the Board of Trustees said, "We trustees are wholeheartedly behind the Readiness Program and have been ever since its establishment." The white student body president said the student government budget would be frozen as of October 30 if money for the CRP weren't produced by the college. Fourteen hundred students signed a petition approving the budget freeze.

The Third World students, most of whom had never been involved in campus protest before, were about to get their first lesson in bureaucracy. Despite the fanfare and rhetoric, nothing was done. Beneath the layer of meetings and committees, nothing real was happening. And the Third World students were impatient. At the time the demands were made, one hundred fifty of them had already dropped out for lack of funds—funds which probably could have been raised locally had the administration allowed it.

On October 13 the CRP students issued an "ultimatum." Said John Brandon, a thirty-three-year-old black ex-convict who had become a tutor in the program: "We do not want to present an ultimatum, but because of the very apparent time warp, or bad communication, which just might be a generation gap, we are forced to do so."

Ewigleben, under TV lights, responded that racism is "an even more important problem than this damnable war we're involved in. . . . We're going to stand behind you. . . . We're not going to leave you out on a limb."

On October 15, about three hundred students staged a non-violent sit-in in the administration building. "We took over the building," Mario Martinez remembers. "We chained all the doors. We had prepared that one. We had thought about it. We went in there and told everybody to get out. The president didn't want to, but finally he did split. All the ladies were asked politely: please leave, this is a student takeover. Some guy didn't want to leave. We told him, 'We're going to have to throw you out, so please leave.' We just gave him his coat and put him out. We were very polite.

"We took care of locking the place up. Now that I think about it, we shouldn't have done it, because it was a bad tactic. But it was a lot of fun. We had people bringing us food. And we let some other people in: Audelith [Audelith Morales, Mario's girlfriend, whom he met in the CRP that summer] came in then.

"After we locked up, we looked around to see what we could find as far as papers and things. We went up to the roof and looked down at all the people. We had a meeting down in the trustees' room.

"It started in the morning and by afternoon it was over. Somebody—I don't know who—took the chains off the back door and the pigs got in. They pushed a couple of brothers, threw them down the stairs. Something was going to start; one of the pigs pulled a gun. We let people know about it, but nothing came out in the newspaper about how they had pulled their guns on us. It doesn't mean anything to me but I know it has some kind of value to people, that they pulled their guns."

The papers said police were called to campus "by mistake" and Ewigleben avoided violence by asking them to leave. The *San Mateo Times* wrote, "Witnesses in the building said the students, mostly black, used threatening language toward female employees in warning them to evacuate their desks and offices."

On October 16 the *San Mateo Times* reported a meeting between administrators, protesting students, and liberal Paul McCloskey, the new Republican congressman in San Mateo County. A photo caption read: " 'What does Delano have to do with this problem?' Congressman Paul McCloskey shouts across crowded table at Ralph Ruiz, firebrand leader of the brown students union on campus. McCloskey was on hand to attempt to mediate Readiness fund problems today but Ruiz wanted to discuss the Vietnam war and the grape strike in Delano."

A few days later the *Palo Alto Times* carried interviews with some CRP students. Mario Martinez was quoted: "I feel that the purpose of high school was to keep us off the street. They treat you like little kids. I want an education. I saw what happened to my parents without an education. I don't want to be oppressed all my life. I want to be able to help my people. We don't want to interfere with people's lives. But we are not going to give up our goals. For most of us, this is a question of survival."

On October 30, Ewigleben reported to the trustees on the administration response to the demands. "We didn't cave in and we didn't say no. Either of these two reactions would have been purely emotional. And neither this country, nor any educational institution in this country, should be ruled by emotion. Reason must prevail." This was already a different Ewigleben from the man who had said three weeks before that "none of the demands will be shelved."

What had happened, after innumerable meetings, was that the administration had agreed to "re-examine" the structure of the financial aids office; "seek funds" for more counselors and tutors; and "develop a minority curriculum . . . in accordance with established procedures. This item has been referred initially to the Committee on Instruction for study and recommendation." Of the two volunteer tutors the CRP had demanded, Pat Sumi was hired but Aaron Manganiello was not. (Pat Sumi was fired shortly thereafter on a technicality.)

The administration made the next move. One day after Ewigleben told the trustees, "Reason must prevail," the following memorandum was delivered to Bob Hoover:

Dear Mr. Hoover:

In as much as Mr. Aaron Manganiello is not a student or an employee of the College of San Mateo, I am ordering that he not be present in the College Readiness Program offices or classrooms. I further order that he not participate in any aspect of the College Readiness Program conducted on this campus.

Sincerely,
Francis W. Pearson Jr.
President, Board of Trustees

In the College Readiness Program the students had traditionally chosen their own staff. Hoover could not have obeyed this order if he had wanted to. He responded:

TO: PRESIDENT EWIGLEBEN
FROM: BOB HOOVER

SUBJECT: We have asked Mr. Manganiello to do volunteer work in the College Readiness Program as long as he can afford to. Until we receive some proof that Aaron Manganiello is damaging our program, the request that Mr. Manganiello be removed from the College Readiness Program is denied.
Yours in Revolution,
Robert S. Hoover
Director, College Readiness Program

Hoover was suspended the next day. The newly elected black Homecoming Queen turned in her crown to protest Hoover's ouster. Such was the outrage, among local blacks as well as white liberals, that Hoover was swiftly reinstated. Ewigleben said that it was "a mistake." But the bad vibes remained.

By demanding Manganiello's removal, the CSM trustees were resorting to outright repression of the Readiness Program, for Manganiello was well known to be an effective political agitator. As the semester wore on, the trustees were to intensify their repression by opening CRP mail, firing Bob Hoover and Jean Wirth, suspending or expelling many of the radical student leaders, and bringing three hundred cops onto the campus, which resulted in numerous arrests, expensive bail, and in at least one case, John Brandon's, a parole violation which meant a return to state prison—even though Brandon was never convicted of any offense in connection with the CSM strike.

Manganiello received a restraining order to stay off campus. The order detailed his part in the October 15 sit-in and added, "On the 14th day of October, a student, Ralph Ruiz, stated [to the Dean of Instruction] in his office that if some action was not taken on the demands above mentioned and that if defendant [Manganiello] was not hired by the following day, guerrilla warfare would take place at San Mateo Junior College campus."

Through November, CRP students continued to drop out for

lack of money. Minor bombings and fistfights became frequent. The *Palo Alto Times* reported that one small bomb in a wastebasket "scorched an American flag hanging above it." Students were suspended or expelled and/or arrested. According to Nelson Rodriguez, he and Ralph Ruiz were simply told not to return to the campus. According to CSM, Nelson "dropped out."

Mario Martinez remembers the mounting frustration: "In the time they were supposed to be working to meet our demands, they had people in courts, they had people in jail, they were kicking all the student leaders out, they were dividing the people, they were expelling people. Most of our meetings they had taped. The other ones, they had infiltrators and spies. The people wanted to discuss things we didn't want the white tutors to know till they were put into action. 'Cause we didn't know who of the white tutors was working for them. We didn't even know out of our own people."

In late November, the accounting firm which had conducted the audit of CRP summer expenditures finally submitted its report to the college trustees. No malfeasance had been discovered in CRP budgeting but the firm included a list of recommendations on how to tighten control over Readiness Program funds. Incoming mail was to be routed to the Dean of Student Personnel office—"checks removed and mail forwarded." As the recommendations put it, "Criteria shall be established by the Assistant Superintendent of Business Affairs which shall determine the purpose of funds received."

The trustees voted unanimously to adopt the recommendations. The next day black students were outraged when a letter from another campus Black Students Union was opened. The entire CRP viewed the opening of mail as an attempt both at censorship and at further obstructing the flow of money into the program.

At their next meeting, on December 11, 1968, the trustees unanimously voted to revise the admission requirements for CSM so that students who were residents of other junior college districts could no longer attend. This eliminated not only latinos from the Mission but Asians from San Francisco and Oakland and

American Indians from all over the Bay Area, many of whom had already been recruited. Later at that meeting Bob Hoover urged the trustees to reconsider, saying, "Those affected most by this policy will be students of color." There was no motion for reconsideration.

The following day, December 12, the Third World students called a strike, reiterating their unmet demands of October 11, and protesting the new rulings and the suspensions and expulsions of over thirty students of color during October and November. They scheduled a rally for the next day, December 13.

II

The rally was held in front of the administration building. Over a thousand students attended. "We called down for the president," Mario remembers. "There was a lot going on, speeches and everything. Some white dudes were screaming while somebody was trying to speak, saying, 'Fuck you, nigger,' and all this. As soon as they called out that word, they got downed. Somebody beat 'em up. Then my brother Tony was trying to speak and this other dude comes up and starts cussing my brother out. So this black brother that was next to him just downed him, too.

"Everybody agreed that we were going to march around the campus. That was the beginning of the strike. So we started marching up the hill a little bit, to Building 19 [electronics—'Whitey's Building']. Some white dudes were there and they started calling names. Just out of nothing—we were just marching. Some white people were with us, supporting us.

"We went into Building 19 and the white dudes started screaming, 'You rotten niggers,' and all this. One girl had a disagreement with this white dude about the strike and he kicked her. As soon as he kicked her, about five black dudes jumped on him and really messed him up. All these little incidents got everybody in a bad mood. Then somebody broke a window. Soon everybody started breaking windows and turning things over. Some teacher called out names. He thought he would get away with it, 'cause he closed the door and locked it. But the doors are made of glass, so they just broke the glass and beat him up.

"That was in the electronics department. See, they had bugged all the places on campus. Every meeting we had, they had a tape. So people were taking out all these grievances. The building that was really damaged was electronics. They're the ones that had set up all the tapes.

"Actually, not too much happened. Just windows broken; a few people got beat up."*

Mario's casual response contrasts with the reaction of administration and press. Almost everyone—almost everyone white, at any rate—condemned the "violence." Twelve injuries were reportedly sustained and property damage was variously estimated at $5,000, $9,000, $15,000, $18,000 and $20,000—the figure increasing as the event receded into the past.

The newspapers spared no effort in describing the vandalism. The *San Francisco Chronicle* reported:

> A mob of 150 shrieking militants, armed with metal pipes and wooden canes, rampaged across the College of San Mateo campus yesterday afternoon.
>
> Behind them they left thousands of students still sitting frozen with terror in their classrooms, and a campus covered with sword-sharp shards of glass. . . .
>
> President Ewigleben, police and faculty associates toured the campus to assess damage and to visit the empty College Readiness Center. . . . On the walls were posters of revolutionary figures, Chairman Mao Tse-tung, Che Gueverra [sic], Malcolm X and others."

Ewigleben was quoted as saying, "I don't know whether [the rioters] wanted to kill or destroy. But the last thing they wanted

---

* Lopate adds: "Although the march made its way through the entire campus, the only buildings where damage occurred were those housing the vocational-technical sciences, [where] occupants attempted to stop the marchers by force, while in other buildings faculty and students made way for them to pass peacefully through."

today was to open up communications." The Third World Liberation Front responded in a leaflet:

> The responsibility for Friday's violence belongs in the hands of white America, namely the administration and the board of trustees. They could have averted all outbursts by recognizing Third World people as human beings in dire trouble and ending the violence that white America has been imposing on Third World people for hundreds of years.
>
> It is only when property is damaged or a white person is injured that the white American will get off his fat ass and act.

One black student added, "We acted out of pure frustration. Frustration from receiving funky checks of $20 or $40 a month to live on. Frustration from knowing over one hundred and fifty of our brothers and sisters had already dropped out of school because of insufficient financial aid."

Audelith Morales said, "Everybody just went nutty and let out all their frustrations because most of the students at the program were from very poor areas . . . and that whole environment was just too much for us to take."

Finally, a black East Palo Alto woman: "I've lived with violence all my life. Don't let a little glass-breaking worry you."

During the riot some students had used steel pipes, pulled out of the campus grass, to break windows. Much was made of this, as Ewigleben later publicly ordered the two-and-one-half-inch pipes removed. A week later, however, he stated, "Most of the weapons had been brought to campus before the rally, indicating the planned nature of the violence." This contradicted the spontaneous steel-pipe theory, but, like it, created an image of "rampaging militants" on which the local residents could ruminate.

The riot of Friday, December 13, lasted less than half an hour. The students, approximately one hundred fifty of them, marched to downtown Redwood City, where they rallied in front of the jail, then dispersed. Meanwhile, police arrived on campus. They were assigned headquarters in the horticulture building. They promptly ripped down the posters and destroyed the radical literature in the CRP center. On Monday, the campus was occupied by three hundred policemen. More closely even than during the simultaneous strike at San Francisco State College, police patrolled the halls and classrooms, and refused to admit anyone without official business.

"A massive show of strength by some three hundred Bay Area policemen yesterday returned an ivory tower calm to the antiseptic hilltop campus of the College of San Mateo," the *San Francisco Chronicle* reported. "A line of autos several blocks long rolled slowly past the police checkpoint at the end of a steep road leading to the campus entrance . . . leaving a pungent smell of burning clutches." Cars carrying Third World students were searched, and IDs were scrupulously checked. Arrests were made on old unserved warrants, unpaid traffic tickets, narcotics charges. With the police checkpoints on campus, and police headquarters close to the Readiness Center, most CRP students found it wise to quit coming to campus. Many others had been suspended or, like Ralph Ruiz and Nelson Rodriguez, told to leave. "It was a complete victory for the pigs," Aaron Manganiello remembers. The December 13 riot, which was a spontaneous act of rage, cost the CRP a good deal of its campus support, and a large-scale student strike never materialized. But more important, the overwhelming police presence physically broke student resistance, and legal or administrative repression soon robbed the Third World students of their leadership.

On December 16, Hoover and Wirth were fired and temporarily barred from campus. The president said they should have prevented the sit-in of October 15 and the violence of December 13 and, presumably, directed the frustrations of their charges into more peaceful channels. The administration announced that the CRP would be "restructured" to include *all* "needy" students, not just students of color.

At this point, it became obvious that the College Readiness Program was being destroyed. The *Palo Alto Times* reported on December 21 that Director of Research Pearce said he and Ewigleben "had been considering a proposal for a central tutorial program to replace College Readiness shortly after the new president came to CSM last summer. His proposal would have been presented even if the near riot of December 13 . . . had not occurred." Hoover and Wirth, it was revealed, were going to get the ax anyway for not directing students into vocational fields.

A later article quoted the Dean of Students as saying of the CRP: "From the very first day, it was a big pain in the neck because it was an exception to all the rules." The head of the Board of Trustees later gave his opinion of the CRP and all minority education to Carol Lopate. As she related it, he said:

> These students should attend the College of San Mateo for a few months, long enough to get vocational training. Then, once they had a full-time job, if they still wanted to go to college for an academic degree they could attend the night school.
>
> It was [his] contention, however, that academic and professional training were unrealistic expectations for these students. The unspoken corollary, one suspects, was that after a brief try at this fancy stuff, they would realize where they belong.

This from the man who said on October 11, "We trustees are wholeheartedly behind the College Readiness Program and have been ever since its establishment."

Violence continued. In January a firebomb destroyed the Dean of Instruction's suburban garage and master bedroom. Each CSM trustee thereafter had bodyguards. The police occupation of the campus lasted for six weeks after the December 13 riot.

CRP tutor John Brandon wrote, "They are destroying our hope and pushing all the people of the Third World up against the wall as if to provoke our limits of control, and then to bring their guns and tactical squad down on us like they were waiting all summer to find any excuse to do. . . . They are destroying our legitimate demands for a place of dignity in this society, and it is just one more act of genocide on all young people of color. . . . They are doing everything they can to provoke violence so they can say to white society: we told you so. We must control these people; we were right in doing what we did to men of color." Brandon's emotion accurately reflected the depth of feeling of most people in the program. As Hoover said, "Now I'm supposed to forget what happened. But there's no way on earth someone like Jean Wirth or me can contribute their flesh and blood to something and then be tossed aside like rag dolls."

After the removals of Wirth and Hoover, one Berkeley educator wrote a letter to the CSM chancellor, a copy of which was sent to Jean Wirth:

> After traveling and consulting throughout the country, it became evident [to me] that the most ambitious and best organized program in the United States was the College Readiness Program of the College of San Mateo. This is the general consensus in Washington, D.C., in the Office of Education, and I believe we all agree that full credit for this honor goes to Miss Jean Wirth and more recently Mr. Robert Hoover.
>
> I have been aware that the College Readiness Program has never had strong support except that given personally by the past president, Dr. Bortolazzi. It is apparent that there has been a shift in commitment to the program and I would suggest that as a result your district will pay a heavy price. . . .
>
> To become involved, as the College of San Mateo did, and then try to disengage, as it is trying to do, is impossible, because the needs of young people do not allow us to back up. For this we are indebted to them. . . .
>
> It is an illusion . . . to feel we have the power to decide the time schedule for another man's fulfillment. It is called racism.

7. Beginning to Get It Together

I

After their expulsion from the College of San Mateo, Nelson Rodriguez and Ralph Ruiz managed to get into the Economic Opportunity Program at San Francisco State, a program similar to the CRP. (Mario and Tony Martinez remained at CSM.) "But," says Nelson, "the strike [at State] was still going on, so there weren't no classes. I registered for the spring semester but things were unstable."

The strike at San Francisco State—later known as the "Mama Strike" because of its many offspring—was one of the most important political events of the sixties for the radical movement. Following the violence at the Democratic National Convention in Chicago, and spanning six months—from November 1968 to April 1969—the S.F. State strike was in many ways a culmination of all the political energy and awareness that had been brewing in ghettoes and on campuses since the early sixties. The strike was also a turning point, since it was crushed and ushered in severe repression on California campuses. Like the young people who went to demonstrate in Chicago the summer before, the striking students learned through painful experience that the state would not hesitate to use massive police power when more sophisticated methods of control broke down. The students threw all their political strength into the strike, in the process attracting much faculty, community, and trade union support. But their strength

123

proved to be very small compared with the combined power of police billyclubs and judicial machinery.

The S.F. State strike was a particularly momentous experience for the Third World students who in fact led it, and around whom it centered. It was as a direct result of the S.F. State strike and others like it that many Third World students decided to begin full-time political organizing in their communities to build a power base among the people—having learned through experience how little power they had without mass community support. The organization of Los Siete de la Raza grew out of the strikes at State and CSM. An organization called Venceremos in Redwood City likewise grew largely out of struggles at Stanford University and CSM.

The struggle at State began ostensibly when Black Panther Minister of Education George Murray was fired from his teaching position on October 31, 1968, allegedly for advocating armed self-defense for blacks. But to the Third World students and faculty at State, Murray's ouster was only one of a series of insults. After months of negotiations and demonstrations, they still had no control over their courses of study or choice of instructors; and they felt they were being made into an elite by their education—forced to abandon their communities and compete with one another.

In the fall of 1968, Third World students presented a series of demands—ten from the Black Students Union and five from the Third World Liberation Front. The demands called primarily for an autonomous Ethnic Studies Department and for open admissions for all local students of color who wished to attend the school. A strike in support of these demands began November 6. The picket line at the campus entrance numbered in the thousands and included students of all colors, faculty, and supporters from unions like the longshoremen, from local ghettoes, and from other colleges. Teamsters refused to cross the picket line. Within a few weeks even administrators admitted attendance at school was down to twenty percent.

The police-student confrontations at State differed from many previous campus uprisings in that the students did not occupy buildings or take other actions which would invite police violence and mass arrest. The students' purpose was to shut the campus down through persistence in maintaining a large picket line, and through mass student support. In the six months of the strike it was almost always the police who initiated violence. Eventually many students learned to fight back with what weapons they could find: chairs, table legs, garbage cans, rocks, and occasional bombings.

The first real violence came on November 13 when, without warning, the Tactical Squad attacked black students near their BSU headquarters. More incidents followed. By December the campus was shut down; but with no prospect of its reopening until the demands were met, the State College Trustees replaced the liberal president, Robert Smith, with the conservative S. I. Hayakawa; Hayakawa's purpose was to reopen the campus, no matter what the cost. His attitude was described by Kay Boyle, one of the striking teachers:

On top of the truck was a whirling, irate little man, wearing a tam o' shanter, a plump little figure who was tugging and leaping and close to foaming at the mouth in his paroxysm of rage. I moved in closer with the students, who were now calling out, "Freedom of speech, Dr. Hayakawa! What about freedom of speech?" Others were laughing at the sight, and admonishing him, "Now remember, no violence, no violence! We can't have anything like that!" But the Acting President of the college was pushing and shoving at those who mounted the truck, including newsmen, and clawing furiously at the sound truck's wires. Once he had jerked them out, he swung around to the crowd, and like a demented orchestra conductor, with arms and hands savagely beating out the rhythm, in furious mockery he led the students in the chant of "On strike! Shut it down!" (Later, still shaken, he told the press: "I can't stand that mindless chanting!")*

* Kay Boyle, *The Long Walk at San Francisco State* (New York: Grove, 1970).

After a long Christmas holiday, heavily armed mounted police developed the tactic of charging at picketing students, sometimes bloodying photographers, reporters and onlookers in their enthusiasm. Nelson remembers, "The cops were on horses, charging around. We were really scared. The horses were coming at us and two press photographers said, 'They're coming after you.' They said they'd stay close by so we wouldn't get beat up so bad. Me and Mario just turned and ran. We hid in some bushes."* Later the police charged Nelson with throwing a rock.

Between December 2, 1968, and January 30, 1969, doctors reported that police had inflicted eighty injuries on strikers who were arrested. Injuries not reported, or of people not arrested, would have significantly boosted this number. The Tac Squad was on permanent campus duty for three months and was reinforced by regular police from San Francisco and nearby cities.

A handful of Community Relations officers held a press conference. They said: "We deplore the carnival of police departments within one hundred miles of San Francisco who now beg to have their policemen permitted to get 'riot training' experience on the heads of San Francisco State students." One of them was promptly relieved of his duties for "unofficerlike conduct." (He publicized the fact and was reinstated a few days later.)

One day during the winter, after the strikers had been caught many times on campus and encircled and beaten by police, Ralph Ruiz suggested they move out of the campus trap and into the middle-class residential area around the campus. This may have been a sensible move but it marked Ralph (and Nelson, who was often with him) as a target for the police. By the end of the State strike, Ralph Ruiz had been identified as a leading brown radical, and Nelson Rodriguez was known to be closely associated with him. When, a few months later, Officer Joseph Brodnik died in a confrontation with an unknown number of latinos, the police already had photos of Nelson and Ralph to show to witnesses.

On January 23, 1969, the students held a mass rally in de-

---

* Mario, like other survivors of the CSM strike, often came to State as a supporter.

fiance of President Hayakawa's orders. Police broke up the rally, blocked avenues of escape, and, in what seemed a conscious attempt finally to break the strike, arrested four hundred thirty-five people. Municipal court judge Laurence Mana, who was later to preside over the trial of Los Siete, refused to release any of the students on their own recognizance, and demanded bail. For many strikers the long struggle then turned to raising bail and fighting court battles.

In March the striking teachers—exhausted, demoralized, many of them broke or in debt—settled their own grievances with the State College trustees. Police billyclubs and legal battles eventually broke the student strike, too. Some ethnic studies programs were established, and Third World students and faculty began arguing over the spoils.

The brown students and teachers had always been divided into two factions. The latinos—in this case mostly Central Americans and mostly from the Mission district—had their own small club, which wanted a campus responsible for and responsive to the community, and which aimed to bring more local young people to school. The chicanos, an equally small group, emphasized recruiting students from farm labor towns fifty or more miles from San Francisco, since the Mission district contained relatively few people of Mexican descent. Apparently their feeling was that since chicanos formed the overwhelming majority of Spanish-speaking people in California and throughout the Southwest, La Raza Studies programs should represent primarily chicanos. But a chicano-dominated program in a city where most Spanish-speaking people were latino would tend to become academic, apolitical, and divorced from the needs of the local barrio.

More important, those students in La Raza Studies who were soon to help form the Los Siete organization felt that government "benevolence," whether through Economic Opportunity programs on campus or Mission Rebels–type organizations in the ghetto, had the effect of setting minority people against each other to fight over the spoils. The small amount of government money and the limited number of college openings made minority students competitive at the same time that it "bought off" many potential leaders with salaries, college degrees, and/or acceptance into the middle class.

In practice what happens is that a united group of students and faculty demand a much-expanded autonomous ethnic studies program responsive to the needs of the local community. After a struggle in which some of the most militant leaders are arrested and caught up in legal battles, the administration compromises, agreeing to create a somewhat autonomous program—as long as it is not too militant or revolutionary. This presents the students and faculty with a dilemma: should they accept the compromise (which certainly looks like an improvement over the current state of affairs), or should they hold out for the ultimate goal—which is probably unattainable without real revolutionary change in the society? Some want to compromise; others want to keep fighting. This works to the college administration's advantage, since it destroys the unity of the group. Eventually the split becomes irrevocable; those willing to compromise take over the offered programs—within the limits established by the administration—while those who want to keep fighting leave or are forced out. In this way many of the most radical minority students and faculty at San Francisco State were eliminated, and the administration could point with pride to the "progressive" new ethnic studies program it had established.

As Aaron Manganiello described it, "At San Francisco State the demands that were won concerning curriculum have now been turned against us. Oh yes, we have more chicano classes—but they're being taught by the biggest Tacos [Uncle Toms] in San Francisco. Roger Alvarado, Donna James, and others who really know their shit aren't teaching.* They've got a guy at State teaching 'Contemporary Chicano Movements' and he has never even been in any movement. . . . He doesn't even have a jail record, which would seem to me one of the first criteria to teach such a class. . . .

"We can never control who or what is being taught at any

* It was not unusual for upper-class students to teach in the ethnic studies programs.

128

institution that is completely owned by the bourgeoisie [meaning not the middle class but the very rich or ruling class]. The only way we will control our education is not through the colleges but only in the streets with workers, in political education classes, breakfast-for-children programs, etc."

It was with these perceptions, gained through a year of college upheavals, that some of the people in La Raza Studies, as well as veterans of the CSM strike, began to commit themselves to full-time community work. José Delgado, who had first gone to State as an Upward Bound recruit, helped start a free breakfast-for-children program in the Mission, modeled after the Black Panther Party's breakfast programs. Tony Martinez, still attending CSM, planned to open a storefront in the Mission to recruit brothers and sisters for school. Nelson and Ralph also tried recruiting.

"Me and Ralph talked to one of the teachers," Nelson remembers. "And we asked him could we do some work in the community and get credit for it. He said yes. We just never went back to class. We tried recruiting kids to go to school—handing out applications for both CSM and State, and running down to them the importance of an education. We had a few—not too many people were interested in going. They would say, 'Yeah, yeah, that sounds just fine. Let me have the application and I'll give it back to you.' I think we got only three or four fully filled out.

"One day we were supposed to meet these brothers to take them to school and talk to a counselor. We were supposed to meet them somewhere but they never showed up. I guess they thought it was only a lot of bullshit. They've been getting a lot of bullshit throughout the years. Anyone comes and tells you without a high school education you can go to college, that sounds like a lie."

The experiences of Nelson, Ralph, Tony and Mario were repeated that year by thousands of Third World students all over California. For these students the strikes marked a turning point. They could no longer believe the liberal promise of free mass higher education in the state. Afterwards, Economic Opportunity Program funds shrank, many of those students and teachers who stood for radical change were fired or expelled, and college admissions became even tighter and more competitive.

The Coordinating Council on Higher Education, implementers of the Master Plan, rejected a proposal for eighteen new junior college campuses—even though the state and junior colleges were already overcrowded and thousands of students were being turned away. "Fewer, larger campuses are more efficient," they explained. At one state college in 1970 there were six hundred places for seven thousand spring semester applicants. The *San Francisco Chronicle* reported, "Thousands of junior college transfers have virtually no place to go for their junior year."

Repression spread from universities down to kindergartens. The State Board of Education established "morality guidelines" for the elementary schools which were derived largely from Navy and Marine manuals. Radical teachers were fired all over the state. The Angela Davis case* was the most publicized, but dozens of other radicals, mostly nonwhite, were dismissed. At Fresno State College, in the middle of the heavily chicano Central Valley, the entire faculty of the La Raza Studies department was fired in May 1970. Six months later many white liberal faculty members were purged.

At San Francisco State, Hayakawa got rid of fifteen American Federation of Teachers members who had been active in the strike; and, after talking of a "reign of terror" in the Black Studies Department, he fired ten aides and all six full-time professors. Later he dismissed the student government, and throughout the 1969–70 school year he exercised strict censorship over the student newspaper.

During that same period, Governor Ronald Reagan pushed through a tuition program for the traditionally free state college and university system, thus underscoring the class nature of the state's higher education. At the same time, university regents and state college trustees moved to centralize their power over hiring

---

* In the fall of 1969 Angela Davis was fired from her teaching job at UCLA for being a member of the Communist Party. A superior court ordered her reinstated on the grounds that the firing was unconstitutional.

130

and firing of faculty, curriculum, and disciplinary procedures; and state legislators raised the penalties for "campus agitators."

In February 1970, California's Coordinating Council on Higher Education became the official boss of the Economic Opportunity Program at universities, state colleges, and junior colleges. This program, combining counseling, financial aid, and a waiving of official admissions standards, supported about fifteen thousand students, the great majority of them black or brown. One state college administrator charged that by taking over the EOP the Coordinating Council, and Governor Reagan, were making the first move toward forcing all EOP students out of four-year schools and into junior colleges. A Reagan official denied this charge but did say he thought junior colleges "would offer the best educational program for a youngster that is behind." At the same time, Reagan vetoed a budget appropriation of $1.6 million to bring new students into the EOP. In 1971 funds were cut from the program.

Newspaper headlines reflected that tightening of financial and political controls:

REGENTS BAR UC DEGREE FOR LINDSAY*
TIGHTER CLAMP ON CAMPUS PAPERS
SAN JOSE STRIKE PROFESSOR OUSTED
LONG COLD ADMISSION VIGIL/THOUSANDS JAM STATE COLLEGE CAMPUSES
A CAMPUS CRACKDOWN/TOUGH NEW REAGAN RULES
FRESNO STATE WON'T HIRE MUSLIM
UC CLAMPS DOWN ON A COURSE IN REPRESSION
HAYAKAWA LIKENED TO SCROOGE

Another headline in December 1969 said simply "THE MASTER PLAN." The article read:

The governor and legislature were officially advised here yesterday that California's Master Plan for Higher Education should continue as the guideline for the state's public colleges and universities. The advice came from the Coordinating Council on Higher Education, which was organized under the Master Plan in 1961 to advise the executive and legislative branches of government on major policy issues in higher education. . . .

* Mayor John Lindsay of New York. The regents considered him too liberal.

131

The Master Plan, which established three independent segments—the universities, state colleges and junior colleges—coordinated by the Council, has been under attack ever since campus disruptions began in 1964.

Yesterday, however . . . the chairman of the Council said he could see no connection between the disruptions and the way higher education is organized in California.

II

Mario and Tony Martinez continued to attend CSM. With many of the old leaders gone, they began to take more responsibility for the Readiness Program. Tempers had cooled: after the strike, some teachers helped students who had missed classes because of the police occupation make up their academic work. Tony participated in panel discussions to improve the program's image and raise funds. He also became head of COBRA, the Confederation of the Brown Race for Action; this group succeeded in getting more counselors hired for the Readiness Program and in establishing the beginnings of an ethnic studies curriculum. COBRA also sponsored the school's first La Raza Week in the spring of 1969.

La Raza Week attracted many people from the Mission, among them Bebe Melendez, who, disgusted with the Mission Rebels, was fishing around for a new direction. Bebe had heard about the Readiness Program from his friend Roberto Vargas, a poet and ex-Brown Beret, then working for an Office of Economic Opportunity program called Horizons Unlimited. "He came up to me and started talking," Bebe said later. " 'Why don't you get involved at the College of San Mateo?' He kept trying to urge me to go down there. One time he was going to take me. . . . Well, I hung him up and I never got there. I did go in April. They were advertising all over the Mission—'Culture Week': they would give some of the brothers and sisters a chance to check out what the real culture was—and I dug what I seen. I got to thinking maybe I should get an education."

Despite the cooling of tensions at CSM, minority enrollment had dropped drastically. In April 1969 only one hundred thirty students were left in the Readiness Program. Mario and Tony turned their efforts once again to recruiting new students or re-recruiting old ones. The emphasis was on street people, mostly high school dropouts. "Once I registered Gio Lopez [the seventh of Los Siete, the one who was never arrested] he would split from college and I would have to find him again," Mario remembers. "He's an out-of-sight guy. I told him he had to do something for himself—he was getting married pretty soon. He started to attend classes but his English was bad so he would get bored and go back to the Mission. I got him into the program twice. Gio didn't enroll for the spring semester. I told him to take his entrance test. He got bored in the middle of the test and walked out."

José Rios, the youngest of Los Siete, was eager to go to CSM. "All my friends—Oscar [José's older brother], Tony, Reynaldo— were going to San Mateo," José remembers. "So I sort of lost interest in high school. My friends and me started rapping about what courses we'd be taking, how to get along in these courses. They'd tell me college was hard work but a lot better than high school. I used to visit them, get familiar with the campus because I was going to be attending the coming semester. I was already accepted. I couldn't wait to start going. 'Cause the education was a lot better and I would be with my old friends again.

"My parents were pretty excited when my brother Oscar started going to the College of San Mateo. And when I brought home my application for them to sign, they were happy too, you know? Mario had gotten me interested in studying medicine, and I still have that ambition. My parents started telling me, 'Your brothers never got to go, 'cause they were older. They really didn't have a choice.' "

Even Pinky Lescallett, who hated school "more than any-thing," and who had been on the streets since he last got out of jail, was ready to try the program. "Tony told me about San Mateo, so I went. But they were having a strike. . . . I came back to the city late one night and the pigs stopped me. They told me I committed an armed robbery. I was ready to cop 'cause five-to-life [the penalty for armed robbery] didn't sound too good to me," Pinky explained. "I wasn't guilty of *nothing*. But the thing is, people in the Mission, we don't have much money. . . . The Man thinks just because we all got black hair, we're all the same. So he picks anybody up and throws him in jail. And your mama feels for you, but she ain't got the money, so what can she do? You ain't got the money to pay a lawyer so all you can do is go and do what the Man tells you. There was a lot of Spanish cats in jail with me. They were swearing to God they didn't do nothing. And these were religious dudes, man; they'd be praying every night."

Pinky copped to petty theft and did sixty days in the county jail. When he got out in April, he visited CSM again at Tony's insistence. "My feeling was that the program was good," Pinky said, " 'cause it was for one thing—to educate the people. . . . The concept was always to bring it back to the barrio, to explain to people like myself. I had my application all filled out and I was going out to school every day, listening to tapes."

Thus all of the seven young latinos who were soon to become Los Siete had been or were about to be involved in the College Readiness Program. Mario and Tony Martinez were still in the program, Nelson Rodriguez had participated for several months, Gio Lopez had been an on-and-off student, and Bebe Melendez, Pinky Lescallett and José Rios were all about to attend. Despite the new restrictions on the program, Tony and Mario continued to recruit, realizing they'd have to use the Man's institutions until they had some of their own.

Something "of their own" eventually came out of the CRP experience. After the strike, Tony, Nelson and Mario participated in the planning for an autonomous Third World college on the peninsula, south of San Francisco. In late 1969 Bob Hoover and Aaron Manganiello jointly founded Nairobi College in East Palo Alto and its brown branch, Venceremos College, in Redwood City. Nairobi/Venceremos used community homes, churches, libraries, and recreation halls as its own facilities. Transfer credits were arranged with some of the more progressive colleges in the country. About a year after its founding, Nairobi/Venceremos got accreditation from the Western College Association. Hoover wrote:

Nairobi College is designed to produce the leaders so desperately needed by communities of color. . . . It is precisely those with the greatest leadership potential who are frequently excluded from education and who therefore come to Nairobi least equipped to pursue their goals. . . . Students will always be in and of the community they intend to serve. No student will be dehumanized by being forced to forget his brothers and sisters while he improves himself. . . .

At Nairobi, classes have been known to redirect their attention for a three-hour session to bring one latecomer up to date. . . . When students cooperate, ask for group rather than individual grading, become genuinely responsible for each other's learning, all members of a class learn more. Even more important, they learn to aid rather than destroy each other.

"I learned a lot from the strike," Mario says. "I learned how to deal with them. Like this thing about petitions—it never works. You either have to do it yourself or force them. I learned things about organizing. I was let down a lot of times, but a lot of times I was happy, 'cause of the things we got through working.

"I was going to school up to that May. I went almost a year. I was getting hip to all these classes. I had talked to more people, teachers and everything. There were some teachers that were pretty liberal. Later on I was going to pick some good courses. I was thinking of eventually going to Berkeley, but then as I read more I liked Stanford better."

In addition to recruiting, Mario tutored in the phonics course he had taken the summer before. "I was so busy I used to miss most of my classes. And people would tell me, 'What kind of example are you setting—cutting your classes?' But there just wasn't time for them.

"Those were good times," Mario says. Like all struggles, the strikes brought people closer together. Donna James, who quit San Francisco State that spring in order to work in the community, remembers, "Ralph, me, Nelson, Mario and Audelith would get together sometimes and spend the day driving around the peninsula in a van, getting stoned and rapping. It would take half the day to pick everyone up—Nelson in South San Francisco, Mario in Daly City, Audelith in San Mateo—and the other half to take everyone home. But it was the only time we had to rap about politics, because on the campuses it was always action. The only politics Nelson was ever involved in was action: throwing rocks, running away from cops. That spring, the brothers were just beginning to get it together."

The personal solidarity that developed from the crucial events of winter 1968 and spring 1969 was partly responsible for the formation of the Los Siete de la Raza organization. Such was the friendship among many people who were involved in the strikes that if it had been Ralph Ruiz or Donna James who were arrested for murder, Mario or Tony Martinez would probably have started Los Siete. (As events were to show, Ralph Ruiz could easily have been arrested.) But more important, the political maturity that strike veterans were beginning to develop paved the way for the Los Siete organization. Survivors of the S.F. State and San Mateo experiences were to form the core of the new organization. The seeds already existed in the movement of students back into the community (as with Venceremos College in Redwood City and the new breakfast program in the Mission), and in the insight and determination that "brothers" like Mario Martinez had developed. "Education is so important for our people," Mario says. "We've been without it so long. In the Mission we hear things like people wanting to join the Green Berets—there are many examples of this kind of ignorance in the streets. You see all these guys turning to drugs. They don't see that this is no help and only oppresses us more.

"We also need education to get the people prepared—to know how they've been oppressed and to deal with it later on. You can't have a bunch of ignorant people running around thinking, 'Get Whitey.' That's not the way it's going to come down. And that's the way a lot of brothers think now. 'Just let me know when the revolution is on and I'll come shoot.' Well, the revolution is on. The time now is for everybody to get mentally prepared."

III

The move toward educational self-determination was so wide-spread in 1968 and early '69 that a brief strike erupted at Mission High. There, even more clearly than at the relatively isolated college campuses, police repression and rising political consciousness in the Mission clashed head-on.

It began when the Tac Squad came to Mission High to stop a race fight—a common occurrence in interracial schools. Both black and brown students immediately united in the demand to keep cops out of their affairs. The latinos circulated a leaflet: "We got ourselves together last week to fight the blacks; now it's time to fight the REAL ENEMY."

The students' demands included black and brown studies, abolition of laminated ID cards, election of hallway monitors, more Third World teachers and counselors, expulsion of under-cover and uniformed cops in school, and abolition of IQ tests. The administration held separate assemblies for each racial group to discuss the demands. When this failed to divide the students, thirty-four of the strikers were arrested, mostly for truancy, after rallies in Dolores Park across the street. The Mission Coalition, recently formed to deal with urban renewal, stepped in with a "compromise" settlement which consisted mainly of replacing one source of irritation, the principal. The student demands were buried in a maze of Board of Education committees.

Detectives Brodnik and McGoran were among the plainclothes-men patrolling their alma mater. According to Nelson's recollection, McGoran told Ralph Ruiz on one occasion, "We know you guys want to overthrow the government. But we don't want to see it in our lifetimes. So we're not gonna let you do it."

"The pigs had declared war on the brothers down in the Mission," Nelson says, remembering the spring of 1969. "About a week before our bust an article came out in the newspaper about how the merchants were being terrorized. Well, nothing like that ever happened. The proof is that this woman who owns a store down on Twentieth and Mission, she came with one of her daughters and apologized to us, because she knew it was all lies."

The article to which Nelson refers appeared on April 25, 1969, on the front page of the *San Francisco Chronicle* and was headlined, "A GANG'S TERROR IN THE MISSION." It began:

A loose-knit gang of idlers and hoodlums are slowly closing a fist of fear around the business life of a once-bustling Mission District neighborhood.

So pervasive has this fear become, it is a virtual act of heroism for merchants to complain to police. Most store owners in the area flatly refuse to talk to outsiders about the situation.

It would still be a skeleton in the neighborhood closet— to be whispered about when no strangers are around—if it weren't for a small lady with dark, frightened eyes.

The article bore the byline of Birney Jarvis, a veteran police reporter. Jarvis's story, like his opening paragraphs, contained more innuendo than fact. The only concrete acts of "terror" were enumerated as follows: "They idle on the sidewalks, making pedestrians walk around them, they lean against buildings and spit, sometimes they fight among themselves. Their language is filthy."

The following day, Jarvis had another front-page story reporting the community outrage over his first article. It began: "A powerful expression of indignation and baffled anger was heard yesterday from the idealistic young men and women who are trying to help Mexican-American youth in San Francisco." A later article reported the distress of most Mission Street merchants over the intemperate language of "A Gang's Terror." After press conferences and apologies, the matter was forgotten. But in the Mission the feeling persisted that "A Gang's Terror" was no accident. Despite the ostensible airing of both sides, the image of dark-skinned hoodlums terrorizing good shopkeepers remained. The article thus set the stage for the announcement of a new one hundred fifty–man "crime-busting" squad which was introduced into the Mission the following week.

"I remember a couple of nights before everything came down," says José Rios. "There was some pig walking by and someone in the group went 'Oink,' and so the pig turned around and started chasing us. They caught this friend of mine and started beating him and beating him. Blood was coming out of his head. They didn't know who said it; they just wanted to get anybody."

José was right. A week later Joseph Brodnik was dead, his partner Paul McGoran was hospitalized, and José Rios and the rest of Los Siete were running for their lives.

8. Mayday

On the morning of May 1, 1969, there was a "Free Huey" rally outside the Federal Building in San Francisco. Inside the building, attorney Charles Garry was unsuccessfully requesting bail for Black Panther Party co-founder Huey Newton while Newton's manslaughter conviction in the death of an Oakland policeman was on appeal. Outside, the crowd was mostly young and black. Some demonstrators were elementary school age—probably brought to the rally from the Panthers' free breakfast-for-children program in the nearby Fillmore district. Older students, both black and brown, had obviously cut classes to attend the rally. Picket signs depicted Newton's head, with beret, superimposed on a big red star. "Red Books" had been distributed, and were hoisted into the air for periodic "Free Huey" or "Power to the People" chants. With the red books and red stars, the scene differed radically from most previous left rallies. It was organized, even disciplined. People marched in step.

Several of the brown radicals who were to form Los Siete were standing in the crowd near a police motorcycle. Donna James remembers that shortly after the speaker announced the death of a policeman in the Mission district, she heard the police radio broadcast the names of three people wanted for the murder. They were Mario Martinez, Nelson Rodriguez, and José Rios.

The killing of forty-one-year-old police officer Joseph Brodnik had taken place in front of 433 Alvarado Street, where José Rios's family had moved three weeks before. It was a pink house with chipped front pillars on a quiet Noe Valley street, three blocks north of Twenty-fourth Street and a half dozen west of Mission Street. The houses on the block ranged from tidy and well repaired, with fences, to shabby, needing paint, worn from frequent tenant turnover.

The population of Alvarado Street was mixed too—mostly brown people and working-class whites. When Irene Jarzyna, a Polish woman who lived across the street at 436 Alvarado, had first seen the Rios boys move in, she became alarmed; but, she later explained, "I felt better when I saw they had parents."

Around nine in the morning of May 1, a twenty-year-old chicano, David Caravantes, drove up to the Jarzyna house, where his girlfriend Diane lived. He had breakfast with the family, then waited for Diane to get dressed so he could drive her to San Francisco City College. As he waited, looking out of the front window, he saw several young people milling around across the street.

All witnesses agree that in the half hour or so that followed, two cars drove up to 433 Alvarado Street. Out of the first, a blue Chevrolet, came a number of young latinos. Out of the second, an unmarked white Dodge which arrived about fifteen minutes later, came Brodnik and McGoran. McGoran had his brown cardigan pulled low to hide the bulge of a holster inside his pants. Brodnik wore a short-sleeved white sport shirt, and carried no gun.

The young latinos were moving furniture which had been stolen from a house in the middle-class Sunset district of the city about an hour before. Definitely present were José Rios, Bebe Melendez, Gary Lescallett, Mario Martinez, and Gio Lopez. Brodnik and McGoran began to investigate. José Rios and two others went upstairs to a second-floor flat at 433 Alvarado. José came down alone a few minutes later with identification.

An exchange of insults led to a fight between McGoran and Gary Lescallett. Someone was knocked down. Two shots from McGoran's .41 Magnum revolver were fired in quick succession.

Joseph Brodnik fell to the sidewalk, a bullet hole in his chest. McGoran, bleeding from the mouth and screaming hysterically, scrambled for cover behind a ledge. The young latinos fled.

David Caravantes, who had been watching from across the street, ran and leaned over Brodnik, who was stretched on his back, one knee up, the foot curled in, a grimace on his lips. "I could feel he wasn't breathing," Caravantes said later, "yet I could see underneath his adam's apple it was still gurgling, so I was thinking of artificial respiration. And then he just turned cold."

One of the first to arrive at the scene was Captain Philip Kiely of Mission Station. He ran to McGoran, who was still hysterical, thinking he had been shot in the mouth. McGoran said two of "them" were still inside, armed and dangerous. Kiely's job, as he said later, was "to take the emergency measure of containing the scene and apprehending the suspects if possible." This meant a full siege: tear gas, M-16s, fire trucks with ladders for police to climb to the roof, helicopters to look for suspects escaping on foot. José Rios heard the shooting and saw the helicopters from his hiding place in a hedge two blocks away.

Mario Martinez later testified he and Gio Lopez were upstairs; they went out the back of the house and caught a bus on Twenty-fourth Street. Bebe Melendez testified he and Pinky [Gary Lescallett] ran toward the Lescallett apartment half a mile away. Bebe said he tossed McGoran's Magnum into a hedge on a side street and threw off his shirt, thinking someone might identify him by it.

TV footage later showed that in the middle of the siege one policeman ventured into the second-floor Rios flat. He knocked on a closed door and was answered by carbine fire. He ducked and shot back, then ran outside to tell the press of his escape. Actually, there was no one left inside. The fire must have come from another policeman shooting into the house from a neighboring rooftop.

When they finally realized there were no suspects inside, police began to pour into the flat. "The pigs were mad," José Rios said later, "because one of their brothers had died, and they had so much anger inside that they just took all the walls and whatever was in front of them and shot them full of holes. They shot fifty or sixty rounds all over the house. Just for the hell of it, just mad 'cause they didn't find who had done it." The flat was wrecked, almost all the furniture destroyed. Fourteen-year-old Dolores Rios was grazed in the hip by a bullet.

Mrs. Rios was found at work, brought home, and questioned with her daughter. When pressured to produce some names, Dolores told police she thought she had heard Nelson Rodriguez's voice upstairs. ("I knew José for about eight years," says Nelson, who, witnesses later testified, was sitting in his girlfriend's Daly City apartment at 10:23 that morning when the bullet passed into Brodnik's chest. "So when they asked his sister Dolores who was there, she naturally thought it was me.")

Stephen Laznibat, the Rios' neighbor, told police he thought he saw several people with guns in their hands, including McGoran. Anna Maria Chavez, a young housewife, saw the tallest boy (Gary Lescallett) and McGoran fighting. Mrs. Jarzyna, when asked to identify the killer, cried, "Was so fast, so fast, I'm not really sure who." David Caravantes asked to talk to McGoran before giving a statement. Later that afternoon he changed his mind about talking to McGoran and said into a tape recorder that he didn't see who fired the fatal shot because McGoran was blocking his view. He said the boys were "rowdy and smart"; McGoran was "excited, pushing, screaming . . . you could see Brodnik was calming him down. . . . If McGoran hadn't gone up after [Gary Lescallett] . . . there would have been no way this could have happened."

At San Francisco General Hospital, McGoran corroborated Dolores Rios's clue about Nelson, whom he knew as a Mission "troublemaker" and who was the same size as Gio Lopez. He also identified Mario Martinez and José Rios—and "possibly" Gary Lescallett and Bebe Melendez—as having been present.

Bebe and Gary changed clothes at the Lescallett apartment; then they split up and waited at two different bus stops for the same

Mission Street bus, which they took north toward the heart of the Mission. They got off at Nineteenth Street and went to the apartment of two girls Bebe knew from the Mission Rebels. A friend, Dennis Calderon, was there. They turned on the radio; it said José Rios had been caught. Just then José walked in; he had taken a different route to the same apartment. They laughed over the inaccuracy, and borrowed money from Dennis. Then they made telephone arrangements to drive out of town. A few minutes later a friend arrived; Bebe, Pinky and José hid on the floor of his car under a blanket while he drove south to Palo Alto.

Meanwhile, Mario later testified, he and Gio took the Greyhound bus to San Mateo. When they arrived, Gio went to the College of San Mateo campus, where he found Tony Martinez walking with his tutor. Excited and half-incomprehensible, Gio told Tony bits of what had happened. A friend at the Readiness Center drove them to meet Mario.

There was no question in the minds of the five who had been at Alvarado Street that they had to flee. Too many black and brown kids had been killed, ostensibly "while trying to escape," whether or not they really meant to surrender.* The five were brown, in the midst of stolen property, with a dead cop on the sidewalk. They felt sure the police who came with their M-16s would not listen to explanations. Perhaps there could be a surrender later, in the presence of lawyers. But their decision to run was not well reasoned anyway. They were simply terrified by the thought of confronting the police.

Tony, Mario, Gio, Bebe, Gary and José met at a friend's house in Palo Alto. They spent the afternoon watching the TV news. Tony, who had not been at Alvarado Street, decided to stay with his brother Mario. "I called my father," Tony remembers, "and told him to call our lawyer, and that we weren't coming

* In 1970 a black teenager was killed in the Hunters Point ghetto of San Francisco by a cop who was chasing him and thought he had a gun. (He didn't.) That same year, two young Mexicans were killed by Los Angeles police who burst into an apartment searching for somebody else. The investigations in both cases concluded that the killings were "justifiable homicide."

145

home. I wasn't thinking about me but about my brother. I was gonna stay with him." In the afternoon Gio Lopez, described by friends as a "stone individualist," went off on his own.* That night Ralph Ruiz drove the remaining five—Tony and Mario Martinez, Bebe Melendez, José Rios and Gary Lescallett—to a house in the Santa Cruz hills about eighty miles south of San Francisco.

II

The police continued their investigation by questioning relatives and friends of the suspects. "May 1 was a nice hot day," Oscar Rios remembers. "Early in the morning we [Oscar and Reynaldo "Ray" Aparicio] went to pick up Mario, but he was still in bed. He said, 'I'll see you later at school.' We just said, 'Okay, punk,' and left.

"At about eleven o'clock we saw Nelson and Ralph at school. We told them we were going to the Huey Newton rally and they said they'd see us in the city. So we bought a couple of beers and split."

Nelson and Ralph were waiting for Mario, who had promised to see about getting them back into CSM. ("I wanted to get Ralph and Nelson back into school because the program lacked leadership," Mario later said.) When Mario didn't show, Nelson and Ralph took off for Palo Alto, where they played pool. At around 4:30, Ralph dropped Nelson off where he had picked him up, at his girlfriend Sandy's apartment in Daly City. Nelson dashed up the stairs because he heard the phone ringing.

---

* Gio Lopez never returned. He was arrested at least three times in various parts of the country during the next year. Each time he gave a false name and was released before the FBI fingerprint check came through. In July 1970 he hijacked a plane to Cuba, where, according to a reliable source, he was accommodated (not imprisoned) in a house with other hijackers. A group of Central Americans living in Cuba took an interest in Gio and tried to educate him politically. At last report he was at work cutting sugar cane.

Oscar and Ray drove from CSM to Mario's "because I wanted to give him some of the homework he had missed," Ray says. "We didn't find him at home, but we did have several undercover pigs chase us. They followed us for a while and then stopped the car. We were really surprised, because not only had we been drinking wine but we had had a little taste of grass. So the smell of grass and wine was on our breath. And all these pigs came out with their flashy-looking guns, and we say, Wow! All this for grass and wine! It blew our minds."

Oscar: "The pigs had their fingers on the triggers. We freaked out. We asked why we had been stopped; they just said, 'Shut up, don't ask any questions.' Finally one of them said, 'There's been a homicide on Alvarado Street. A policeman has been shot to death. It was your friends.' "

Ray: "They began telling us we better come up with some information. If not, it was going to be the end of the brothers. We would not be squealers, they said, but we would be heroes for saving them. They had Mrs. Rios with them in a squad car, asking her to recognize friends of the brothers, because we were all suspects. Mrs. Rios and her daughter and Mrs. Martinez were all in shock. Especially Mrs. Martinez—she was ill for the next two or three months.

"When we arrived at 850 Bryant [the San Francisco Hall of Justice] they took us to the floor where they make interrogations. The officer in charge was a fat-looking pig, and a bigot and a half. He first asked Oscar to come in. He told Oscar all the many good things he would do to his brother and his friends if he was to turn them in. Then he told Oscar the kind of dirty things he would do to Oscar if he didn't turn the guys in. He told him what the family could go through if they did not find the brothers.

"He started telling me again how the best thing I could do was to turn the brothers in. And that if I didn't want them to get shot like dogs, it would be best to tell where they were, so they would go there and bargain with them and finally have them throw down their guns, give in peacefully. I told him he was lying.

"Then he told me and Oscar we should be glad that none of

147

the good friends of the police officer who had been killed had gotten their hands on us."

Ray and Oscar were finally released and found their way back to the car where it had been stopped near Daly City. With police trailing them, they drove to see Mrs. Martinez. "We heard she was really sick," Oscar says. "But as soon as we got outside the car and went in the house, as soon as we closed the gate, man, four cars came. 'Just hold it right there! Come on, tell us where they are.' They searched the whole house.

"Ray says, 'Don't you have any respect for a sick woman?'

"The pig goes, 'Don't talk to me about that shit.' "

Inside the house, Homicide Inspector Jack Cleary—who was now in charge of the case—found Mrs. Martinez in bed. He sat down at the vanity and questioned her, resting his feet on the bedspread. Another cop pressed his gun to the stomach of the third son, Orlando Martinez, aged fifteen, and asked where his brother was; then he said, according to Mrs. Martinez, "When we find them we'll shoot them down like dogs."*

Nelson Rodriguez, who had been dropped off at his girlfriend's apartment in Daly City, picked up the phone on the twelfth ring. "It was José. He said, 'Haven't you heard the news?'

"I said, 'No, what news?' The car we were in had no radio, so I had no idea what was happening.

"José said, 'Turn on the radio.' Just as I turned it on, they were saying a policeman had been killed, and they ran down the names of the suspects: first José, then Mario, then me!

"I called home. My brother answered. He said, 'They're here.'

"I said, 'Who's there?'

"He said, 'The FBI. They're looking for you.' I just told him to tell my parents I was okay, and hung up."

Police were busy on Mission Street that night. "We see the pigs following us," Oscar says, "so we stop and let them pass. They find out I'm José's brother. They phoned right away and this pig

* Cleary denied this in court.

148

comes, Pig Ellis [Lt. Charles Ellis, head of the homicide detail]. He pulls me to the side and says, 'I know where your brother's at. And I know *you* know where your brother's at. And I know you're gonna tell me. Because if you don't tell me, he's going to tell me when we catch him. I promise you, I'm going to give you five years in jail. If that's the last thing I do, I will give you five years in jail. It's not a trick; it's only a promise. Just remember!' ''

The night of May 3, Ralph Ruiz took Nelson—the last of the seven fugitives—to the Santa Cruz hideout. There, for the first time, Nelson met Bebe Melendez. He was not overcome with affection for Bebe, who said he had been the one to wrestle with McGoran over the gun and finally take it away from him.

Ralph told the six to hang tight—he would get legal advice and contact them. But on May 3, Ralph himself was arrested in San Mateo. He was a possible suspect in the killing because one eyewitness (who was never called to testify) identified his picture, others got the name "Rios" and "Ruiz" confused, and, of course, he was known to the police as a political troublemaker and a friend of some of the suspects. To establish his innocence, Ralph gave a statement of his whereabouts on May 1 to the inspector in charge, Jack Cleary (who was a close friend of Brodnik's, having been sworn into the police force on the same day in 1956).

Ralph told Cleary he had cooked breakfast for his father early that morning, called Nelson's house and talked to his father, then picked Nelson up around 10:30 at "Sandy and Alex's" (Sandy Domdoma was Nelson's girlfriend; Alex is Sandy's brother). Ralph said he was with Nelson for six and a half hours, mostly in San Mateo. He told Cleary about a ticket they got from a highway patrolman at 12:30. Around 5:00 P.M. he dropped Nelson off at Sandy's. He mentioned the name "Winkle," which Cleary wrote down, with a description.*

* According to Cleary's own notes of his interview with Ralph, which were introduced as evidence in the trial.

The police released Ralph. The highway patrolman was contacted: he identified both Ralph and Nelson as being in the car when he gave the ticket. Police also questioned Nelson's father: he had gotten two phone calls early in the morning of May 1—one from Ralph and one from Mario, both looking for Nelson.

Ralph's statement, supported by the highway patrolman and Nelson's father, established both his and Nelson's alibis. Yet Cleary either didn't believe the statement or didn't care. Sandy Domdoma and "Winkle"—Donald Wilson, who had been with Nelson in Sandy's apartment when Brodnik was killed—were never even contacted by police. Nelson remained a prime suspect.

For Ralph this arrest was the beginning of a continuous police tail. He knew he was being followed and couldn't return to Santa Cruz. So he began to gather evidence for Nelson, including a statement from Barbara Fuller, the secretary at the Readiness Center, that she had received three phone calls from Mario on May 1, all looking for Nelson. These calls, like the one Mr. Rodriguez received, indicated Mario and Nelson were not together that morning. Ralph also convinced his lawyer from CSM strike days, R. Jay Engel, to represent Nelson. He brought Sandy Domdoma and Donald Wilson to Engel's office to confirm Nelson's alibi.

III

What newspapers called "the biggest manhunt in the history of Northern California" was under way. Police were searching as far away as New Mexico's Rio Arriba County, scene of the June 1967 Tierra Amarilla courthouse raid, where it was rumored the fugitives had fled.

In Santa Cruz, Nelson told the others that police had already staked out the Palo Alto house where the fugitives had spent the afternoon of May 1. The next step might be Santa Cruz. The six decided to set out for the beach. "We were so freaked out, we really didn't know what to do," José remembers. "I mean, 'cause when you're running like that, you really can't think straight. You're always jumping whenever you hear a funny noise."

They camped on Pescadero Beach, north of the city of Santa

Cruz. Across the highway were a gas station and grocery store. There the little money they had was spent on food.

On May 3, Bebe had called the Mission Rebels and spoken to President Edlo Powell about arranging a surrender. Powell promised to find a lawyer. Bebe called back the next day but Powell wasn't there; the phone calls became an open secret in the street. Through adult members of the Rebels' board, Powell contacted Jack Berman, a successful criminal lawyer and former assistant D.A. Berman called San Francisco Police Chief Cahill and said he was in contact with people who were in contact with the suspects, who wished to surrender, if they could be guaranteed they wouldn't be harmed. He told the same to Chief of Inspectors Martin Lee. The brass listened cordially to Berman, and continued their investigation. Bebe and the Rebels never made contact again.

May 6 found the six fugitives still frightened, despairing of negotiations, and very hungry. They determined to steal a car and head south. First they tried to hold up an old man, but he called their bluff by pulling out a shotgun as he opened his car door. They prudently retreated.

The second time they did better. Daniel Goodell, assistant manager of a Redwood City grocery, was sunbathing at the beach with his fiancée, Karen Turiello. They saw the young latinos walk past near the ocean, talking and laughing. A few minutes later one of them reappeared with a rifle and, according to Goodell, said, "How would you like to get shot?" The six took Goodell's watch, wallet, car keys and lunch, which they swiftly devoured. Turiello remembered one saying, "We don't want to hurt you; we just need your car." Without touching the couple, the fugitives took their Buick Riviera. Five minutes later, Goodell walked across the highway to the gas station and called the police.

A roadblock was waiting in Santa Cruz. When the police ordered the six suspects out, they hesitated, wondering if the first one would be shot. Finally, Nelson recalls, he took the lead. They remembered one Santa Cruz cop saying as they were being fingerprinted, "You're lucky the San Francisco police didn't get you."

Mario, Pinky and José had been charged with murder, attempted murder, and burglary on May 5, the day before they were caught. At that time, according to the *San Francisco Examiner,* Bebe and Nelson were no longer suspects, being sought only for "questioning." But on May 8, Bebe, Nelson and Tony—not previously a suspect at all—were charged too. Later Gio Lopez was also charged.

At the lineup the night of May 6, when the suspects had been brought back to San Francisco, Irene Jarzyna identified Mario and Tony (in her testimony it became clear she was mistaking Tony for José). David Caravantes identified Pinky, Mario and José; Anna Diaz, a seventeen-year-old witness, identified Bebe. The eyewitnesses picked out almost as many plants in the lineup as suspects.

Before the lineup, attorney Jack Berman asked Chief of Inspectors Martin Lee, "What's all this about, Marty? You know one of them wasn't even there."

Lee replied, according to Berman: "You mean Rodriguez? I know." (According to Lee, all he said was "I know.") Later Lee insisted he meant his response sarcastically.

But in fact, if he was at all familiar with the investigation, Lee knew about Ralph Ruiz's statement, which put Nelson miles from Alvarado Street the morning of May 1. The police hadn't bothered to contact Sandy Domdoma or Donald Wilson, for whom Ralph had given addresses and descriptions, to investigate the alibi. (Tony Martinez also had an alibi witness—his tutor at CSM.)

"In Santa Cruz," Nelson says, "I was the only one who was questioned. They said, 'We know you weren't there, but why don't you give us a little information? You were wanted anyway for S.F. State.'

"I says, 'Why?'

"And he says, 'Well, you threw a rock at one of the officers.' Well, I didn't know about that. When I came up here they served me with a warrant and I never knew anything about it. If they wanted me that bad, like, I wasn't hiding. I was always on the street. They could have picked me up anytime."

IV

In the week between Brodnik's death and the capture of the six, the news media played a crucial role—spreading the police version of the incident, lauding the achievements of Mission Eleven, and solemnly mourning the death of a "heroic" cop.

The night of May 1, TV networks described the suspects as "four or five latin hippie types." Brodnik and McGoran were "the best . . . specialists in catching burglars in the act. Their success in police work was amazing."

The *San Francisco Chronicle*'s banner headline on May 2 read, "GANG ESCAPES SIEGE." The story began, "One of San Francisco's most highly decorated police officers met sudden death at the hands of at least three young hoodlums. . . ."

Laudotories followed. "HEROIC OFFICERS . . . VICTIMS LIVED WITH DANGER," was the *Examiner's* head; the *Chronicle* settled for " THE END OF A CRACK TEAM" and enumerated Mission Eleven's more than four hundred burglary arrests and dozens of bravery medals. The May 2 *Chronicle* also carried a bedside interview: "McGoran, speaking painfully through swaths of bandages, said from his hospital bed yesterday that the gang that killed his partner turned the smoking gun on him and emptied it at pointblank range . . . Incredibly, the heavy slugs from the .41 Magnum revolver . . . missed the beaten, bloodied officer as he tried to crawl to safety." Days later, when the gun was found with four slugs left in it, the police had to revise McGoran's story.

The *Examiner* said, "Intimates of Police Chief Tom Cahill say they've never seen him so upset as he is over the killing of policeman Joseph Brodnik. They look for a tougher policy." Mayor Alioto was out of town that week—in Washington, D.C., as it happened, discussing the Panthers and other security problems with Attorney General John Mitchell. Alioto rushed home for the funeral—an official day of mourning in the city—and promptly offered a $5,000 reward for information leading to the capture of each suspect.

On the night of May 2, the special hundred fifty-man crime-busting detail, for which the original "Gang's Terror in the

Mission" article had set the scene, went into action. "Most of their job," the *Chronicle* reported, "centers around stopping suspicious characters and making sure they are not involved in illegal activity." Close to a thousand arrests were made in the next few days, mostly on outstanding warrants or traffic violations. Many of those arrested went to jail because they couldn't make bail.

Brodnik's funeral sermon was generously quoted by the newspapers: "In an era when it isn't safe for people to walk the streets of our cities in broad daylight, Officer Brodnik was one of the thin blue line saving this country from anarchy. . . . If we go back two or three generations, we might see the beginnings of the whirlwind we reap today. The complete permissiveness of parents, the fracture and collapse of so many families, so many neglected children . . . In the old days, fathers of families were the symbols of authority, but today the word 'punish' is a dirty word. . . . Perhaps, my dear friends, Officer Joseph Brodnik will not have died in vain if his sacrifice opens the eyes of the community to what we need."

Colleen Crosby, daughter of Jessie Brodnik's brother, did not cry at the funeral. "Up to the time of my uncle's funeral, I wasn't political at all," she says. "I took part in a few anti-Vietnam [war] actions at San Jose City College. But I was just a typical American student, not very aware of politics. The political ceremony the police made out of my uncle's funeral made me very uptight. Hundreds of them came from the Bay Area and as far away as Los Angeles to join the pig parade. They were as cold as the rest of the cops that had come to my aunt's house during the nights after my uncle's death. Most of them had never known my uncle. They talked about the 'dirty pigs and filthy latinos' who they had already decided killed my uncle. They came up to my aunt and said, 'It was the dirty latinos who killed your husband. You should call for the death penalty.' I had been raised to believe a person was innocent until proven guilty. But the police had their own interpretation of justice. I was disturbed, totally confused, that my uncle had associated himself with such racists."

On May 7, an interview with José Rios appeared in the *Examiner*. "It was really the fault of the pig who didn't die," José said.

"He was calling us punks and hitting us." A police inspector responded: "We have no information indicating that either police officer acted in this manner." (Actually, most of the eyewitnesses said at least that Pinky Lescallett and McGoran were fighting.)

"We're not criminals," seventeen-year-old José went on. "The newspaper said we were wanted dead or alive." He was asked if he would testify for the prosecution if he were cleared of firing the shot (the interviewer later explained that it was a "joking question"). But José answered, "These are my friends. We will stick together."

The same day the *Examiner* printed a letter: "Profound sorrow and shame are felt amongst the Salvadorian communities in California because of the horrible crime committed by some young hoodlums described by our news media as Salvadorians."

"The press didn't say one single word of truth," Mrs. Martinez later said. "All lies. Starting with, not one of them bothered to find out what kind of families these boys came from or what they did, what was their mission. I saw a picture of my son where it said, 'one of the suspects.' Why didn't they say, 'One who is trying to help his Raza, who is trying to bring La Raza out of the darkness, trying to serve humanity?' . . . They are more criminal than anyone else for what they have done."

Sensationalism no doubt had the effect of trying and convicting the six in the minds of the public. But in addition, by depersonalizing the suspects, projecting an essentially racist image of undifferentiated dark-skinned hoodlums, the media set Los Siete up: had the cops been able to trap them in hiding, there could easily have been a massacre.

In June a memorial ceremony for Brodnik was held at his daughter's high school, St. Paul's, in Noe Valley. A tree was planted and a plaque laid outside the school. Mayor Alioto spoke about ending the ghetto conditions "which breed such senseless crimes."

"The mayor's words were not received enthusiastically by the predominantly police or police-oriented assembly of some 500 persons," the *Examiner* reported. Jessie Brodnik spoke after

Alioto, saying simply, "Capital punishment must be done." The audience cheered. Right-wingers distributed anti–Mission Coalition propaganda. The *Examiner* concluded, "What was intended as a touching tribute to a fallen hero turned into a political scene."

Two factions were already competing for the right to use Brodnik's death for their own purposes. One was the law-and-order faction represented by the Police Officers Association, some of the small Mission and Noe Valley merchants, and, on a larger scale, by Governor Reagan. The other was the "liberal" faction represented by the top echelons of organized labor, the redevelopment interests who would be all too happy to end ghetto conditions "which breed such senseless crimes," and Mayor Alioto.

Mrs. Brodnik became an instrument of the right-wing faction. On June 30 she spoke at a Sons of Italy "Law 'n Order" brunch. "We voted for capital punishment in California," she said. "Please, please see that it's carried out." Later that summer she went to Sacramento to lobby for a bill that would have imposed a mandatory death sentence on anyone convicted of killing a cop. The bill was passed by the Assembly but died in Senate committee.

When seven months later another policeman was killed, his widow told the press, "I can't hate the two men who did this. . . . I don't believe anyone should be killed, and that includes these two men." Mrs. Brodnik expressed her disagreement with this philosophy in a letter to the *Chronicle.* "The Lord didn't waste time when he saw how evil man had become," she wrote. "He sacrificed man by causing the great flood. If capital sacrifice sounds better than capital punishment, by all means change the wording."

9. Serving the People Doesn't Mean Being a Waitress

I

Oscar Rios remembers how the Los Siete de la Raza defense organization began: "On Tuesday they were caught. We went down to Santa Cruz to see if we could catch them there. We came back and they were already in jail. We saw them on television. That same night we had a meeting at Horizons Unlimited [a youth counseling program]. About three hundred people showed up. A lot of radical people came and tried to take over. But after the meeting, man, they would just go home, and we would stay there and wonder: what're we going to do? What're we going to do? Ralph Ruiz started bringing order and discipline to the meetings. We started organizing committees. Then we got an office. We were sitting around and decided we needed a name, and someone said, 'Los Siete de la Raza,' in case the seventh guy, Gio Lopez, got caught."

The office was a small storefront in the inner Mission, a short walk from San Francisco General Hospital. To raise money for legal defense, the new group* began turning out leaflets and fund

---

* Among the original members were Ralph Ruiz, Donna James, Roger Alvarado, Roberto Vargas, Oscar Rios, Reynaldo Aparicio, Francisco Flores, José Delgado, and other students from La Raza Studies; Al Martinet, a community organizer for the city's Economic Opportunity Council; and several street people.

appeals saying that Los Siete were victims of a police frame-up.
One such leaflet began:

A Bunch of Punks—Crime in the Streets
For years a gang of hoodlums have been running around
the Mission terrorizing and killing our people. They have
beaten our children and women, shot our men, stolen our
meager belongings and are getting paid with our stolen
money. The hoodlums run around on bikes and hopped-up
cars, cruising at reckless speeds through our streets, and there
is no one to stop them, not even the police, because these
gangsters *are* the police.

In informal talk, street organizing, and eventually the underground press, the line was tougher. The seven "brothers" were
seven revolutionary heroes, seven Huey Newtons, for having defended themselves. This rhetoric, somewhat confusing to outsiders, continued through the next two years. In the Los Siete
organization, however, there was no confusion. If the police were
"gangsters," this only gave the "brothers" an obligation to defend
themselves.
Initially, the families and friends of the six who were in jail
were uncertain about what kind of defense they should attempt.
The Martinez family had asked their lawyer to defend Tony and
Mario. Ralph Ruiz got R. Jay Engel, who had defended many
black and brown radicals on charges stemming from the San Mateo
strike, to represent Nelson. Oscar Rios, somewhat wary of left
rhetoric, hired a local chicano lawyer for his brother José. The
Lescallett and Melendez families allowed the Mission Rebels, in
the persons of Ed Powell and a white member of the board of
directors, to hire Jack Berman. According to Donna James, the
director promised to give the Los Siete defense $50,000 on one
condition: that "politics" be kept out of the case. Politics, he said,
would kill the brothers.
"I had a doubt in my mind about having this a political case,"
Bebe Melendez remembers, "because I had this lackey bourgeois
Uncle Tom [Powell] telling me that we shouldn't have a political

case, that all the Man was going to do was slap me in the joint right away. Well, that's not the point. This is a political case from the beginning, whether we like it or not. I wasn't righteously aware of what a political case this was, so I wanted a hush-hush thing with little publicity, and this Tom was telling me that if you have a political case the judge is going to hang you. Tony, Mario and Nelson were rapping to me about how in hell is that man going to tell you something when he's working for the Man? And that's true, 'cause he's nothing but a pig. He doesn't have a badge, but he's still nothing but a pig.''

The first step in the search for alternatives to the Mission Rebels took Oscar Rios and Donna James through the Southwest to talk to leaders in the chicano movement. "I took off to Denver, New Mexico, and Texas," Oscar says, "trying to get help from all these big latinos, supposed to be. In Denver, man, I spoke there and I got about $28. They have their own problems. I went to New Mexico, to Reies Tijerina, and I talked to him. He told me all he was doing, but when it came to money, they didn't have nothing. I went to San Antonio, Texas, and talked to Pete Tijerina [Reies's cousin], who got I don't know how many millions of dollars from the Ford Foundation. He was sitting in a big leather seat, big rug on the floor. He said, 'I'm sorry, man, I can't help you.' He recommended me to this lawyer. I came over here to see him. He said, 'I like your ideas, but this is my price.' And we didn't have the bread.

"Then we went across the Bay to talk to the Panthers. Ralph got hold of Bobby Seale and David Hilliard and they set up a meeting. Right away Bobby came out and said, 'Okay, this is what we can give you: we'll give you one side of our paper. . . .' He just settled everything. 'We'll give you space at rallies, anything you want. We'll see if you can work out with us.' They were a real help. Right away Bobby started talking: he had an interview on Channel 9, and he mentioned Los Siete—'los saytay,' he said; he couldn't even pronounce it. He came over to the parents and talked to them about Huey P. Newton.

"The Panthers said, 'We're going to clear everything from Garry, and you can have him,' 'cause they could see the unity, man. This was the biggest chance they had—to unite brown and black people. Bobby could see this was the time."

Los Siete held its first rally in late May, outside the Hall of Justice, with the support of the Black Panthers and the Brown Berets.

Allying with the Black Panther Party was a gamble for Los Siete, but a necessary one. Despite the negative image many barrio people—especially older ones—had of the Panthers, the only alternative for Los Siete in terms of alliances and political direction was the poverty program approach which had dominated the Mission for the last few years—an approach which consisted essentially of "keeping politics out of the case."

The Panthers and Los Siete had political education classes together. Part of the Panther newspaper was turned over to Los Siete and the new Los Siete paper *Basta Ya!* (roughly translated by one member: "Enough of this shit!") carried messages from Huey Newton, still in jail, and news of the Panthers and other movement groups. From the beginning Los Siete saw itself as a group of political organizers whose purpose was far broader than legal defense of the six who were in jail. And *Basta Ya!* reflected this.

The first issues of *Basta Ya!*, while making the basic facts about the case familiar, isolated the new Los Siete organization from many people in the Mission. "We were trying to get our own thing together," Oscar says. "A lot of people got turned off. Didn't dig that theory we were talking. Too radical. So people said, 'No, this thing is turning people off.' But we didn't care, you know. That was the only thing we had in our minds. And when we started talking to the people, we didn't know what to say. They would say, 'Aw, hang those punks!' We used to get so frustrated 'cause people would just shut us off. We started with all this militant thing. Mao—who read Mao? I couldn't understand who he was. At school Mario used to wear a Mao button. But I never could get the urge to wear one. But we started getting educated, started having political classes, reading a little of the red book, man. And all that added up to for me was, we were trying to organize on a big level, up here, when we were supposed to be down on the ground."

In talking to people about the case, Oscar and others learned that the revolutionary rhetoric of the last few years had far outdistanced real political work. The Los Siete organization wanted to close that gap. "Serving the people" became a philosophy with Los Siete, as it had with the Panthers. The free breakfast-for-children program at St. Peter's Church, begun by students from La Raza Studies, became a Los Siete project. A second breakfast program was begun at St. John's Church in the north Mission, a mixed neighborhood of latinos, native Americans, poor whites, and blacks.

The founding of Los Siete and its merger with the breakfast program precipitated a split that had long been brewing in La Raza Studies at San Francisco State. Some members of the program feared that supporting the "cop-killers" would endanger their position on campus and objected when Roger Alvarado, the charismatic leader of the Third World Liberation Front during the strike, spoke out in favor of the six defendants. Other, more radical, students rejected this attitude. The strike had taught them that education came through struggle, and, as Donna James said, for the kind of work they wanted to do there was no use remaining in school. Roger Alvarado, José Delgado, Ralph Ruiz and several others began to work with Los Siete full time. "Roger was really a lot of help," Oscar says. "He knew how to organize. He was the one that really got the paper together." The first issue of the paper, a mimeographed pamphlet, was dated *17 de junio de 1969.* Like all future issues of *Basta Ya!* it was both in English and Spanish. The major article in the first issue, by Alvarado, was an emotional pledge of commitment to the brown struggle and an explanation of why he and others like him could not remain at school, pursuing personal success:

Under those in power, La Raza conditions are so inhumane that minerals are taken from our lands to place someone on the moon while young Raza sisters have babies on dirt floors of cardboard shacks in Gilroy, California. We have lived as a conquered people, struggling in the mouth of the lion, a lion we are told loves us while taking our sons to Vietnam to fight and die in a war against a people that are as poor as us. . . . We like to think of ourselves as individuals accepting our situation individually and letting the rest of La Raza get along as it can. We have forgotten and ignored so much of what was once La Raza, the communal living, the spirit and character of *los pueblos,* in favor of this middle-class thing called individuality. . . .

II

That summer of 1969, while the six defendants waited in jail, Los Siete's storefront became the center for a number of community services—the breakfast programs, draft counseling, an emergency ambulance pool, the *Basta Ya!* newspaper, recruitment for college. Along with stacks of movement newspapers there were cartons of *Venceremos,* John Gerassi's collection of speeches and writings by Che Guevara, and of Che's diary, several cartons of which *Ramparts* magazine had given the organization. Medical services were discussed: the first attempt in this direction was a program of checkups and innoculations for children in the breakfast program. (This was not always successful, as attendance fell off at the breakfast on the days the doctors were there.)

By standards of radical rhetoric, the new organization's programs seemed tame. A sympathizer working at the Mission Rebels remarked that if it weren't for the fact that Los Siete had been founded to defend the "cop-killers," most of its programs would qualify for OEO money. The differences became clearer as time wore on and federal monies dwindled. A year later the same sympathizer was working at Los Siete's free medical clinic.

As Mario, now in jail, said, "There were things before this— Horizons Unlimited, other little programs. Out of our arrest and the occupation of the community [by the police looking for suspects] , things were just hurried along. Los Siete has done a lot more than groups that were trying to get established before this happened. Most important of all is that it is a project of the people. The other projects were being financed by the government, and they always had to do what the government said."

In the fall of 1969 Los Siete acquired a small restaurant in the north Mission. It was just across the street from the large Levi-Strauss factory, where over four hundred latin women, many of them recent immigrants who spoke no English, worked long hours for low wages.* Los Siete renamed the restaurant "El Basta Ya." They hoped to attract the women workers to come in for lunch.

There was a back room for meetings and a small office next door for paperwork, but the office was not to be the center of activity. "Target areas"—parks, busy streets—were designated as places where Los Siete members should hang out. These early attempts at organizing were sometimes naive: in one instance two attractive teenage girls were supposed to hang out in a certain park and "rap to the brothers"; the latin youth, predictably, only wanted to flirt. The concept of organizing was gradually broadened. The women became involved in the breakfast program, welfare rights organizing, and later in La Raza legal defense.

People in Los Siete also began to work with Horizons Unlimited, the Mexican American Political Association, the Mission Coalition, the hospital workers union (which had set up a radical caucus called Workers Defense), and even with Centro Social Obrero, the latin caucus in the laborers' union. Most of these groups already had a handful of dissident members hungry for political information. Los Siete began to develop these allies and contacts, while remaining a small organization whose members knew and trusted each other.

III

A few members of Centro Social Obrero had become upset at what they considered dictatorial methods President Abel Gonzalez was using to run their organization. They complained to Fernando Herrera, who had been an officer of the club and written its constitution. In mid-1969 Herrera began an anti-Gonzalez campaign. In leaflets passed out at the Centro and at Local 261 he accused

* Hourly base rates in 1970 ranged from $1.94 to $2.09, with bonuses for workers who produced one hundred percent or more of their quota.

Gonzalez of "selling jobs and . . . stealing money from our organization." Herrera was expelled from Centro Social soon after for "bringing disrepute and lack of respect to the organization."

Herrera also accused Gonzales of using Local 261 funds for political purposes. New members of the union paid, in addition to high initiation fees, a "voluntary" $20 contribution to the Laborers Political League, which had donated five thousand dollars to Mayor Alioto's 1967 campaign.* *Basta Ya!* consistently pointed out that beneath these accusations of corruption lay an attack on Gonzalez's prime function: to maintain political control, especially of the workers, for Alioto; and to pave the way for redevelopment in the Mission.

Gonzalez had, by mid-1969, extended his influence to the Mission Coalition. He succeeded in becoming one of their community representatives on a committee that was supposed to represent the community in redevelopment negotiations with City Hall—this despite the fact that he had been in Alioto's cabinet. "In the beginning, several sincere people were involved in MCO," said a realtor who quit in 1969 after Gonzalez's appointment to this committee. "But these people gradually got disgusted and dropped out, leaving Gonzalez, etc., in charge, as was planned in the first place. In addition, the existence of the Mission Coalition kept other truly serious social organizers, potentially dangerous to Alioto, out of the area."

In the fall of 1969 MCO held its second annual convention. The delegates refused to pass two resolutions in support of the four hundred thirty-five San Francisco State strikers then on trial for their mass rally on campus, but did come out in favor of peace in Vietnam, draft "alternatives," and the grape boycott (Hubert Humphrey and Robert Kennedy had also endorsed the boycott). The convention refused to pass a resolution supporting the Los Siete defendants, though it went on record as hoping they would get a fair trial. Another resolution requesting more police protection for the Mission, with vague mention of recruiting minority

---

* *San Francisco Examiner* columnist Dick Nolan also put the "voluntary" in quotes in a March 14, 1969, article discussing the contributions.

cops, almost tore the convention apart. When it passed, several Mission Rebels stormed out in disgust.

The uproar at the MCO convention was just one example of how the May 1 incident had been a catalyst, making police oppression the foremost issue in Mission district politics. When the MCO failed to deal with this issue—except in a sugar-coated but basically reactionary way—by requesting more police, if possible from minorities—its moderate-center coalition began to fall apart. Through the May 1 incident and the subsequent organizing efforts of the Los Siete organization, people were becoming alienated from MCO-style politics. How to transform this alienation into effective political action—and extend it to the majority of the latin community—was the task facing Los Siete.

Meanwhile, the group found itself caught up in an ambitious volume of day-to-day work running the restaurant and the breakfast program. Food had to be gotten and distributed. Los Siete leafleted Mission district grocers about their moral responsibility to return some profits to the community in the form of food for hungry children. (They took a few children along for added effect, and also to educate the kids.) Merchants varied in their responses, but many were cooperative, even enthusiastic about the breakfast. Several storekeepers, particularly along Twenty-fourth Street, began to stock *Basta Ya!*

An article in the paper by José Delgado laid out some of the ideas behind the breakfast:

Truckloads of bananas spoil and are dumped every week from the South San Francisco Produce Market during the height of the fruit season. Tons of other fruits and vegetables are dumped as overripe too. The price is high so the produce moves slowly. It's a crime. The system will throw away food before the businesses will lower their prices. . . .

At least 100,000 people (by EOC standards) in San Francisco go hungry each day. . . . We, who do not have the billions of dollars this government has, are able to feed our hungry children. This is something which shows the people they can start meeting their needs without having to come under the welfare-type attitude this government has when it throws a few dollars into any oppressed community.

The breakfast program had its ups and downs. There were days when only one worker showed up. Others overslept or forgot. There would be no syrup one week, no bacon or sausage the next. Weeks went by without butter, months without fruit. When supplies and workers fell off, the children got restless and wild. The St. John's breakfast program was discontinued after slightly less than a year.

These problems were due partly to lack of discipline among breakfast workers, partly to harassment from church officials. But the most important problem was a lack of community enthusiasm for the program. La Raza families are usually close-knit and eat together whatever breakfast they can afford. Either because free breakfasts were not a major need in the Mission or because Los Siete went about organizing the breakfasts without mass support, the project floundered.

No one in Los Siete had had experience running a restaurant. There were always last-minute supply needs that had to be met at the local grocery, where food was most expensive. El Basta Ya served good lunches for fifty cents and dinners for a dollar, but never broke even. It was popular among young people, especially white radicals, but older latinos kept away. Despite a good deal of muckraking around the conditions at Levi-Strauss, Los Siete did not attract many of the women workers to the restaurant. Operating the place also required enormous amounts of energy, which could otherwise have been used for more aggressive organizing.

As Donna James said, "We began to learn that serving the people doesn't mean being a waitress." The restaurant was re-evaluated and in the spring of 1970 Joe Romero, an experienced cook, and his wife agreed to take the place over. The name was changed from the clenched-fisted El Basta Ya to the more leisurely Las Sirenitas (the mermaids) in honor of Romero's daughter's dancing group. The posters of Mao, Che and Geronimo came down. In their place appeared reproductions of Latin American historical scenes, portraits of Hidalgo, Juarez and Zapata. The groovy but unstable tables with red-and-white checkered cloths were replaced by sturdier formica. A cigarette machine, pinball machine, and beer sign which lit up completed the decor. These changes effectively turned off longhairs, who in turn had been turning off Levi-Strauss workers and other latin adults. But unfortunately Romero and Los Siete gradually drifted apart.

Although almost all Los Siete's first programs were revised or dropped (the St. Peter's breakfast program ended after about a year), the group's early experience was important both to its members and to the community. The college students, at least some of them, had come home, rejecting the kind of token success which traditionally drains ghettoes and barrios of radical leadership. Although it was still feeling its way—analyzing the district to determine what programs would serve the people's needs and win their support—Los Siete had at least demonstrated to the community its commitment, its willingness to learn from what Che Guevara called "that great source of wisdom that is the people."

Like the six who were now in jail, the young latins who formed Los Siete began with little actual organizing experience— much rhetoric, some literature, many inspiring examples, but little practice, and, as José Delgado later pointed out, "not enough mass basis built." Tony, Mario, Nelson and Ralph had begun to do some organizing of street brothers, with the goal of getting them into college and making them politically aware. The Los Siete organization, growing from these efforts, also emphasized street organizing at first. In their first year they recognized the need to move away from organizing primarily street brothers and toward organizing families and working people; but it would take longer to accomplish the move in practice—to adjust, as José put it, "to a new style of work."

As winter 1969 turned to spring 1970 and the trial seemed as far away as ever, the changes in Los Siete's emphasis could be seen through the issues of *Basta Ya!* The exchange agreement with the Panthers had ended. Los Siete's message was now directed to brown people, not to the blacks or white radicals who read the *Black Panther.* One early issue included the full text of a resolution supporting Los Siete passed at the latest SDS convention. Nothing could have had less meaning to most people in the Mission. Early issues of *Basta Ya!* had said on the masthead, "San Francisco, Califas, Aztlán." But nobody except the radicals even knew what Aztlán meant (see page 51). After eight months the heading became "Mission Community Newspaper." And while originally *Basta Ya!* had concentrated heavily on police harassment, later issues explored family problems, medicine, food, housing, labor conditions, and urban renewal.

Los Siete was not without its casualties. Ralph Ruiz, who had done so much to start the organization, went underground less than a year later, before the actual trial began. He had felony charges to face, some stemming from the San Mateo strike. But more important, he couldn't stand the constant police harassment. "He wasn't afraid of doing time," Donna said; "he was afraid for his life." Roger Alvarado dropped out too, though he didn't disappear. Having been the public man for years, he suddenly went private, whether temporarily or permanently remained unclear.

The loss of two strong leaders was healthy in the sense that it left authority divided. Quieter people began to speak up. Women demanded equal respect. Like the Young Lords in New York, Los Siete was learning to fight *machismo,* the latin version of male chauvinism. In this respect, as in their rejection of cultural nationalism, Los Siete and the Young Lords were vanguard groups within the brown movement. (The Young Lords, a Puerto Rican group whose organizing stressed both "serve-the-people" programs and support of Puerto Rican independence, had been established in Chicago shortly before Los Siete was formed, and later spread to New York and other eastern cities—where it was called the Young Lords Party to distinguish it from the Young Lords Organization, the Chicago group.)

The Los Siete organization itself had no single leader. Eventually a central committee with rotating membership was formed to evaluate the various projects and analyze Los Siete's overall direction. Los Siete members formed small groups which studied together; there were also many supporters who weren't actually members but who worked on Los Siete's programs or provided helpful publicity. Newsreel, a film collective, made a movie about the "brothers." A local group called the Research Organizing Co-operative produced a pamphlet explaining the arrest, the tracking system, urban renewal and political repression; the San Francisco Mime Troupe created a Los Siete "cranky"—a moving scroll accompanied by commentary (see following pages).

By December of 1969, "Los Siete" was a familiar phrase in the Mission. Rallies, posters, leaflets and bumper stickers were common. "Free Los Siete" buttons in several styles began to compete with, then overtake, "Viva la Huelga" buttons on the lapels of black leather jackets and the straps of soft leather handbags. This didn't indicate a reduction in support for the grape boycott but simply an understanding that Los Siete was closer to home.

Graffiti appeared all over the Mission district. Persistently, the authorities would paint over these slogans, until the base of the Mexican liberty bell in Dolores Park and the walls of Mission High were thickened with many different shades of tan. Small stickers were printed up and pasted on walls and lampposts throughout the city. One of them, which remained for years stuck to a Mission High blackboard, read: "THE BROWN FLEA CAN HARASS THE DOG TO DEATH. FREE LOS SIETE!"

"Something in the community is different now," Oscar Rios said a year after Los Siete's founding. "People's ideas. Signs on the wall mean something. People are beginning to buy the paper. People can change; I'm sure of it now. If I can change, why can't anybody? I used to be an acid freak, you know? And I lived in Daly City, man, so I was better than these people. This place—the Mission—was more dirty. I had the stereotype of the *pachuco* in my mind.* I was brainwashed. I would spend my time goofing

---

* A *pachuco* was a chicano youth, originally characterized by a "zoot suit" style of dress. In the early 1940s in what became known as the "Zoot Suit Riots," white sailors attacked the barrio in Los Angeles and pachucos fought back. The pachuco stereotype which many whites had at the time was of a violent young Mexican hoodlum.

171

around, watching that lousy TV like I was hypnotized.

"I think if this wouldn't have happened, I'd still be tripping. I'd just be going to college, thinking I'm better, and not coming to the community. But this experience of your mind opening is really good. I couldn't see it until the bust. When it happened—wow! It was like a wall in front of me that disappeared."

i there! My name is
ART and I'm here to
rve you. You are in-
ted to enjoy the
ducational murals which
ne my walls as I aid your
njoyment with a com-
entary on the points of
terest . . .

At the outset of the Mural of Progress we see the San Francisco of yesteryear—financial capital of the west coast, yet somehow still provincial. Oh, it has its towers of commerce, but . . .

lacks executive living quarters for the young movers and shakers of high finance. They're rced to live in faraway suburbs and the inner city decays—a tragic situation . . .

But with the coming of me, BART, luxury apartments—the Dolores Towers, the Bernal Arms, the Hanging Gardens of Guerrero—sprout like sequoias from the garbage heaps. A new Manhattan rises from the slums!

Now all this was not achieved without sacrifice and struggle. There were those who attempted to halt San Francisco's progress. They were known as latinos. Please do not misunderstand. BART has nothing against persons of Hispano-American persuasion. . .

We employ more than our quota of them in responsible positions.

But living where you can't afford to live creates dangerous anxieties and illusions and often leads to violence in the streets. Once there was violence in the Mission District, and the ringleaders of it were the notorious Los Siete de la Raza ...

These seven latin hippie types didn't think much of our high schools . . .

So they set up their own so-called College Readiness Program. Well, yo can imagine what that led to. A sen less attack on the American system education. If everyone went to coll who'd pacify Cambodia? Why do y think we have a tracking system?

THE TRACKING SYSTEM

us   home

Nosotros   casa   escuela

school

who is this man?

The father of our country a gringo.

ONE DOLLAR

END

FIN

But back to our story. Imagine if you will two selfless dedicated officers of the law, two men who heard themselves called pigs and did not flinch but merely smiled and toyed with the rubber hoses in their pockets. Their assignment: follow Los Siete, but go in disguise . . .

These two officers saw the sinister Los Siete actually carrying a TV set. They approached the surly youths for questioning. Let us not dwell on the lurid details. Suffice it to say that during the ensuing scuffle one of those brave officers was shot with his partner's gun. . .

But let me make one thing perfectly clear. That officer was shot, with his partner's gun, by Los Siete.

Oh, they got away at first but your police department reacted swiftly and in due time got six of them.

GRAND OPENING

You can relax now; our story is almost over. You see, I am the first BART train to enter the Mission, and there will be an opening ceremony. Los Siete and their families and the 29 latinos who still live in the Mission . . .

SPLAT!

. . . will be privileged to stand on the tracks as I arrive. Life is short! BART is long!

We are approaching the station. Do you hear the people cheering? This is the Daly City express. You will enjoy the new Daly City—it is now one building, 57 square blocks. It also forms the northern city limits of Los Angeles . . .

Los Siete fought, but you wanted security. And now you've got security, courtesy of the Total State.

10. In the
Halls of Justice

On May 19, 1969, Los Siete were indicted by the grand jury for murder, assault with intent to murder, and burglary. In the thirteen months between this indictment and the beginning of the trial in June 1970, the six defendants waited on the seventh floor of the San Francisco Hall of Justice, in the county jail. Even Bebe, who was used to Youth Authority prisons, was disgusted by the conditions there.

"Me and brother Pinky, we didn't have nothing in our cells," Bebe relates. "But the pigs planted a couple of shirts, and something else, you know? I didn't dig it. I told one of them, 'Look, man, I didn't have this shit in my room.' And he's telling me, 'Well, we found it under your bed.' I said, 'One of us is lying and I know I'm not.'

"Now, brother Pinky, he was pretty hot because the pigs had come into our room and they threw his letters and everything all over the floor. So Pinky said, 'Look, man, if you're going to search me, at least you could have the courtesy to put things back in their proper order.'

"The pig puts his hand on the oppressor stick and says, 'You gonna shut up.'

"Now, brother Pinky, he comes from a long line of 'I ain't taking nothing.' So Pinky told him, 'You got to shut me up.' So the pig got scared and he went and got three other pigs that all looked like giant polar bears, and Pinky went to the hole.

"There are five or six pigs who jump on brothers," Bebe

continues. "One brother, they shoved a billyclub up his ass. He yelled out, 'No, not that!' but they just shoved it up his ass."

One guard always made a big fuss about going into the elevator with the six. "I can't stand the smell," he would say, or, "I don't want to drown, with so many wetbacks in there." Another guard liked to harass Nelson, saying, "How is the revolutionary wetback greaser today? ... What's the matter with you, *spic,*—can't you talk, or are you thinking of having your revolutionary friends kill me the way you killed Detective Brodnik?"*

Like many other "political" prisoners, the six refused to take such treatment for granted. Through their lawyers, they complained during their court appearances about harassment in jail. "In the streets they were known for their big mouths," Donna James said. "And in prison they're known for their big mouths. The guards have names for them—the 'Burrito Bandidos' and the 'Unholy Six.'"

In June of 1970, after scattered reports of brutality, harassment and bad sanitation, a committee of lawyers released a study that condemned the San Francisco County Jail as "brutalizing" and "deplorable ... beneath the standards of the State Department of Corrections and in violation of the U.S. Civil Rights Act" and the Eighth Amendment to the Constitution, which bans cruel and unusual punishment.

The study went on: "Food is unfit, and kitchen conditions are unsanitary. There is a lack of emergency care and prisoners have been punished for even asking to see a doctor ... men with tuberculosis and syphilis are allowed to mingle with non-infected inmates, and bedding is not sanitized before being used by other prisoners." (José Rios picked up hepatitis almost as soon as he was put in jail.)

"Rehabilitative care is so lacking," the lawyers went on, "that inmates are brutalized and their anti-social attitudes reinforced, so that they tend to return to a life of crime."

"The trip they got is psychological," Pinky says. "I hear people yelling, 'I'm sick of this place. I'm gonna cop!'"

* From a petition written by Nelson and filed in court during the trial.

At pre-trial hearings, the one hundred–person capacity courtroom was invariably filled. Occupying the front row, directly behind the defendants, were Mrs. Martinez and her youngest child; Mr. Martinez, whose eye injury kept him off work; Audelith Morales, who translated for the parents; and, less regularly, Mrs. Melendez and Mrs. Lescallett. The Rios parents and one or two older brothers were also regulars. The rest of the courtroom was filled with young supporters drawn by the Los Siete organization.

There was a great deal of love in the courtroom. Even strangers to Los Siete would remark how much the trial seemed a family thing. Oscar and Ruth Rios and Ray and Esperanza Aparicio brought their new babies, who were passed admiringly from arm to arm while the defendants twisted their heads to see them. The four defense attorneys soon joined in this family feeling.

Charles Garry had brought two young lawyers into the case in addition to R. Jay Engel, who continued to represent Nelson. Richard Hodge, who represented Pinky, is a partner in a firm which handles many political and dope cases, rock bands, and hip writers. With his calm, relatively businesslike style, Hodge is a good complement to the more emotional Garry. In early 1969 they and a third lawyer won acquittal for the Oakland Seven— seven white radicals charged with conspiracy to commit misdemeanors during Stop the Draft Week in Oakland in October 1967. Michael Kennedy, who represented Bebe, had worked for the Emergency Civil Liberties Committee in New York, taught draft law and defended draft resisters in Puerto Rico, and represented Timothy Leary and various Weathermen. With his sharp tongue, rimless glasses, and near-shoulder-length hair, Kennedy cultivates the image of the unconventional attorney.

Charles Garry, who represented the Martinez brothers and José Rios, has a political history which began in the 1930s, when, as a tailor in San Francisco, he worked in Upton Sinclair's 1934 gubernatorial campaign and participated in the General Strike. He started practicing law in 1938; by 1943 he represented sixteen unions, and in the 1950s he handled over eighty McCarthy era loyalty fights. He ran for Congress on the Progressive ticket in '48 and '49. In 1968 he defended Black Panther Party Minister of Defense Huey Newton on charges of murdering an Oakland policeman. He has been the Panthers' chief counsel ever since.

Joseph Karesh, the superior court judge who presided over the pre-trial hearings, was a liberal, so everyone said—and so he showed by countless gestures: admitting standing-room crowds, listening at length to arguments, letting Garry out a few minutes early to debate William Buckley. But it was an odd sort of liberalism. Several months before the Alvarado Street incident, Karesh had presided over a trial in which police officer Michael O'Brien was charged with killing a black man. At that trial, defense attorney Jake W. Ehrlich, chief counsel for the Police Officers Association, had attacked the black witnesses appearing against O'Brien as "hyenas [living in] a hellhole . . . people of little or no moral honesty or integrity." The one white prosecution witness he called "a vicious punk who wants to destroy our government . . . our homes, our children, two hundred years of American democracy and the flag and all it stands for. . . . I can realize our black brethren sticking together . . . what I can't understand is [this witness] coming apparently from a good home and selling his soul to prove his hatred for a policeman." O'Brien was acquitted.

Liberal reporters were offended by the racist atmosphere of the trial and criticized Judge Karesh—who hails from South Carolina—for allowing Ehrlich free rein. Although Karesh frequently said he had nothing to apologize for in his handling of the O'Brien case, the press censure certainly did not please him, and probably made him wary of future highly publicized, racially charged trials.

The man who prosecuted Los Siete, Assistant District Attorney Thomas Norman, had a rather prim courtroom style which he apparently adopted on the assumption that a jury would be put off by Garry's earthiness, Kennedy's acid wit, and the radical politics of the defense. But this primness was only part of his repertory, and every lawyer has one. When one day Huey Newton, just released from jail, came to the trial, Garry introduced Norman to Newton as "one of the nicer pigs."

Homicide Inspector Jack Cleary, who was in charge of the

police investigation of the case, sat beside Norman throughout the trial and personally escorted witnesses to and from the Hall of Justice. Cleary had an affable-Irish-cop exterior, but it was deceptive, for as inspector in charge he was largely responsible for the police portion of the alleged case against Los Siete. As it later became clear, the police, under Cleary, tried to pick and choose—following up and using that evidence that would be useful to the prosecution case, and ignoring anything that might prove the innocence of the defendants. (For example, Ralph Ruiz's statement to Cleary on May 3 clearly indicated that Nelson Rodriguez could not have been at Alvarado Street at the time of the shooting. Police under Cleary's command checked out two of the four alibi witnesses Ruiz mentioned, who verified what he had said. However, neither Cleary nor any other inspector ever contacted Nelson's two most vital alibi witnesses.)

III

During the thirteen months between the arrest and the beginning of the trial, the defense presented a series of pre-trial motions designed to safeguard every one of the defendants' rights and to challenge every judicial procedure they considered illegal. Unfortunately the indictments were not about to be dismissed. The pre-trial motions for the most part turned out to be exercises in futility whose only practical function, aside from political education, was to make a record for a possible appeal.

The defense moved to suppress the burglary evidence on the grounds of illegal search and seizure. They showed that the police had conducted their investigation without warrants and in some cases without "probable cause." McGoran was called to testify. Kennedy asked him, "Weren't you really suspicious because they were *latins* moving furniture?"

McGoran responded, "I would stop anyone moving furniture like that—black, latin or Chinese." Months later he explained, "I thought I had white in there too." Karesh eventually ruled that "Even if it *was* a violation of the law, under the circumstances what they [the police] did was reasonable."

The defense moved to quash the grand jury indictment because grand jury members were not peers of the defendants. According to a survey conducted by law students which Garry introduced as evidence, San Francisco judges nominate personal friends to the grand jury sixty percent of the time and professional contacts another fifteen percent. In the nine years from 1960–1969, the defense showed, the average income of grand jury nominees was $20,000, while the Mission district's average was around $4,300. Furthermore, the fact that the grand jury which indicted Los Siete was one hundred percent white, Richard Hodge argued, was *prima facie* evidence of illegality. The motion to quash was denied.

The defense also attacked the petit jury panel, which is picked from voter registration lists. As a rule these lists tend to exclude the young, the transient, the illiterate, the ignorant, and the disaffected. But the particular complaint of defense counsel was that until March 1970 jury panels also excluded the many latinos who couldn't read or write English. Then, two days before the defense was to challenge the constitutionality of the petit jury panel, the California Supreme Court decided it was illegal to exclude Spanish-speaking citizens from voting simply because they weren't literate in English. The jurists noted that Spanish-speaking people "are the heirs and founders of this state . . . and contributed in no small part to its growth."

Karesh would have quickly denied the motion to invalidate the jury panel—as judges usually do—were it not for the fortuitous State Supreme Court decision. He admitted that the current jury panel was now technically invalid, but rejected the defense's suggestion that names of Spanish-speaking citizens be gotten from "respectable" latin organizations and thrown into the hopper along with names from voter lists. With no alternative but to wait for a new jury panel, Karesh shrugged his shoulders and the defense threw up its hands.

By law, jurors who oppose capital punishment cannot sit in first-degree murder cases, since they would presumably vote against the death penalty even if the evidence "required" it. Garry argued that a jury composed only of supporters of capital punishment was a hanging jury, likely to convict on less evidence than a jury which fairly represented the community. To support his contention, he called Professor Hans Zeisel of the University of Chicago Law School.

Zeisel said fifty-eight percent of the U.S. population opposes capital punishment. In one study he interviewed jurors from over four hundred criminal cases in which the first ballot was split. Since all jurors in each case had heard the same evidence, Zeisel explained, it must have been personal differences that accounted for the split ballot. He found that those who supported capital punishment were generally the same ones who voted guilty on the first ballot, whether or not they were involved in cases calling for the death sentence. Judge Karesh denied Garry's motion that death penalty opponents be allowed on the jury.

It was during the next hearing, in late May 1970, that the O'Brien case was first mentioned. The defense was arguing for latitude in questioning prospective jurors on their political and racial opinions. "In the O'Brien case you allowed a racist lawyer to ramble on," Mike Kennedy said. "The least you can do is allow us the same latitude from the other direction." When he noted the pallor on Karesh's face, Kennedy added, "I am not suggesting you erred in the O'Brien case."

Karesh was visibly shaken. "In view of your mentioning the O'Brien case, I don't know if I should sit in this trial," he said. But Garry successfully soothed his ruffled feathers.

At the next hearing, in June, Garry was arguing for access to McGoran's personnel file. He said it would reveal a "pattern of conduct" from which the jurors could infer McGoran's behavior on May 1, 1969. McGoran was "a racist, a liar, and a drunk," Garry argued. Something in Karesh's subsequent comments said Garry had gone too far. When Garry said McGoran had called black people niggers, Karesh argued, "A man may be prejudiced against Negroes without being prejudiced against Spanish people." When Hodge said the violent character of the victim of an alleged assault is always admissible in court, Karesh snapped back, "Racism is not related to traits of violence."

Rumors that Karesh would withdraw from the trial began leaking two days before the next scheduled hearing. At this hearing, Karesh explained at great length that he was *withdrawing,* not disqualifying himself, because disqualification implied prejudice and "I am not prejudiced . . . despite the laughter in this courtroom." Karesh said he was withdrawing because of Kennedy's reference to the O'Brien trial. "When the defense counsel themselves say it, I don't think it fair to the defense, the prosecution, or the people that the O'Brien case be retried," he said.

But it was an excuse; Karesh had long wanted out. By June 1970, the political pressures on him must have become very great. Judgeships are political appointments,* and both political parties seemed to want to hang Los Siete. Much as Karesh may have wanted to please the politically powerful, he could see, especially after Garry's "racist, liar and drunk" remark about McGoran, that the defense had an excellent case.

The defense understood the reasons for Karesh's withdrawal but nevertheless tried to appeal to his integrity, asking him not to bow to political pressure. Each defendant took the stand and swore he wanted Karesh to remain in the case and believed he could get a "fair trial" in his court. Michael Kennedy apologized: "Take my statement in context. If it was untoward, remember I was trying desperately to change Your Honor's mind about a question I think is fundamental [*voir dire,* the questioning of prospective jurors]. Don't farm us out to someone who has no history with us, no understanding of what has come down these last four hundred days [since the arrest]. . . . I will under no circumstances make any references to O'Brien in the future."

Karesh took it all in, especially the flattery, and adjourned till the next day. Although the lawyers had argued partly to make a record for appeal, they also sincerely wanted Karesh to stay. Ex-

* By custom most judges retire in mid-term, giving the governor the opportunity to appoint a replacement. If he behaves well, the replacement rarely has much competition when he comes up for election. All but four of San Francisco's twenty-four superior court judges active in 1969 were first appointed.

plained Garry: "At least Karesh can be reached. When I look at the other judges available, I throw up."

Next day the courtroom was packed. Reporters and cameramen added to the confusion. Karesh waited a good long time to come out. He was uncharacteristically brief: "After the assurances I got yesterday . . . I see no reason why I cannot try this case." Applause. He continued: "But I already told the presiding judge last week that I was withdrawing, so the case has been resubmitted to the Master Calendar." He directed the defense down the hall to straighten it out. Most people thought the defense merely had to tell the presiding judge, Robert Drewes, that Karesh was taking the case after all. They stayed in the courtroom, expecting the lawyers to return directly. But Karesh had left, and as the minutes passed, more spectators got up to leave. Soon Drewes's courtroom was as jammed as Karesh's had been.

Again the TV cameras, the anxious faces. When Drewes entered, Garry began, "Your Honor, I would like to object . . ."

"Your objection will be noted for the record," interrupted Drewes in a cool, otherworldly voice. "This matter has been assigned to Department 23, Judge Laurence Mana, for trial Wednesday, June 17." He shut his book and fled.

Everyone sat stunned. "Clear the court," the bailiffs ordered. "There is another matter before this court."

In the hall, young Los Siete women tried to explain to parents in rapid Spanish what had happened. Brothers and sisters leaned against the walls, looking gloomy. Garry told the press: "In thirty-one years of practice I have never seen such a cop-out on the part of the judiciary. . . . Karesh is a coward."

For most supporters of the six, the judicial machinations culminating in Karesh's withdrawal produced a feeling of utter hopelessness. Something was going on "up there" over which they had no control. But for members of the Los Siete organization, powerlessness in the halls of justice was just another reason to continue building power within the community.

11. The Community
Must Take Control

As the pre-trial hearings came to an end, the spring of 1970 found the Los Siete organization analyzing its first year of community organizing and preparing for its second. The two projects which were to dominate its second year—El Centro de Salud and La Raza Legal Defense—emerged in that spring, directly from events in the community.

Tony Herrera, a member of Los Siete who had attended San Francisco State, later wrote a history of El Centro de Salud:

Our clinic El Centro de Salud has a long and beautiful history which goes back to the beginning of our organization, Los Siete de la Raza. In those early days we would look around and see that our people were suffering from lack of health care. We could see that many people lacked jobs and we knew that as a result they did not have enough to eat, and the ones we saw immediately affected were our children. We knew that the lack of nourishment directly affected their ability to learn. So our first health program began, focusing its attention on our children. We had two free breakfast programs, one at St. Peter's Church and one at St. John's. We knew that if our children had a balanced meal before going to school, at least their minds would not be on their hungry stomachs.

The program grew to feed more than two hundred children daily. It lasted over one year, but because we were young and inexperienced and this was our first attempt to begin to deal with our people's problems, we could not mobilize the people to take the breakfast program over. Without the support of the people the breakfast program was destined to fail.

During that time we began to expand our understanding of ways to deal with our people's health problems. We knew some doctors and other medical professionals who had volunteered to help us. So we arranged for the doctors to come once a week and examine the children. Some parents came forward and helped us in initiating the project. We did urine tests, ear and throat exams, and made startling discoveries. We discovered that our children were suffering from nutritional problems: infections which their bodies could not combat, rashes, blisters, bad teeth; children who felt weak and tired. We found anemia, ear infections, throat infections. We began to see exactly how immense the problem we had to deal with really was. We began to see that before we could have a real understanding of what problems affected our people, we would have to do serious investigation about our community.

So with this in mind we started to go door to door, to people's houses, giving families medical exams, paying close attention to all that we saw and learned. We learned that the problem extended beyond the children to their mothers and fathers and to the health facilities that were available to our people. We learned about San Francisco General Hospital and how people hated to go there. We learned that at General Hospital there were no translators and that many times people would leave discouraged because they could not communicate with anybody there. We learned that people were afraid to go there because they knew that if they had immigration troubles they could be reported to the immigration department. We learned that Welfare was not supplying people with enough money to receive proper medical treatment. We learned of doctors in our community who charged fantastic rates, who had taken people to court simply because they could not pay the tremendous prices. So, slowly, the people began to open our eyes. Everything that we learned we published in our newspaper *Basta Ya!** because we knew that although at the time we could not do anything about the problems, we had to let people know the truth, because the news they heard did not.

Late in 1969 a number of hospital workers from San Francisco General came together and formed a group called Workers Defense. . . . They fought for job security, better working conditions, patient demands such as translators, child care, adequate equipment and staff . . . So we worked closely with Workers Defense and we supported each other and ran articles of their struggles in *Basta Ya!*

In March 1970 a strike of city workers paralyzed San Francisco. The workers went on strike for better conditions, fringe benefits, etc. The city, rather than meet the workers' demands, closed the hospital down. Then the media carried a series of articles about how the workers were responsible for leaving the people with no health care. We saw how the city really didn't care if the patients had a place to go or not. So we met with the Workers Defense, got together doctors and professionals and other community people, and opened the clinic for the first time. For those first few days the clinic was open twenty-four hours a day; it was called the Strike Support Clinic. Then the strike ended. Nothing was changed—except that we had succeeded in creating a health center dedicated to stopping the miserable health conditions in our community.

---

* Maternity care was a particularly sore point. The paper reported that women often had their babies in the emergency or X-ray room; that women with difficult labors had to be transported through dirty tunnels in order to get to a different part of the hospital; and that once, when an elevator failed, a baby was lost. Another problem was the lack of facilities for drug addicts. In the summer of 1970 there were only eleven beds for junkies who wanted to quit, even though the Mission and neighboring Potrero Hill are heavy drug areas. Addicts were turned away and told to return in a few months.

When the city strike ended, El Centro de Salud was on its own. A staff of volunteers began to raise funds, set up books, paint walls, build cabinets, gather supplies, canvas the neighborhood, and deal with patients. The clinic was open four nights a week from 6:30 to 10:00 P.M. A pool of about twenty doctors, most of them young and white, served on different nights; many were interns. As their year of internship ended, two of these doctors began to work at the clinic full time.

Prescriptions were filled minutes after the appointment ended, usually with free drugs garnered from the countless samples with which drug companies inundate doctors. (Workers at the University of California Medical Center—which supplies doctors and interns to San Francisco General—and other hospitals rounded up these samples and routed them to the handful of free clinics in the city.) A small lab in the back of the clinic did routine tests. By June, three radical pharmacists had emerged and were working in the prescription department. Clinic workers requested, and were denied, permission to use San Francisco General's X-ray machines.

The clinic was a small operation able to offer only fairly unsophisticated medical services. Its ultimate purpose was not to replace San Francisco General but to show people the necessity of seizing control of the institutions they use—in this case, hospitals, but in a broader context, schools, the police force, and so on.

One of the clinic's earliest and most persistent problems was convincing people the place was professional and trustworthy with all those "hippie types" working inside. The doctors were young and usually bearded, and in order to break down the professional caste system most chose not to wear white coats. Only gradually did neighborhood people develop confidence in the clinic, finding it was responsible, free, friendly, homey, and clean but not offensively sterile. Many Los Siete members became community workers, talking with the patients, usually in Spanish, while they waited to see a doctor. There were no long financial or personal questionnaires. Patients were asked to leave a contribution if they could afford to do so; otherwise the services were free.

A few months after its founding, the clinic started afternoon classes to begin to train "paraprofessionals" in taking blood, translating medical histories and performing simple tests. Ex-convicts, welfare mothers, and dopers participated in the program. Young latinos who had known mostly street drugs found themselves on the dispensing side of the pills; along with their experience went a unique ability to communicate the hazards of drugs.

In May 1970, a fiesta—called *El Año de Los Siete*—was held on the clinic block. The week before, workers at the clinic had canvassed residents of the block for their approval. People had liked the idea and agreed to put up streamers and posters on their houses. The day was scorching hot, and the block was jammed with food stands, rummage sales, and sweaty people. For entertainment, there were bands, films, speakers, and *Las Sirenitas* ("The Mermaids"—a dancing group), in dark stockings and emerald green bathing suits. Afterwards, the neighbors brought out their brooms and helped clean up.

"Very few of us had had experience in medicines or clinics," Tony Herrera ended his history of the clinic:

> We learned the hard way what it means to run a clinic. We made mistakes but we learned from them and they helped us grow. But the one mistake we could not afford to make again was to fail to get the support of the people. We learned at the expense of the breakfast program that without the support of the people anything we did was bound to fail. We trained community people in medicine. We taught people how to do tests, how to spot symptoms; we trained people in nursing, and to use laboratory techniques. Because if this is to be truly a community clinic then the community must take control of it.
>
> Our clinic has been an example to other people of the things that can be accomplished by struggle and hard work. People have told us our clinic is one of a kind because we truly care for our people's health. We have gone with people to the Immigration Department to insure their rights. We have gone with people to General Hospital to make sure they get the care and medicine they need, translating and putting pressure on the hospital to help people out. We have helped

195

people win their disability cases before boards and in court. People have come to us from other communities to seek help in starting clinics like ours. One that is dedicated heart and soul to serving the people.

II

By its second year the Los Siete organization no longer centered its activities around the trial of the six, but legal defense remained one of its priorities. The clearest everyday reminders of oppression in the ghetto are the police, and whenever what seemed like a particularly outrageous example of police brutality came to Los Siete's attention, they would publicize it. Between fall 1969 and spring 1970 a series of such events provided the impetus for the formation of La Raza Legal Defense.

According to the police version of the first incident, at about 1:00 A.M. on November 29, 1969, two police officers tried to stop a fight between two brothers, Felipe and Alfonso Alcaraz. In the process a third Alcaraz brother was shot and all three brothers were arrested, two of them for attempted murder. When their mother went to the station to inquire about the arrests, she was arrested for assault. Bail for the family came to more than $11,000—or $1,100 to a bondsman. The family never got this money back even though some of the charges against them were dropped.*

The Alcaraz family had a different version of the incident. They said the police interfered in a private argument (even the officers admitted being told it was a family dispute) and started bullying the brothers, who fought back in self-defense. Their contention was supported by the fact that the third brother was shot

* Bail punishes poor people who can't put up the entire amount by obliging them to pay ten percent to a bondsman, which is not returned even if they are never convicted or brought to trial. And those who can't pay the bondsman must wait in jail. A recent *Time* magazine survey showed fifty-two percent of the prisoners in city and county jails throughout the country have not been convicted of any crime—most just can't make bail.

in the back, buttocks and foot—five times in all—and thus could not have been engaged in an exchange of gunfire, as one cop asserted.

Los Siete got Richard Hodge's law firm to defend the Alcaraz brothers; the firm promptly filed suit on behalf of the family for false arrest, false imprisonment, damage to their good name, and, for the third brother, for gunshot injuries. When the Alcaraz case came to trial in August 1971, the jury compromised, finding the Alcaraz brothers guilty of misdemeanors only: disturbing the peace and wielding a weapon.

Five months later, on April 19, 1970, a warm Sunday afternoon, two plainclothesmen approached a mixed group of whites and latinos picnicking in Sigmund Stern Grove, a park in a middle-class, mostly white neighborhood near San Francisco State College. In the melee which followed, two youths, one of them handcuffed, escaped custody. Police reinforcements arrived and eventually eight young men were charged with assault, resisting arrest, disturbing the peace, and lynching—"taking a prisoner by riotous means from lawful custody."

The district attorney charged that "there had been many complaints about the area as a trouble spot. The officers observed a rowdy, screaming, yelling crowd of about one hundred and fifty persons—passing plastic bags of apparent marijuana, puffing hand-rolled cigars, and drinking. . . . The officers observed a knife fight going on between two parties." The police attempted to arrest the two, but "a struggle ensued involving . . . approximately forty to fifty people." Police said someone yelled, "Let's do him in like Brodnik."

"There is probably not a person in San Francisco today who does not know that Officer Joseph Brodnik was the victim of a lawless event," the D.A. concluded. "The People submit that . . . this group knew that their victims were police officers . . . and worked together in a riotous frenzy with the specific idea that they would add one more officer to that long list of those killed this year."*

* Four policemen were killed in 1970.

The young men asserted that they, not the police, were the victims. They said the policemen did not identify themselves to more than two members of the group and the rest didn't know they were officers. "It would have been so easy for either officer to yell, 'Police, stand back,' " the defense argued in a pre-trial brief. "Why didn't they? If there is any fault it lies with these officers for their gross lack of professionalism." It might be added that if a crowd of fifty people seriously wanted to kill the cops "like Brodnik," they could have done so. After the incident, no drugs or knives were found, so that the only charges against the young men—assault, resisting arrest, disturbing the peace, and lynching—resulted from police interference in the picnic.

Three of the defendants, two of them disabled Vietnam veterans, subsequently filed $440,000 in damage suits against the city and eighteen unnamed officers for beatings allegedly administered both at Stern Grove and in jail.

Although the young men did not consider themselves radicals, and some of their parents didn't particularly want to be associated with Los Siete, it was largely through Los Siete's efforts that they were released on their own recognizance, and—as in the Alcaraz case—that damage suits were filed and some effort was made to counter the police version of the incident.

A month later, on May 19, 1970, came the death of Vincent Gutierrez, the catalyst for the formation of La Raza Legal Defense. At about four in the morning, eighteen-year-old Vincent left his house. He had been drinking for the past day or two, celebrating the arrival of his and his wife Maria's newborn daughter; he had also been taking barbiturates. Maria got worried and called police. Two cops found Vincent on a street corner a few blocks from home. They tried to arrest him; he fled. One officer caught him in a running tackle and shoved him up against the wall while the other struck the left side of Vincent's neck with his billyclub. Vincent was put in a paddy wagon. As the driver stopped the wagon to investigate another situation, he heard a thud "emanating from the interior of the vehicle," as the police report put it. When the driver looked in back, Vincent Gutierrez was dead.

Police claimed Maria Gutierrez had told them Vincent left

home "carrying a knife, threatening harm to his mother." Maria denied this, adding, "I told them not to hurt him. I said I know what he has on his face [he had one scratch from a fall taken the day before]. I warned them . . . I said, 'You killed my uncle [Luis Gutierrez had died in jail three weeks before], and he said, 'Oh, we didn't do that.' I said, 'Yes you did, you guys did. . . . You killed him at the Valencia Street station' [the Mission district police station]."

At first the police said Vincent had died as a result of his fall the day before. Later they changed the cause of death to barbiturate overdose. When in the coroner's office Maria asked about "a big purple bruise down to [Vincent's] ear," she was told, "That's how they get when they die."

Los Siete conducted a massive leafleting campaign, saying the police had murdered Vincent and urging attendance at his funeral, to be held at St. Peter's Church. The Gutierrez family did not object to the political use to which Los Siete was putting Vincent's death, especially since Luis Gutierrez had died in jail just three weeks before, also from "barbiturate overdose." (A cousin who viewed Luis's body remembered, "One ear was completely swollen and purple. He looked just like Vincent. . . . The police said that was natural because when you die you change color. And I said, not after only a few hours of death. He said, 'Well, an overdose brings it on faster.' ")

With Los Siete's help, the Gutierrez family had two private autopsies performed on Vincent's body. Both showed that the level of barbiturates in Vincent's blood was not lethal. The laboratory which analyzed samples of Vincent's brain tissue found "foci of hemorrhage." Although the hemorrhaging was not sufficient in itself to cause death, neither was the barbiturate level. It seemed that the combination of the two had been fatal. On the basis of these reports, a $400,000 damage suit was filed in behalf of Maria Gutierrez. "I shouldn't have called the police," the young widow said later. "I should have went to get him myself."

A long protest march and funeral procession wound through the Mission. Graffiti appeared: "Vicente Asesinado" ("Vincent Murdered"). A few days after the funeral one of the district's best known people's poets, Bebe Melendez's old friend Roberto Vargas, wrote and distributed a poem in response to Vincent's death.

> Look back
> Look back Chente . . . si puedes
> Remember the Roach Pad hunger
> Joys . . . highs, sorrows?
> Mission sidewalks (BART raped)
> Hum goodbye pa' siempre carnal
> But the genocide trail begins su fin
> Trembling with the weight of our guns. . .
> Chente 18 brown and dead
> In the land of E Pluribus Unum
> Dead in the land of the Apollo 13
> Edsel . . . Titanic . . . U-2 and Gary Powers
> Mission Hi . . . State College and business as usual.

III

A month later, in June 1970, La Raza Legal Defense opened on Twenty-fourth Street. Its purpose was to assemble enough skills and manpower to be able to respond to any incident like the Alcaraz, Stern Grove or Gutierrez affairs—to help people get good lawyers, file damage suits, and publicize police brutality. The office was soon swamped. Complaints of police brutality came in every few days. People needing help in eviction cases, dope busts, and hassles with Immigration or Selective Service contacted the office. The young Legal Defense workers—all from the community (among them Bebe's sixteen-year-old sister, Rosa Melendez)—contacted lawyers, acted as translators and liaisons, investigated arrests, and got people out of jail on their own recognizance. If people had trouble getting to court, Legal Defense would arrange for rides and baby sitters. Some of the young people began working for Legal Defense after they themselves had come for help. Legal Defense gradually built up relationships with about thirty lawyers. Some of the younger attorneys moved their offices into the Mission district and began occasionally to accept payments in kind: a dinner repair of a car.

The office produced weekly leaflets describing the latest confrontations between police and Mission district residents. They explained constitutional rights and handed out legal advice supplied by the local office of the National Lawyers Guild ("Don't carry more dope than you can eat," etc.). Police brutality remained the burning issue, and in the succeeding months Legal Defense helped file suits on behalf of many young men who said they had been harassed, beaten, or "challenged" to fight in station houses; in one case they filed suit for a whole family who said they had been beaten with billyclubs and dragged down a flight of stairs. In a one-year period, over one hundred cases of alleged police brutality were received by the office, and fifteen damage suits were filed.

"Our aim," a Legal Defense leaflet explained, "is to provide educational materials that inform people of what is happening in the Mission. We are not an alternative to a lawyer's office. Not every case can be handled, but everyone who comes in is advised of community and other legal services that are available." An article in *Basta Ya!* elaborated:

La Raza Legal Defense is struggling to put an end to police brutality, to bring pressure on Mission police stations to demand that officers who are sadistic and violent be released from police service. Through reporting police harassment and brutality to La Raza Legal Defense, we can become united and inform the community of these acts. As a united people we can begin to move to put an end to this form of oppression once and for all. We can demand community control of the police and organize street patrols.

Like the clinic, La Raza Legal Defense was an effort to show people why—and eventually how—they must take control of their lives.

In addition to its clinic and legal defense work, Los Siete became deeply involved in the issue of urban renewal, the decisive issue for the Mission district, for if the community did not fight redevelopment, most of its residents would be forced out by increased rents. *Basta Ya!* had analyzed and attacked urban renewal in almost every issue. BART's effect on property values, the role of the Mission Coalition in legitimizing redevelopment, the role of Abel Gonzalez as Mayor Alioto's "man" in the Mission, were all explored. Many groups in the MCO were beginning to doubt its usefulness after all, now that the all-important veto power over Model Cities had been bargained away.

Before the third annual MCO convention, Los Siete allied with the League of United Latin-American Citizens, the Welfare Rights Organization, and some education, health and block committees, to propagandize against the continued reign of MCO President Ben Martinez, and against certain by-law changes Martinez had proposed which would open MCO to "Irish-American," "Italian-American," and "European-American" power blocs, and allow MCO officers to live outside the district. The day before the convention the names of Mayor Alioto's twenty-one appointees to the Mission Model Cities Neighborhood Corporation were announced. The creation of this board took urban renewal out of MCO's hands: it was now, it would seem, merely a matter of time before the changes the Redevelopment Agency desired were under way.

The actual convention, in October 1970, was tense from the start. Any pretensions to democracy were dissolved by the blunt way in which floor microphones were cut off with audience speakers still in mid-sentence. Typical of MCO's role in ghetto politics were the vote appeals by aspiring Democratic Party politicians which appeared in the MCO yearbook—with slogans like "Power to the People" and "Right On." When the first by-law change—allowing Martinez a third term as president—was approved by a narrow margin, the dissident groups challenged the vote's legality. The chairman ignored them and tried to push on. But dissidents began to crowd the stage, shouting, "*Vendido! Oppor-*

tunista!" ("Sell-out! Opportunist!"). Then they walked out, vowing to form a new coalition which would not sell out the needs of most people in the Mission.

Despite the elated feelings of solidarity among those who had walked out, the auguries for this new group were not very good. Its politics were much too diverse; many of the well-intentioned liberals who walked out appreciated Los Siete's help but considered the organization too radical. But at least it was a beginning. The people inside Centro Obrero Hall, as well as those who were still, out of boredom or disgust, filtering out, had at least begun to see how MCO—and ghetto politics in general—was controlled. Although Martinez resigned a few months later, and the media ran stories to bolster the MCO image, the organization's reputation in the barrio had been badly hurt. This discrediting of the MCO was a hopeful sign—but as Los Siete had discovered, it was a long way from consciousness to effective political work. And for poor people in the Mission there wasn't much time. Four months after the convention, the city was already installing palm trees and decorative tile near the recently completed BART stations on Mission Street. Would piñata stands be far behind?

IV

Los Siete de la Raza began as a group of students and ex-students attempting to organize street youth around issues like police brutality. By the time the clinic and legal defense office were established in the spring of 1970, Los Siete was beginning to represent the interests of working families, the basic social unit in the Mission district. Coming out of a movement which consisted of students, radicals, and some street people, this was an essential transition.

People within Los Siete were trying to develop the historical understanding and self-discipline they considered necessary attributes of true revolutionaries. In developing this understanding and discipline they had to struggle with anti-intellectualism. As with the Young Lords in New York, members of Los Siete were supposed to read each day; the books were then discussed in political education classes. This reading, in addition to work at the clinic or legal defense, writing for and selling *Basta Ya!*, raising money, leafleting, public speaking, and, for some, school, jobs, or children to care for, imposed a heavy schedule. As a result, Los Siete remained small, with an increasing number of friends who worked with Los Siete projects but weren't actually members of the organization.

One of the most impressive aspects of Los Siete was the personal changes in many of its members. Although some people left to form new groups, or just to give up politics for a while, those who remained grew more responsible, articulate, dedicated, and mellow. Almost everyone in the group learned to speak convincingly in public, to read carefully and think analytically, and to shoulder responsibility.

The women in Los Siete grew stronger and more independent. Like the Young Lords, Los Siete fought *machismo* in political work as well as in personal relations. This was no easy fight, since some young men who were fairly sophisticated radicals and good workers still wanted their wives or girlfriends to stay home and keep out of political work. Stronger women in the organization made a conscious effort to step aside and let other women take the lead.

People in Los Siete were trying to become revolutionaries, which necessarily required defining what "revolutionary" meant for brown people in the United States. Clearly it meant solidarity with wars of liberation such as the war in Indochina; and Los Siete, through *Basta Ya!*, tried to show people in the Mission that they, the Indochinese and many guerrillas in Latin America had a common enemy: Yankee imperialism.

"Revolutionary" also meant devoted to changing the entire social and economic system. Los Siete members believed—partly because of their experience in poverty programs—that in the long run reforms were not going to improve conditions for the masses of latin people. But they realized they were at the beginning of a long revolutionary process. Their immediate goal was not to "start the revolution then and there," as Bebe Melendez once put it, but to organize, educate, and learn from the people.

"Revolutionary" for Los Siete also meant "internationalist"—that is, rejecting cultural nationalism in favor of a class struggle which crossed racial and even national boundaries. But despite this opposition to cultural nationalism, Los Siete remained a brown organization. Its precise appeal was its concern for the needs of latin people in a predominantly latin area. Its members felt there was no use combining with other groups to form a multiracial organization until a significant number of brown people had been united around revolutionary demands. It was also important to Los Siete to remain within the brown movement which, despite its fragmented nature and the diversity of its political ideologies, held a tremendous appeal for chicano and latin youth—an appeal stemming from its proud, assertive new spirit, a spirit so important to people who have been discriminated against and taught they are inferior.

It's hard to say what success Los Siete has had after its first two years. The hostility of the powerful mass media has made its message difficult to spread; Los Siete's available avenues of communication with its people aren't nearly so powerful: a small, street-vended newspaper and day-to-day contacts at the clinic or legal defense office with people who often have little time to get involved in politics. But a few events toward the middle of 1971 indicated that people were beginning to make time.

Meetings, leafleting and picketing around a threatened eviction of the clinic in the early summer of 1971 mobilized neighborhood people and developed a strong core of Los Siete partisans. The landlord, who owned a pharmacy on the ground floor of the building, wanted to get rid of the clinic and rent to some "real doctors with real patients and real money," as he put it, who would send people downstairs to buy at his store. (El Centro de Salud dispensed free drugs whenever possible and so didn't provide any clients for the drug store.)

When the landlord said he wouldn't renew the lease, Los Siete called meetings with people who had used the clinic, asking them to pass the word and boycott the pharmacy. In the week that followed the pharmacy lost fifty percent of its business. When the landlord still didn't give in, picketing was begun. Insisting that community people must fight for the clinic or it wasn't worth saving, Los Siete resisted the temptation to use outside pressure from friendly doctors or other, mostly white, health professionals. Enough community people responded—a number of them housewives—to convince the landlord to reconsider after only one day of picketing. The women who had come to the clinic's defense would hopefully remain organized as a pressure group on health care issues in the Mission.

It would seem that after two years Los Siete was at least moving in the right direction; that more genuine contacts had been made, more trust established, than by radical organizations in the past—especially in the Mission district, where political activity has been dominated either by the Democratic Party and its Mexican-American friends, or by Office of Economic Opportunity–funded groups which are often full of opportunists. Los Siete is indigenous; it is not being paid by anyone to exist, and its members work mainly from idealistic motives—as Tony Herrera put it, "dedicated heart and soul to serving the people."

12. Mind If
I Call You Piggy?

I

Judge Laurence Mana had just returned from a vacation in Italy in June 1970 when the political hot potato the Los Siete trial had become was dumped in his lap. "You should've seen him the first day in chambers," Mario Martinez later said. "He was dropping everything."

Mana didn't have Karesh's thirteen months of background in the case, and often during arguments seemed to be bored or confused. Sometimes he would lean back in his chair, nodding; you could hardly see the slight, graying judge behind his huge desk, flag and books. Once he mumbled "sustained" when an objection hadn't even been made. "Force of habit," attorney Hodge called it. Privately, both sides complained he was wishy-washy. Both sides tried—with success—to push him around, and both discovered that where logic in an argument with Mana often failed, persistence might win.

In February 1969 Mana and other municipal court judges had been invited to Sacramento to meet with Republican State Assemblyman Don Mulford concerning judicial response to mass arrests—specifically to the upcoming trials of four hundred thirty-five demonstrators arrested at the January rally at San Francisco State. According to the *San Francisco Chronicle*, Mulford, "after conferring with two members of [Governor Reagan's] official family . . . threatened" that the judges would find themselves up against "heavily financed opposition" for re-election if they weren't tough on the S.F. State strikers. Mana, who had set high bail for the strikers in January, was apparently considered sufficiently tough. He was elevated to superior court by Governor Reagan in the fall of 1969, just eight months before the Los Siete trial began.

Mana sometimes seemed to resent the defense lawyers, who got so much attention. He would often warn Garry that he needn't shout so loud—the jury wasn't present. Once when Mana threatened to issue contempt citations, Garry asked, "Why are you looking at me when you say that?"

Mana responded, "Maybe it's because you're so glamorous."

Prosecutor Tom Norman was even more obvious. "I think there's a press conference," I heard him say one day. "Where's Charlie? Oh, there he is: you can see the bright lights."

The jury of seven women and five men was selected in only two weeks, more swiftly than expected. If it contained no peers of the defendants, at least it had people under forty. Most of the women were housewives, clerical employees or in low-level management; the men worked for the government or for banks. There was one black man, one brown woman, and one long-haired Mexican.

Probably the two most important jurors were Kenneth Heck, a balding, middle-aged bank investment counselor who was later elected foreman; and Robert Hijar, a post office worker with shoulder-length hair whose real vocation was painting. Hijar was a middle-class Mexican who later said he felt somewhat privileged, and remote from the average street brother. Supporters of Los Siete were pleased and somewhat amazed that a "longhair" had gotten on the jury. But there just seemed to be too many longhairs on the jury panel for the prosecutor to exclude them all. In addition, Norman was no doubt afraid the defense would use its peremptory challenges (i.e., its right to dismiss without stating the cause) on jurors who seemed conservative, such as Kenneth Heck. So Norman compromised and accepted Robert Hijar.

Other jurors who added interest to the proceedings or played significant roles during deliberations were Leslie Houck, an attractive corporate secretary who inspired many sexist comments from male reporters; Lawrence Lewis, a young black nuclear weapons technician for the Defense Department; Gilbert Gates, a nervous insurance man who, *after* he had been chosen as a juror, wore an American flag pin on his lapel, as if to taunt the defense; Mary Girard, a quiet chicana employed as a switchboard operator and office clerk; Bonnie Cancienne, a young white Bank of America employee who turned out to be one of the defense's strongest supporters; and Pamela Budd, a self-reliant young secretary who, because of her somewhat irreverent manner, was one of the defense attorneys' favorites.

Norman's opening statement contained one surprise: he said an unidentified person fired the first shot, which killed Brodnik; then McGoran looked up to see Pinky Lescallett point the gun at him and fire. "That Paul McGoran wasn't struck by that second bullet is a miracle," Norman said. "The same person fired both shots."

Both Norman and the defense knew that most witnesses who said they saw one of the defendants with a gun described him as a short boy, about five-four. Pinky Lescallett, at six-one, towered over the other defendants. How Norman intended to prove it was Pinky remained a mystery—until it became clear he didn't intend to prove it at all. He had to accuse Pinky of firing the second shot because McGoran had accused him, and without McGoran's testimony the case would fall apart. And since there was only a three- to five-second interval between the two shots—too short a time logically for the gun to change hands—he had to accuse Pinky of firing the first shot, too.

The first prosecution witness was the burglary victim, Mrs. Ruth Horenstein. She described leaving her house at 8:30 A.M. on May 1 after carefully locking her miniature black poodle inside. Norman asked if she had noticed anything unusual as she left. "I did notice somebody," she answered stiffly. (She had previously identified the person as Gio Lopez.) "He was standing on the wrong side of the street for the bus and I couldn't understand why he was loitering there." The defense objected to the word "loitering" and it was stricken from the record.

At 3:00 P.M., Mrs. Horenstein said, her husband called and told her to come home. "I found my whole house a mess," she told the jury. "Everything was in complete disarray. My living room was a shambles, furniture all over, light bulbs broken. . . . I sustained a very great loss."

"When you got to your house did you find your little poodle dog?"

"Yes. She was very badly hurt. She had been bleeding all day."

Kennedy objected: "No one is charged here with brutality to a dog, nor is it included in the crime of burglary. . . . It was elicited and is totally immaterial and should be stricken."

"Motion to strike is denied."

The star prosecution witness, Paul McGoran, was an enormous, brooding man. The strangest, most upsetting thing about him was the deadness of his face. The many lines all pointed down, accentuating a perpetual frown and small, sad eyes. It soon became apparent that part of the deadness was caused by the fifteen milligrams of valium (a strong tranquilizer) he took every day.

McGoran told how Mission Eleven began in March 1966 as a daytime burglary detail: "I worked with [Brodnik] and with the record of arrests we had made, the good work—" It was the first of many comments the defense demanded be stricken as "self-serving."

On May 1, a little after ten A.M., driving with Brodnik down Alvarado Street, McGoran said, he saw "a young man walking fast toward the basement area of a home . . . carrying an item into the basement that looked like either a turntable or stereo amplifier . . . [which] came from the rear of an automobile parked at the curb. . . . I saw a young man take a television set out of the driver's side, [then] walk to the same place I saw the first man go." Asked how many young men were there, McGoran answered, "There was five altogether, including Gary Lescallett, plus the one I saw went into the basement [he meant José Rios]." He then

212

identified Nelson Rodriguez, Bebe Melendez and Mario Martinez.

Norman looked confused. "What about Rodolfo Martinez—Tony?"

McGoran: "I recognized him as being there but I'm not one hundred percent sure of him. . . .

"I went over to the driver's side of the Chevrolet and I looked in. On the front seat I saw a metal cashbox, bluish; it appeared to have a number of fresh pry marks." Inside he found an envelope addressed to Laurence Horenstein. "I asked if anyone there was named Laurence Horenstein. [As] I was asking this question, there were three that were heading toward the stairway upstairs." He identified the three as José, Bebe and Tony—"I believe" (actually José, Mario, and Gio Lopez, according to the defense).

"Mario" (Bebe, according to the defense) was at the rear of the blue Chevy. "He went to the front steps and sat down. Nelson Rodriguez was at the stairway of 429 with Joe [Brodnik]; Gary Lescallett had gone to the porch of the house next door; he was sitting on the ledge. José Rios came from the doorway of 433 Alvarado and he gave me his social security card. . . . He headed toward the basement; I told him to stay. He said, 'Fuck you, I'm going where I want to go.' I told Joe to go to the basement and bring the party back. I heard some loud talking. Then both of them emerged from the basement area and stayed in the sidewalk area. The other two hadn't returned from the house and they were under investigation for burglary. I called in on the walkie-talkie to find if the radio car had been sent.

"Mario Martinez made some wisecracks which I don't recall at this time. Gary Lescallett said, 'I'm gonna go upstairs.' I just told him everyone was going to stay at the scene here. He said, 'What are you gonna do, shoot me?' I told him, 'No, I'm not gonna shoot anybody.' He jumped on the ledge and I jumped up on the ledge with him. I grabbed him and tried to shake him free from the pillar. He said, 'Now you've had it,' and he let me have it right in the mouth. We tussled and went down to an area between the pillar and the post near the sidewalk. We exchanged a number of blows. The next thing I knew I was going over to the sidewalk area and my eyesight became dark. I was being hit and kicked when I

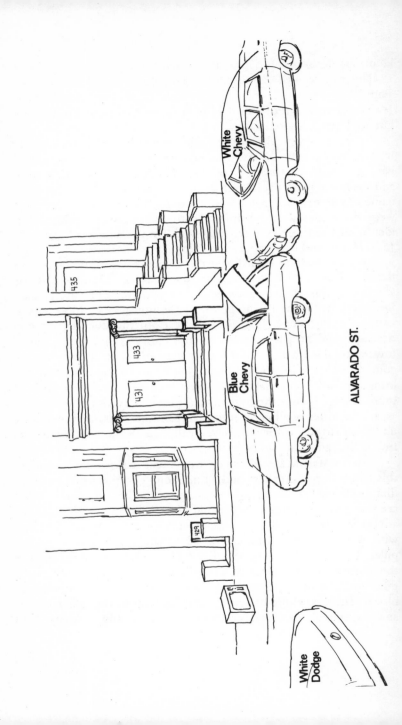

White Chevy

Blue Chevy

White Dodge

ALVARADO ST.

435

433

431

429

was on the ground. Next thing I recall was I heard Joe holler, 'Look out, Paul, he's got your gun!' Then I heard a loud report right in front of me. All I could think of was taking cover.

"I remember moving around the feet of Joe and behind the pillar. Then I looked over and saw Joe. I saw a burn mark on his chest. I saw Gary Lescallett in the car pointing the gun at me—it was my gun. He fired the gun at me as I was reaching for the walkie-talkie."

Norman asked, "Do the defendants look the same today as they did on May 1, 1969?"

McGoran responded, with a nod toward each one: "No, he looks much cleaner today. His hair is shorter. . . . He was wearing different clothes, much dirtier clothes. . . . He has on a nice suit today." Mario later remarked, "He sure enjoyed calling us greasers from the stand."

Norman introduced into evidence the police tape of the radio messages sent by Brodnik and McGoran between 10:15 and 10:30 A.M. on May 1. It started with the businesslike requests of Mission Eleven for help: "Can I have a 904 [meet an officer] at 433 Alvarado?"

"We're trying to get somebody now. . . . Is that Elverano or Alvarado?"

McGoran, more excitedly: "Alvarado."

Brodnik: "Mission Eleven, will you code 2 that—904 code 2?" (Meaning "urgent, respond immediately; red light and siren not recommended.")

Seconds later, McGoran, shouting hysterically: "Mission Eleven, a shooting; I've been shot!" Then, "Two of us, two police officers shot, an ambulance please! . . . Hurry, I've been shot in the face; my partner's shot in the chest!"

Seconds later: "My partner's dead!"

"Did you tell Officer Brodnik, 'Go get that son of a bitch'?" Charles Garry began his cross-examination.

"No," McGoran said.

"You realize you're under oath?" Objection sustained. "Why is it that you have a .41-caliber weapon?"

"I bought a new gun in 1966. The department was going in for larger guns."

"Didn't you buy this gun before the department issued any such directive?"

"I don't remember."

"Do you have any trouble with your memory?" Objection sustained. "Don't you have a tab at the Lamplighter?" (a bar next door to McGoran's apartment in the Mission district—he had moved away from his family in Pacifica some years before).

"On May 1, didn't you go to the Lamplighter for several belts before going on duty?"

McGoran looked first to Norman and then to Judge Mana. When no objection was made, he answered, "I waited for Joe at the Lamplighter because my doorbell wasn't working. I drank a cup of coffee."

"Were you in any of your favorite bars—Lamplighter's, Lefty O'Doul's, the Circle, Duke and Larry's—after midnight on May 1?"

"I don't recall where I was the night before."

"You had something to drink the night before?"

"I may have."

"Did you have an alcoholic breath on May 1?"

"No."

"Were you carrying breath sweeteners?"

"Yes."

"That was to cover your alcoholic breath so your superiors wouldn't know you were boozing it up?"

"No sir."

"Did one of the defendants tell you you smelled like a brewery?"

"I don't recall that."

"Sure?"

"Positive."

"Just as positive as when you told Brodnik, 'Go get that son of a bitch'?"

"Yes sir."

"You're also positive you didn't call the defendants greasers, punks or motherfuckers?"

"Yes."

"Or any form of obscene or degrading language?"

"Yes."

"Didn't you get angry when José Rios said, 'Fuck you'?"

"No sir."

"You were happy about it?"

"No, I've heard it before."

"You have a pretty calm temper?"

"I would say yes."

Garry continued the grilling: "On the morning of May 1, did you use the terminology, 'Make like a rabbit'?"

"No."

"You've used that terminology on many occasions, have you not?"

"No sir."

"You haven't?" Garry read a portion of the motion to suppress evidence hearing before Judge Karesh the previous December in which McGoran had admitted using the term. "And you have done so on many occasions, isn't that right, sir?"

"I can't recall how many. At first I thought he meant a sex term."

"Did you tell Gary Lescallett to make like a rabbit?"

"No."

"Did he say to you, 'Go ahead and shoot me'?" Garry repeated it very loud, three times: " 'GO AHEAD AND SHOOT ME! GO AHEAD AND SHOOT ME! GO AHEAD AND SHOOT ME!' Didn't he say that loud enough for everyone in the neighborhood to hear?" McGoran admitted Pinky had said something like that. Garry, more softly now: "And you didn't have your gun out? *How did he know you had a gun?*"

Objection sustained.

"Did you at any time tell Gary Lescallett or anyone else that they were under arrest?"

"No."

"Did Gary Lescallett ever hit the ground?"

"Yes." (Much of the defense case was to rest on this admission by McGoran that he knocked Pinky Lescallett down.)

"He stayed down?"

"I don't know."

"Because the next thing you knew you had the gun in your hand and you were waving it around, and you fired the gun and it killed Brodnik?"

"No."

Over the weekend break, word of McGoran's address got out. "Free Los Siete Que Viva" was spray-painted in large letters on the side of his apartment building; it was never painted over.

After the weekend, Garry started in with renewed vigor. "Let's talk about Joseph Brodnik. You didn't think he was a very good cop, did you?" Objection sustained. "Didn't you think Joseph Brodnik was too soft and he shouldn't be a police officer?" Objection sustained.

"You've been bragging about how well you're doing on the witness stand, haven't you?" Objection sustained. "You were so drunk Saturday night you couldn't even take your father home." Objection sustained. "Your Honor," Garry complained, "it goes to his being an alcoholic and a bum."

Norman: "He [Garry] should be cited for misconduct." Judge Mana ignored the suggestion, which Norman was to make frequently during the course of the trial.

"Do you remember the time you were tried in South San Francisco for assault and battery?" Garry continued. Objection sustained. "Don't you have a vile and atrocious temper?" Objection sustained. "Didn't you have a vile and atrocious temper on May 1?"

"No sir."

Garry began to ask about a "heart condition," tachycardia, which McGoran had mentioned to a doctor at San Francisco General Hospital on the day of Brodnik's death. The witness explained, "I can tell you what I feel, that under tension, any kind of physical exertion, my heartbeat goes up to as high as one hun-

218

dred eighty counts per minute." McGoran said he took three drugs for his tachycardia: digitoxin, ponesterol and valium, the last one three times a day in five milligram tablets.

"How was your tachycardia about the time you asked Gary Lescallett not to go upstairs?"

"I don't know," said McGoran.

"On May 1 you told the doctors at General Hospital you were not knocked down?" Garry read from the hospital record: "Was hit in face . . . was not knocked down. Not unconscious." This was an important point. At the crucial moment, McGoran had testified, he was on the ground, dizzy, blacking out. Now he answered: "I don't recall . . . I didn't see him write anything down. I didn't state to him that I was not knocked down."

"What did you say your name was?" Michael Kennedy began his cross-examination. When McGoran answered, Kennedy went on, rapidfire: "You're sure of that, are you? Have you taken any more tranquilizers? You feel okay? Hearing okay? Sight okay? Feel calm and relaxed, do you? Mind if I call you piggy?"

"Objection!" Norman screamed. "And counsel should be cited for contempt!"

Kennedy: "Joe Brodnik would never operate as the bad guy?"

"Yes, he did."

"When?"

"I can't recall."

"Of course you can't, because he never did. . . . You enjoyed being a bad guy?"

Norman: "Objection. It's argumentative and degrading."

Kennedy: "There's no way I could degrade him. . . . You were jealous of Officer Brodnik on May 1, weren't you?" Objection sustained.

"Your Honor, this goes directly to why he shot him. You knew Joe Brodnik was a good deal smarter than you?" Objection sustained. "The fact is, you and Joe Brodnik quarreled on May 1 right before this incident."

"No, I never quarreled with Joe."

"Didn't Joe Brodnik always admonish you—I won't use such a big word, strike that—tell you to stop being so vicious and brutal?"

"No."

"But you were vicious and brutal?" Objection sustained.

"You were a coward and that's why you carried that big gun?" Objection sustained.

"Did you take valium on May 1?"

"Yes. It was prescribed for me and I took it on that day. I tried to avoid physical exertion because it makes my heart go up."

"And one way you could avoid exertion was to pull that revolver and tell people to stay away from you? It was your habit to draw your gun whenever you went up to a group of latinos and to line them up against the wall?"

"No."

"Didn't you pull that revolver and say, 'Don't move!'? Wouldn't that be the sensible thing for a man with a heart condition to do?" Objection sustained.

"After you got hit you pulled the gun. Wouldn't that have been the intelligent thing?" Objection sustained. "You weren't really worried about your heart condition, were you?" Objection sustained.

"Isn't it a fact that Joe Brodnik never took his gun into an unarmed group because he was afraid of just the thing that happened? . . . Because he's smarter than you?" Objection sustained.

"Isn't it a fact—now really, officer—that you do not know how many shots were fired?" Richard Hodge began his cross-examination in a much less aggressive style than either Charles Garry or Michael Kennedy.

"Yes sir, I know—I know there were two shots," McGoran answered.

"You're not sure there were not three?"

"No, I'm not sure there were not three. I know there were [at least] two."

"Weren't you trying to mislead the jury when you told them two? ... Can we have the question read back so the officer can have a better opportunity to explain it?"

McGoran: "When you're on the receiving end of a .41 Magnum the report is very loud, almost deafening, so there may have been three."

"So there could have been three, four, or even five?"

"I don't know, sir."

"Did you tell anyone you believed that gun had been emptied at you?"

"I don't recall making that statement." (It had appeared in the *San Francisco Chronicle,* however, as part of a bedside interview with McGoran.)

"Did you seriously think you were shot in the face with a .41 Magnum and still alive to put your finger in your mouth?"

"Yes."

"Where was Gio Lopez that morning?"

"I don't know."

"Well, he's charged with murder. Did you see him that morning?"

"No."

"I want to ask you—and take your time and think carefully—look at Danilo [Bebe] Melendez and Mario Martinez, and tell me if the person who made the wisecrack ['You smell like a brewery,' according to the defense] was not Danilo Melendez?"

"No, it was Mario Martinez."

"You're absolutely sure?"

"Positive, sir."

"Do you recall telling him—and I want you to think about this—'You fucking Mexican, I could wash my hands on your back'?"

"No, I didn't know he was Mexican. I understand that he's not."

"Go ahead and grab me the way you grabbed Gary Lescallett."
McGoran touched Hodge's lapels. "Just like that?"

"Yes." Nervous laughter from the spectators.

"Did you have to shake him repeatedly to get him loose?"

"I didn't shake him. He let go and hit me in the face."

Hodge read from the motion-to-suppress-evidence transcript:
"I grabbed him and tried to shake him free from the pillar."

"Isn't it true that the individual you saw with the gun was kneeling by the open car door?"

"No."

"He was latin?"

"He was Gary Lescallett."

"He had long hair?"

"Yes sir."

"He had medium build—five foot three to five foot six?"

"It was Gary Lescallett."

"Isn't it true that the individual took the gun from your hand after you shot Officer Brodnik?"

"I never had the gun out of my holster."

"Would you be willing to take a lie detector test to prove you didn't kill Officer Brodnik?" Norman objected, but Hodge had his finale well planned. He turned to Pinky Lescallett: "Would you be willing to take a lie detector test?"

Pinky jumped up, shouting, "Yes!" Mana and Norman began to squeal: "Mr. Hodge, you know that's improper!" "Cite him for misconduct!" Later, Mana said, "Mr. Hodge, that was gross misconduct, and I've got to warn you. It was highly improper for you to make that grandiose gesture in the presence of the jury."

"However that may be," Hodge said, "I'd like to offer to the district attorney to submit my client to a lie detector test."

Mana: "The court will note your silence on that other matter."

R. Jay Engel, Nelson's attorney, began: "Have you made any report on the May 1 incident?"

"No official report."

"After eighteen years as a police officer, how many days have you worked that you haven't filed a report?" Objection sustained.

"Isn't it highly irregular not to make a report?" Objection sustained.

"There are no records you prepared?"

"I remember what happened. I won't forget it. I got a very vivid memory of this here incident."

"You reported only five suspects?"

"No sir."

"Up to the arrest, there was no account in the paper of there ever being more than five?"

"I knew there were six."

"Any account in the paper?"

"As I recall . . . they only had pictures of five."

"The police fliers went out with five suspects, in response to information you gave."

"I guess that could be possible."

"You have no heart problem, you have tachycardia?"

"I have a heart problem."

"Your heart problem is tachycardia."

"Whatever it is I have."

"On May 2, you told the doctor the last time you had tachycardia was three years ago in 1966 when you had to take a lie detector test?"

"I don't recall telling him; I may have."

"You have no doubts you took a lie detector test?"

"I didn't take a lie detector test."

"Did you have an episode of tachycardia in connection with taking a lie detector test?"

"I didn't take a lie detector test."

"Whether you took it or not—in connection with taking one?"

"I would say no, because I didn't take one."

"In San Francisco General Hospital, you mentioned a lie detector test to the doctor?"

"I may have mentioned it but I didn't take the test."

"*The* test? Which test are you talking about?"

"The one in Redwood City."*

Engel went on: "Isn't it a fact that they told you you didn't have a heart problem but that you were imagining the whole thing—it was psychosomatic?"

"No sir, I could feel it."

"Hasn't your lawyer advised you that one reason you might *not* get a retirement [McGoran was requesting, and later received, retirement with pay] is that your heart problem is psychosomatic?"

"No."

Engel referred to a thick medical file. "On May 15, 1966 [the doctor] told you they were psychosomatic?"

"No. It's a very real experience."

Engel read from the file: " 'A number of complaints he tends to attribute to his heart, whether correctly or incorrectly, are in fact psychosomatic.' Didn't the doctor tell you that?"

"No, I don't recall that."

Engel pressed on: "Didn't [your] doctors feel in June 1966 that you should quit the police force because you couldn't deal with situations under pressure?" Objection sustained. (Mana: "I don't see the relevance.")

"Did they tell you to quit for any reason?"

"No."

"Didn't you request a transfer because you couldn't handle

---

* McGoran had, in fact, been about to take a lie detector test in 1966 when his heartbeat began to go up. He had accused a neighbor's son of throwing a rock at his Pacifica house. The judge was sufficiently impressed with the boy's denial to ask both him and McGoran to take lie detector tests. After his attack, McGoran changed his story and said he had only seen the boy make a motion to throw the rock. This information came from the San Francisco General Hospital medical report and the Pacifica Police Department's file on McGoran, both of which were entered in evidence.

the pressure in the communications department?"

"I would say the pressures were pretty great. . . . I requested a change to Mission Station. You could call it that, yes sir."

"Isn't digitoxin the drug for the heart and valium just a tranquilizer like any other?"

"It's a tranquilizer that tranquilizes the heart."

"It doesn't work on the rest of your system?"

"I don't feel any different. I don't feel high or anything after I take it."

"Hasn't Dr. Mintz told you to take valium up to three a day for nervousness?"

"He prescribed it."

"Has he used the word 'anxiety'—valium to control anxiety?"

"I don't recall that terminology."

"Your valium jar, doesn't it say three times a day for nervousness?"

"I don't know."

"Could you bring it tomorrow?"

"Yes sir."

Next day McGoran handed Engel the pill bottle. "Does that refresh your recollection that the doctor prescribed the valium 'as needed' for nervousness?"

"No sir."

"For nervousness."

"For whatever reason he prescribed it."

"Did he prescribe it for nervousness?"

"I can't remember the exact wording he used."

"Did he prescribe it for nervousness?"

"I don't know why; I thought it was for the heart."

"Didn't he prescribe it as necessary for nervousness?"

"I don't know the reason why he put it."

"Well it says here, 'as needed.' He must have told you what you needed it *for.*"

"I got the prescription."

"He must have told you what you needed it for."

"It was for the heart. That was my understanding."

Engel read from the medical file:

"As necessary for control of nervousness."*

"Did you tell Dr. Mintz you were frightened of being a witness?"

"I related to him that I had been threatened and I was upset about it. . . . I didn't say I was frightened to testify. I was frightened because I had been threatened."

On re-cross-examination (after re-direct examination by Norman), Garry asked, "How were you threatened?"

"The audience. They made motions that they were gonna get me. I could read their lips."

---

* The file was entered in evidence. It included periodic letters from physicians to the retirement board. Each letter would end with the recommended treatment—including "valium . . . as necessary for control of nervousness" or "anxiety."

13. Nobody Walk Every Day the Same

I

The first eyewitness, Mrs. Irene Jarzyna, had been watching TV in her bedroom on May 1, 1969, when her daughter Elizabeth called her to the window. "I saw six boys and two men—one in white shirt, one in brown," she testified. "A TV and radio some boys were bringing from the basement.* One sat down. One was start talking with the man with the brown jacket [McGoran]. The biggest one start telling, 'Hit me, hit me.' The man in brown was grab the boy in the front of the jacket and pull—push him to the wall. The boy was hit in the head with the hand."

"Well," said Norman, "who hit whom?"

Mrs. Jarzyna thought a moment. "The boy was—hit this man. It all happened so fast, all the boys was jump on him. Was fight . . . all six of them beating him." She repeated the number six several times, as if she had memorized it. "Man in white [Brodnik] was there by TV and radio and then he turned fast and he ran to the group of boys and was like separating them, and then I saw one with the gun. The boy was have the gun and Brodnik was have hands up . . . and the boy just shot him."

Norman: "Did you actually see the gun in the boy's hand?"

Jarzyna: "Yah. . . . He was shooting once and then again." She

* The direction in which the property was being moved proved later to be a crucial point.

couldn't point out the gunman, but did identify Tony and Mario as being there. Tony, she said, "was showing a card to the man in brown." (Both McGoran and the defense agreed José Rios had shown identification.)

"Anyone else you can identify?" Norman asked.

"All the boys. All of them—six."

"At 2:51 P.M. on May 1 the police asked you some questions into a tape recorder?" Garry began his cross-examination.

"Yes."

"You told the man you did not see the gun."

"I was so nervous, so crying, so upset. It was a very shock for me."

"You told him"—Garry read from the transcript of the May 1 tape—" 'Was so fast, so fast, I just heard the shot. I'm not really sure who.' "

"To who?" asked Mrs. Jarzyna.

"To the policeman with the tape recorder."

"I saw what was happened."

"How many times had you seen these boys before May 1, 1969?"

She answered automatically, "Six."

"All the time you were sitting at the lineup you had your glasses on?"

"Yes." Garry showed her a photo of the lineup in which she was sitting in the audience with her glasses off. "Show me where your glasses are in this picture."

"No, I don't have here. . . . The boys weren't on the line."

"So when you told me you had your glasses on all the time you weren't telling the truth?"

"What you mean not telling the truth?" Then with a cute smile: "You didn't say what time."

Next trial day Garry showed her the same photo of the lineup. By this time Mrs. Jarzyna no longer enjoyed being cute. She made exaggerated faces—bored or sarcastic—and flung her eyes ceilingward to show her exasperation. "That's not the same picture you showed me Thursday."

"Are you sure?"

"Yes."

"Would you bet your life on it?"

"Yes, I would bet my life."

"Can we have a stipulation, counsel," Garry turned to Norman, "that this is the identical picture we showed her Thursday?" Reluctantly, Norman stipulated. Garry turned to the witness. "You don't have a good memory today?"

"Oh, I have a good remember today. It all depends what you be ask me."

"Madam, how is it that six days afterwards [at the lineup] you remember just two people and in the courtroom now you say you remember all six of them?"

She thought for a moment. "Their movements, how they are walking."

"What is it about the walk of these six young men that reminds you of the people that were there?"

"How they walk and how they act to each other. They are boys. . . . Old woman walk different. In the first of May they was walking the same almost like they was walking today from the beginning. When the fight started there again was another movement and this was different too. . . ."

Garry asked her to demonstrate. She did so, talking—"He jumped up fast . . . he was kind of shuffling . . . he was all nervous"—and prancing across the courtroom floor. In her tight dress and high heels, with her shoulders twitching, she tried to imitate, as one reporter put it, "Huey Newton's soul."

Kennedy began his cross-examination gently. "At some point you phoned the police. After all of the events were over?"

"No, that was when they start fight. I have telephone very close to my bed and I was just grab the telephone when start fight."

"You took your attention away from the street activity and looked at your phone?"

"Phone, yes. I was screaming, I was crying, and I was talking real fast."

"You picked up the phone at the beginning of the fight?"

"When I saw this man was standing, the high man, and then the boy was hit him in the head, then I grabbed the telephone."

Norman began to make an objection. Kennedy turned and directed a very audible pop in his direction. He explained: "That was just a little pop to the district attorney. He was making an objection when no objection was called for, in an effort to prevent the witness from saying something he didn't want her to say. I merely wanted to let the prosecutor know I knew what his game was."

Mana: "In all my nearly eight years as a judge it is the first time I have heard an attorney use that kind of tactic to express some kind of a retort to the court. I am a little perturbed with some of the things that have been going on. The record will indicate your explanation is in the record for subsequent review by certain parties."

Garry: "I don't know what that means."

Mana smirked: "Well, you just keep wondering about it." It seemed Mana was threatening Kennedy with a contempt citation. But when Kennedy called him on it, Mana backed down.

Mrs. Jarzyna continued: "When I put the telephone down, that was already man was shot."

"By the time you hung up the phone after talking to the operator the incident was all over, isn't that true?"

"Almost. Only the two boys was still in the car."

"Mrs. Jarzyna, you could not identify Danilo [Bebe] Melendez on May 6, 1969 [at the lineup], could you?"

"No."

"And now fourteen months later you see a person walk from his chair thirty-five feet to the holding cell and, bingo, it triggers in your mind that you have seen that walk before?"

"Yah."

"Now that has got to be a very distinctive walk, right?"

"It have to be when I remember. It was close."

"Are you prepared to identify a man, madam, whose face,

height, build [and] voice you cannot identify, in a murder case, because his walk is close to a walk you saw?"

"The measure of something was in my eye no can come [sic]. I am sorry."

"So am I." Kennedy asked her to demonstrate again. She did so. "Keep walking, please."

"You like my walk?"

"One more time around, please." Then, with a perfectly straight face: "Maybe I'm confused. But I thought the walk you made now was the walk you made for Mario Martinez yesterday."

"Could be," said Mrs. Jarzyna with a shrug. "Nobody walk every day the same."

"You didn't see Danilo Melendez at all on May 1, did you?"

"Sure, like I said, it reminded me by his walk."

"Did you see him on May 1 or did you see someone whose walk resembles his?"

"Yes, that's right. I see somebody that walk like him."

Mrs. Jarzyna's sixteen-year-old daughter Elizabeth Kossowski repeated her mother's story but did not venture any identifications, having chosen incorrectly at the lineup. Norman was very solicitous of Elizabeth, a student at St. Paul's, and when during a recess I approached to ask her a question, the D.A. nervously said, "Elizabeth, come here. You don't have to answer anything. This lady's a reporter. Do you read the *Berkeley Tribe*?" (I was covering the trial for the *Tribe*.)

II

Norman's nervousness about his witness was a sign of growing tension. It was about this time that Brodnik's widow started showing up. She would come escorted by one or more plainclothesmen and be shown to a seat in the rows reserved for press or lawyers. Her hands shook so violently at one of these appearances that she had to leave the courtroom. Partly it was being near all these dark-skinned longhaired kids; as she told me later, "They're all leftists. They never worked a day in their lives. You know they were planted."*

The jurors stole glances in Mrs. Brodnik's direction. She stared at Charles Garry with all the hate she could muster. The *Chronicle* reporter wrote of her chic apparel and expressionless face.

The defense countered with appearances by Tom Hayden and John Froines of the Chicago Seven, and later, when he got out of jail following reversal of his manslaughter conviction, by Huey Newton. Colleen Crosby, Brodnik's niece, also showed up in support of Los Siete, and got her picture in the paper. Afterwards, Colleen said, Mrs. Brodnik called her parents in San Jose and told them to control their daughter.

The Marin County Courthouse kidnap attempt** occurred around this time and resulted in increased security at Halls of Justice throughout the Bay Area. Everyone now had to show identification, submit to a search, and state his or her business on entering. This included attorneys and led to protests from Garry that the material in his briefcase was "a sacred matter between my client and myself" and no guard was going to see it. (When Kennedy complained to Judge Mana that being searched was degrading, Norman argued, "I let them search my briefcase," and Kennedy responded, "He doesn't mind being degraded.") The judge finally gave the defense attorneys passes which allowed them to enter the hall without being searched.

Chronicle columnist Herb Caen wrote during the trial, as if to stir up old prejudices against the six defendants, "PEOPLE ARE WONDERFUL, but on the other hand: after Police Officer

---

* In a phone conversation after the trial in which she expressed disapproval of an article on Los Siete which I had written for *Ramparts* magazine.

** On August 7, 1970, Jonathan Jackson, the younger brother of Geroge Jackson, attempted to free three black San Quentin inmates and kidnap a superior court judge, a district attorney, and three women jurors from the Marin County Courthouse in San Rafael, California. Police opened fire on the getaway truck and in the ensuing gun battle Jonathan Jackson, the judge, and two of the black inmates were killed.

Joseph Brodnik was killed in a street brawl, the Upper Noe Valley Neighborhood Council planted a tree in his memory at Twenty-ninth and Church, over a simple sidewalk plaque bearing his name. Street gangs have twice ripped the plaque out of the concrete—and as for the tree, a new one had to be planted the other day . . . the original one had been destroyed."

In early August the Los Siete organization and the Soledad Brothers Defense Committee held a national rally which attracted more local police than national attention, and which led to scattered violence. The violent image did not endear the defendants to the jurors—nor did the assassination of a Berkeley policeman shortly after: the papers asserted that the assassin had engaged the cop in a discussion of the Los Siete case before killing him.

College, high school and even elementary school classes came to watch the trial. Sometimes they couldn't get in because the courtroom was already filled with undercover police, elderly trial-watchers and an assortment of white radicals and hippies. Members of Los Siete, meanwhile, tried to save seats for brown people, both to observe the judicial operation and to show community support for the brothers. Although this led to some conflict with white trial fans, Los Siete did succeed in providing moral support and a spirited antidote to the oppressive courtroom atmosphere.

Those of us who didn't want to buy lunch used to bring our brown paper bags to a small restaurant/bar near the Hall of Justice where the friendly waitress didn't mind our taking up space. One day the waitress, who was always eager for trial news but no doubt sensed the tension in the air, confided to us that she thought Charles Garry must be very brave to work for the Panthers, because if he ever lost a case they'd surely kill him!

III

David Caravantes was a young chicano with short curly hair and a three-piece suit, a student at a labor relations school in Berkeley funded by the Ford Foundation to train union leadership.

Caravantes testified that on May 1 he was sitting on the back of the living room sofa in the Jarzyna house at 436 Alvarado for about half an hour, waiting for his girlfriend Diane to get dressed. Around 10:30 A.M., to his recollection, "There was a couple of people across the street from where I was situated at. They were just standing around there . . . maybe three. I saw a Chevy drive up. The people in the automobile proceeded to unload some stuff . . . between five and seven of them, either four or five males and a young lady.* Between six and nine [were on the sidewalk altogether]. A minute or two after this activity had started another car approached—Chrysler product. Two male adults got out of the car and walked over to these youths and identified themselves as police officers. One of the parties involved went upstairs and got some identification. I can identify him, I think, by sight."

Garry to Mana: "Have him come down and put his hands on the man."

Caravantes: "I'd rather not, Your Honor; I don't see why I should." He finally agreed to stand behind the persons he wanted to identify—José, and later Mario and Pinky—without touching them.

"Mr. Rios [José] went back downstairs; McGoran told Brodnik to go get the son of a bitch. McGoran had gotten into a verbal exchange with the tallest of the young men. [There was] swearing back and forth between these two gentlemen. The young man took off his glasses. This officer got real angry. He went to where the young man was, grabbed the young man, and threw [him] against the wall. Then it looked like the young man grabbed the officer's gun."

"Now, just a moment!" shouted Garry. "This is not a magic show, and this is not a whodunit. For him to make a remark like that is prejudicial."

Mana ordered the answer stricken. "Admonish the jury to disregard the answer. Advise the witness, if you didn't see something you can't testify to it."

"Mr. Caravantes, having the court's admonition in mind, what was it that you saw take place between those two persons?"

"The shorter of the two grabbed the gun."

* Caravantes was the only prosecution witness to mention a woman.

"Did you actually see a gun in somebody's hand?"

"Yes. It was a man about six feet tall. They went to the ground. The rest of the people that were there jumped in a big fist fight."

"Do you know how many were involved in this fist fight?"

"Seven or eight. A shot was fired. . . . [Brodnik] fell on his knees with his hands in the air."

"Do you remember where Officer McGoran was?"

"He was on the ground."

"Did you see the person who fired the shot?"

"No, I didn't see the person's face. I couldn't [describe him]. They were beating the hell out of [McGoran]. . . . Then another shot came. Someone pointed a gun from the immediate area of the curb and a shot was fired in the direction of Officer McGoran. He was laying down screaming."

Just before the recess Garry asked Mana "to permit me to sign warrant for the arrest of Officer McGoran for perjury. I asked him over and over again whether he said to Officer Brodnik, 'Go get that son of a bitch.' He denied it."

"That motion is denied," said Mana. "I'm not going to get involved in it."

Garry asked the witness if he had ever lived in Marin County (north of San Francisco). Caravantes was silent for more than twenty seconds, licking his lips, looking mournful. Finally he said, "Your Honor, by answering this question I'd be incriminating myself, leaving myself open to prosecution for other things under which you could not provide protection."

Mana: "Let the record indicate he has taken the Fifth Amendment." It later came out that Caravantes—and his girlfriend Diane—had used a phony address to get into the College of Marin as non tuition-paying residents of the county.

"You've got five to seven people in this automobile, is that right?" Garry asked.

"Yes."

"There would hardly be any room to take anything inside?"

"Well, it's fairly crowded."

237

"You did not see any property in the hands of anybody?"

"I did see the stuff carried out but I can't specifically say who carried what with the exception that I saw the TV put down and saw the young lady carrying the radio."

"How long had you known Officer McGoran prior to May 1, 1969?"

"I never knew him personally. . . . I had no personal contact with Officer McGoran."

"Didn't you tell the police: 'There's people that I know that know him real well' [in Caravantes's May 1 statement]?"

"He worked where I was working for a while—over at White Front [a discount department store] last year."

"Isn't it a fact you've spent time with Paul McGoran, talked to him about the case and asked him is there any way you could help him?"

"No. The only thing I ever said to him was, 'How are you?' "

"What did he say?"

"Something about he was still sick . . . his mouth was wired." (McGoran's jaw had been broken during the incident on May 1.)

"Didn't you make a statement that there were certain things you'd like to find out, at 1:51 P.M. on Thursday, May 1, 1969, you'd like to be able to talk to him about it?"

"I was concerned on how he was, what shape he was in."

Garry read large portions of Caravantes's May 1 statement, which was much less damning to the defense than his trial testimony: " 'McGoran got shot in the mouth. I'm sure of that. I did not see Brodnik get killed. McGoran was in front of him. . . . couldn't see because both policemen were in my way. . . . I really didn't see.

" 'You could see Brodnik was calming him down,' " the statement continued. " 'If McGoran hadn't gone up after the guy, had just waited on the stairs, there would have been no way this could have happened. Brodnik was really casual about it. He took the situation calmly. McGoran was excited, pushing and screaming.' "

Garry: "Remember telling the police officers and reporters around there that Paul McGoran went too far this time, and got what he was entitled to?"

"No."

"Did you make a statement that would be similar in substance—that Paul McGoran went too far?"

"No, I don't think so."

Kennedy began: "Last time you saw Brodnik before he was shot, he was moving [towards] McGoran and the young man?"

"I saw him start to run over there."

"And at that moment you didn't see a gun in anybody's hand?"

"No, I didn't."

"So for all you know, McGoran shot him, right?"

"Well, I was looking at McGoran at that moment, so from what I could see, he didn't shoot him."

"McGoran's back was to you, wasn't it?"

"McGoran was on the ground then."

Kennedy reread the May 1 statement: "Q: 'You seen him actually shoot, right?' A: 'You see, McGoran was in front of him. . . . I couldn't see because both policemen were in my way. McGoran was directly in front of me.' "

Caravantes denied that police or law enforcement agencies had ever done him any favors. But when R. Jay Engel asked about his union leadership training course—"In order to get into that program you have to be recommended, don't you?"—Caravantes admitted getting a recommendation from the chief of police of San Rafael, in Marin County.

"And you're telling us that this was not in tribute for your coming here to testify?"

"That's right, I'll tell you that any time you ask it."

"I just asked it. Right now there is a letter on file from the chief of police of San Rafael recommending you for this very special program, and this is not for your testifying here?"

"That's right."

The next witness, Stephen Laznibat, was a thirty-four-year-old Yugoslav immigrant who worked as a shop mechanic. Sometime after May 1, Laznibat found on his doorstep a leaflet produced by the Los Siete committee describing the May 1 incident as having taken place in front of 438 Alvarado Street. The error was typographical but it happened to be Laznibat's address. In court Laznibat explained, "I wanted to see someone within the law about it because it bothered me so much that a paper goes around like this bearing my address. To me it is important, and I carried it with me and I showed it to whoever asked me about what happened to me at 438 Alvarado—that this is not true." He pulled the crumpled leaflet from his pocket and showed it to the judge.

Laznibat testified that he saw a fight; a short young man with black hair pulled a gun and stretched out his arm. Laznibat said the young man fired and the man in front of him fell back. Then he fired again in the direction of another man hiding behind a pillar.

"Didn't you tell the police officer at 11:10 A.M. [on May 1] that the man who was hiding had a gun in his hand?" Garry asked on cross-examination.

"I might have. . . . I don't remember," said Laznibat.

Garry read from the witness's May 1 statement: " 'I think the man who was hiding had a gun.' "

On re–direct examination by the prosecution (after cross-examination was completed) Laznibat explained, "I went outside after and saw it was radio, not gun."

After the weekend break, before the jury came in Norman said Laznibat had been threatened. "I think the general public should know," he said. "Friday Mr. Laznibat testified in this case—"

"Wait a minute," Hodge interrupted. "The district attorney is now consciously attempting to get before the jury this particular data through the press in the hopes they are going to disobey the court's admonition [and read the papers] . It has no other purpose and will have no other effect."

Norman persisted: "I think Your Honor should be concerned in the interests of a fair trial that our witness has been intimidated. . . . He received a threat to his life!"

Hodge: "I hold the district attorney's actions here as a breach of good faith. He is conniving and scheming. He is pulling every trick he knows how to pull."

Garry: "Since we're talking about threats, I received twenty-two phone calls last night. I finally disengaged my phone. This has been going on daily, hourly. We haven't come here crying about it. How about the state of siege in this courtroom? I don't care if he's been intimidated or not; we're all being intimidated."

On re-cross-examination, Kennedy picked up the crucial question of whether McGoran had a gun in his hand, as Laznibat had said, on May 1. He asked Laznibat, "Did you talk to police officers after you went to the scene?" (Whispering to his colleagues): "What's that idiot's name?" (Then loud, to Laznibat): "Kracke?"

Norman: "Objection to that aside."

Kennedy: "Nobody heard it but you, so you can eat your objection."

Norman: "Jack Cleary heard it too. He referred to that inspector as an idiot."

Engel: "If the district attorney thinks it's so objectionable that we call one of his inspectors an idiot, why does he make a point of putting it in the record?"

"Nor should he be eavesdropping," Kennedy added.

The point—which was lost in all the put-downs—was: If, on May 1, Laznibat *did* discover it was only a radio and not a gun McGoran had in his hand, he never told Inspector Kracke (Cleary's partner in the investigation), or else Kracke never amended the May 1 statement. The defense argued further that the scene had been too chaotic for Laznibat possibly to have gone forty minutes later and seen it was a radio, not a gun. On May 1, Laznibat said only two suspects were on the sidewalk and that they, like McGoran, had guns. He was not called to the lineup or to the grand jury hearing. On the stand he said, "Yesterday was first time I found out that I am going to have to come in the court and testify for sure and I haven't been with this for over a year now. I asked [Norman], 'Gee, I don't remember anything I have said. What do I do if someone asks me if you said this or that?' "

Engel remarked later: "He doesn't remember anything. He is just buying anything that the police have been telling him."

The next witness, Anna Maria Chavez, said she saw four men fighting. A "tall thin person" shot the policeman. The killer was "almost the same size as the one who was shot. He was dressed in a T-shirt. He was clean and neat." "Tall and thin" seemed to describe Pinky Lescallett; yet other witnesses said Pinky had been wearing a jacket, not a T-shirt, and was far from clean and neat. Mrs. Chavez's testimony seemed only to increase the confusion of the already muddy prosecution case.

Anna Diaz, a nineteen-year-old college sophomore who had lived next door to the Rios family, was called to the witness stand to establish Bebe's presence at the scene—she had identified him at the lineup and in front of the grand jury. She testified that she had seen only the end of the incident: "I went to the window. . . . [One boy's] arm was extended from the car and he had a gun in his hand. McGoran was down on the ground. . . . There was [another] boy running, with long dark hair; he wasn't very tall." After some uncertainty, Anna Diaz said she couldn't identify him.

Norman asked, "Did you attend the lineup? . . . Do you re- member who you identified from these photos?" She pointed out Bebe. "I want to draw an X over this person's head. What was this person doing on May 1?"

"He was the one that turned and ran down the street."

Getting this identification in court was a pyrrhic victory for Norman. Anna Diaz's statement that Bebe was *not* the one with the gun turned out to be crucial.

Anna's father, Alejandro Diaz, gave one of the more damning pieces of evidence in the prosecution case: "I heard a banging sound. I looked out and saw a young man running from the house . . . to the other side of the car and he was yelling in Spanish,

'Vamanos de aqui. Yo creo que lo mataste.' ['Let's get out of here. I think you killed him.'] His eyes were very bright, like anger or tears."

Norman asked Diaz to identify the young man who made this exclamation. Diaz looked miserably unhappy to be testifying at all. "He won't bite you," Garry said; "come down and pick him out."

"It isn't a question of biting; it's a question of conscience!" Diaz almost sobbed. He pointed out Mario.

The confusion among the prosecution witnesses' stories was now so great that even the most diligent trial-watchers had trouble keeping score. Mrs. Jarzyna, her daughter Elizabeth, and Stephen Laznibat said they had seen a short boy shoot Brodnik. David Caravantes hadn't seen who fired the shot but thought the tall boy (Pinky) took the gun from McGoran. Anna Chavez said a tall person did the shooting, but he was clean and neat—while McGoran and most other witnesses said all the young men present were long-haired and messy. Anna and Alejandro Diaz hadn't seen the incident but saw people on the sidewalk afterwards: Anna thought she saw a short boy, Bebe, without the gun; Alejandro thought he saw a different short boy, Mario (who is Bebe's height), also without the gun, yelling to someone else, "I think you killed him." McGoran, of course, said he didn't see who shot Brodnik but swore the second shot was fired by Pinky Lescallett.

Aside from the fact that most of them had amplified their May 1 statements, these witnesses were obviously confusing the identities of various defendants, especially Mario and Bebe. The only person who stuck in everyone's mind was Pinky; but McGoran was sure he had the gun, while Mrs. Jarzyna, her daughter Elizabeth, and Laznibat were sure it was a short boy who had it. Caravantes backed up McGoran but in so doing directly contradicted his own May 1 statement—for reasons which became somewhat clearer as the trial proceeded.

Every witness was *sure*, until cross-examination began. Then it turned out they had been discussing the case, reading the papers, expanding their statements each time they talked to police. Two of the witnesses most damaging to the defendants, Irene Jarzyna and David Caravantes, had been thoroughly discredited in the eyes of many trial-watchers because of their open hostility to the defense, the frequent contradictions in their testimony, the extraordinary amplification of their May 1 statements, and, for Mrs. Jarzyna, more than a touch of the absurd in her performance.

The last eyewitness, Della McKinney, did little to clear things up. Her testimony seemed to have no value except for her identification of Nelson. "I heard a noise," she began. "I went to the front door. There was another shot about the time I reached the front door. Across the street there was a scuffle going on and a man was falling. Another person was back behind this pillar. He was bleeding from the mouth. I saw two other people. One of them had a car at the curb and the other one was on the other side of the car. The one on the passenger side had a white T-shirt on. He had a mustache, wavy brown hair, medium dark. He ran back to the person lying on the sidewalk and he either made a kicking motion with his foot or bent towards him a little bit. . . . The boy sitting over there with the striped tie and mustache [she indicated Nelson] looks very similar."

"How far is your house from where this scene is?" Garry asked.

"About two hundred feet, I think." (Later, the jury was taken to Alvarado Street to examine the scene of the crime. They walked to Mrs. McKinney's porch and saw that faces were just not identifiable at two hundred feet.)

"What does your husband do?"

"He's an auto wrecker."

"And your husband as an auto wrecker deals with the police department constantly?"

"Sometimes he deals with them."

"He has to deal with them because he has to get clearances on licenses and check hot cars?"

"I don't think he works too closely with them."

Della McKinney was the only witness besides McGoran who identified Nelson. In May 1969 she had identified Bebe and José but only called Nelson "similar." At the grand jury she said of Nelson, "*if* this is the person" (emphasis added). On further cross-examination Garry brought out the fact that Mrs. McKinney had refused to see R. Jay Engel about her tentative identification of Nelson at the grand jury hearing. Mrs. McKinney explained: "My husband said, 'I don't think you should discuss this with anybody.' I said [to Engel] I didn't know if I should discuss it. He said I was the only one [at the grand jury hearing] that had mentioned his client's name and he would like to show me a picture. I said I was scared. I didn't want to meet him; if he wanted he could leave off a picture at my house." (The picture was of Gio Lopez.)

Engel cross-examined Mrs. McKinney regarding their telephone conversation. "I said to you, 'Well, what do you think?' [of the photo of Gio] and your response to me was, 'You're right.' "

"No, I think my response was, 'The hair looks very much like his.' "

"You said, 'Don't worry, Mr. Engel, I can't possibly identify your client.' "

"No."

"You don't recall that?"

"No."

"Do you recall that I said, 'Well, but I am worried and I do want to come over and talk to you.' And you said to me, 'I have been telling them I cannot identify that man. Don't worry about it.' Isn't that what you said to me?"

"Yes, " Mrs. McKinney admitted.

IV

So the trial wore on. Finally the eyewitness testimony was over and all that remained was a tedious series of police witnesses. One had found the gun on a side street, with no usable fingerprints on it and four slugs left. Another had examined much of the stolen property. He found in José's car a letter to Ray Aparicio, Mario's textbooks, and a copy of CSM Research Director Pearce's report on the academic success of the College Readiness Program; also gloves and tools, and, in José's bedroom, a jacket with Horenstein's wallet and another pair of gloves. He found fingerprints of Dennis Calderon, Ray Aparicio and Gio Lopez on the cars. But he had originally reported Calderon's prints as belonging to Nelson; this error wasn't corrected until ten months after the incident.

"How many other bonehead blunders have you pulled in this case?" Garry asked.

"It was not a mistake in identification. I mistakenly read the name of Nelson Rodriguez instead of Calderon in dictation."

"Isn't it a fact that by making this false identification of Nelson Rodriguez you instilled into Paul McGoran a confidence that Nelson Rodriguez was at the scene?" Objection sustained.

Another crime lab officer testified he found Lescallett's fingerprints on the Horenstein's big brass lamp in the storeroom at 429 Alvarado. He produced several enormous diagrams of Pinky's print pattern and explained them in minute detail. He also found Tony Martinez's prints on forty percent of the blue Chevy's steering wheel. This was the only evidence against Tony other than Mrs. Jarzyna's identification. Norman asked, "If a person drove with gloves on, would there be prints on the wheel?"

"No, gloves would wipe them out."

Garry (who has studied fingerprints): "That's ridiculous."

Crime lab officer: "It would generally destroy or make impossible to get usable prints"—implying that Tony must have been the last driver.

Garry: "It's a fallacious statement. Anyone knows that fingerprints can last for years."

Engel: "Besides, there's another sixty percent of the wheel anyone else could've driven on with or without gloves."

Garry, whispering to his colleagues: "This is the worst piece of shit I've ever heard."

Norman: "Excuse me, did someone use a vulgarity? I heard something alarming. . . ."

One of Inspector Jack Cleary's functions as a witness was to clear up Stephen Laznibat's May 1 statement that he had seen a gun in McGoran's hand.

"Did you have an opportunity at any time during this year to have an interview with Mr. Stephen Laznibat?" Norman asked Cleary.

Garry objected: "It's a well-known rule of evidence that if a witness makes a statement and subsequently makes another statement, the subsequent statement cannot be used to rehabilitate what he [originally] said."

Mana began to argue about it. "I'm not going to argue," Garry said. "If Your Honor wants to violate all the rules of evidence, go ahead." Mana finally admitted Cleary's statement, admonishing the jury that it might not be the truth of the matter—in other words, Laznibat might not have seen that the "gun" was only a radio; what was admitted in evidence was Cleary's assertion that Laznibat later changed his May 1 statement.

Cleary: "[Laznibat] said there was a correction in his statement. It mentioned he thought he saw something like a gun but he walked over shortly after giving his statement and found out it was a walkie-talkie."

Describing the scene at 433 Alvarado when he arrived, Cleary said, "I didn't see any police officers shooting"—this despite the fact that many pictures of policemen aiming guns and rifles had been entered in evidence.

Cleary also testified he had no knowledge of complaints against McGoran—after he, Norman, and defense counsel had spent many hours in chambers arguing over defense access to McGoran's thick complaint file. "Only good reports," Cleary said with a straight face. Even the defense lawyers were amazed at this blunt denial.

"Were you worried about the fact that McGoran had been accused of having a gun [in his hand]?" Garry asked.

"No sir."

Kennedy: "He tailored the investigation to frame these kids when all the while he had information that McGoran had a gun and he didn't follow up on it."

Norman: "I submit that statement by Mr. Kennedy is misconduct."

Garry: "Well, here we go again. It is baby talk again. Here we are trying a serious case, making serious arguments, and he is right away saying, 'Teacher, he's guilty of misconduct.' Other than McGoran, on May 1 no one else placed a gun in anyone's hand. Yet you knew on May 1 at least one witness, forty minutes after the event, said he saw what appeared to be a handgun in McGoran's hand. The neutron activation test [which determines if a person has recently fired a gun] is ninety-eight percent foolproof if a person has not washed his hands. The test is valid up to twenty-four hours. Why didn't you give a neutron activation test to Paul McGoran?"

Cleary: "We knew that Mr. McGoran didn't fire a gun, didn't have the gun in his hand."

"Isn't that just your judgment?"

"That wasn't my judgment. It was the witness's statement."

"The witness's statement was that he had a gun in his hand and you knew that on the day you were investigating this case."

"No sir, he never had his gun out. You can check it," Cleary insisted.

"I am referring to Mr. Laznibat's statement: 'I think the man who was hiding had a handgun.'"

"He corrected it when Mr. Norman referred the statement to him."

"How many months later, Inspector?"

"February [1970]," Cleary admitted.

"We're talking about *May 1* [1969]. You had a duty to see if McGoran fired a weapon." Objection—argumentative. Sustained.

Engel asked Cleary if a statement had been taken from Paul McGoran on May 1. "I think a tape was taken but it didn't come out," he replied. "There was some malfunction of batteries or something."

"I assume you told him [the inspector] to go back [to the hospital] and do it again."

"I did not."

Garry had questioned Cleary's integrity in not investigating McGoran as a suspect. Engel questioned it for not investigating Nelson Rodriguez's alibi as given in Ralph Ruiz's statement to him on May 3. "Isn't it a fact that Mr. Ruiz told you he picked up Mr. Nelson Rodriguez, before this incident occurred, at 377 Peoria [Sandy Domdoma's apartment]? Didn't Mr. Ruiz tell you that when he saw Nelson Rodriguez the morning of May 1 [he] was with a man named Winkle?"

"No sir."

"Did you get the name Winkle from Mr. Ruiz?"

"Is it on that statement there? I don't recall the name of Winkle."

Engel handed Cleary his own handwritten statement of what Ralph had told him. The statement, which Engel had Cleary read to the jury, included a description: "Winkle, one hundred seventy pounds, nineteen to twenty years."

"Did you ever contact anybody by the name of Winkle that fit that description?"

"No sir."

"Did you ever go to 377 Peoria Street to find out who lived there?"

"I myself didn't. I'm sure all of the addresses were checked."

"Do you know if anybody did?"

"I'm sure they did. I don't recall."

"Isn't it a fact that Mr. Ralph Ruiz told you that he had been with Nelson Rodriguez for approximatley six and a half hours on May 1, 1969?"

"No sir."

"Did Mr. Ruiz say to you that he took Nelson Rodriguez back to Daly City, dropped him off at Sandy and Alex's at about 4:45 P.M. and Mr. Nelson Rodriguez was with him for approximatley six and a half hours?"

"May I see that statement again, sir? . . . Yes . . . correct."

On re-direct examination Norman tried to introduce a mug shot of Ralph Ruiz. Still smelling of fixer from the lab, this photo showed Ralph with long scraggly hair and a black eye, and was obviously intended to demonstrate that Ralph—and his statement —were unreliable. Heated debate followed; Mana finally agreed the photo had "no probative value" as evidence.

Norman's last card was Daniel Goodell, victim of the May 6 car theft near Santa Cruz. The defense argued that Goodell's testimony had nothing to do with the incident of May 1 and was highly prejudicial. They had not been hired to defend the six on armed robbery charges. Norman said—and Mana agreed—that it was admissible because it showed "consciousness of guilt . . . identity . . . their intent that they operated together." The defense then offered to stipulate Goodell's testimony—to admit that the substance of it was true. But Norman would have none of it. He wanted Goodell on the stand.

Goodell turned out to be as pliable as Della McKinney. The young man who held the gun on him and said, "How would you like to get shot?"—whom he had identified on May 6 as José Rios—he now pointed out in court as Tony Martinez. On cross-examination he stubbornly denied he had identified Rios; Norman finally had to stipulate to a Santa Cruz sheriff's report which said Goodell identified Rios as having the gun.

Goodell's then-fiancée—now his wife—also testified. In her version the six were somewhat less sinister. "We don't want to hurt you; we just want the car," she remembered one of them saying—after hungrily consuming the couple's picnic lunch.

14. Power to the People, Streeter

I

By the time the defense case began in late September, three months after the start of the trial, almost all the mass media had stopped sending daily reporters. Those TV newsmen and women who had begun to feel sympathetic to the defendants explained that their stations hadn't anticipated so long a trial and couldn't afford to keep sending them. The *San Francisco Chronicle*'s police reporter told us, as he rushed in at the end of each day to find out if anything important had happened, that his paper was simply "inert": it was an unfortunate accident that coverage was letting up just as the defense case was beginning. But it was hard to agree; the *Chronicle,* which had so vigorously condemned Los Siete and praised the police eighteen months before, had suddenly cut way down on its coverage just when evidence damaging to the police began to come out in court.

Among the "establishment" reporters only the *San Francisco Examiner*'s elderly Harold Streeter remained a regular. Despite a certain paternalism (he described female supporters as "brown-skinned beauties with dark, dazzling eyes"), Streeter was conscientious. But the *Examiner* persisted in calling it the "Brodnik case" long after everyone else had accepted "Los Siete." By September, Streeter had become an anomaly and a fixture in the courtroom. Nelson Rodriguez sometimes grinned at him, or whispered as he passed, "Power to the people, Streeter!" Streeter, bewildered, wondered what Nelson had against him.

Streeter was too serious and perhaps too old to be part of the cynical camaraderie that sometimes filled the press section—affectionate put-downs, witty exchanges with the lawyers, sexist or racist jokes. Notes would go back and forth: one reporter responded to Donna James's complaint that the sheriff would not allow books to be delivered to the "brothers" by scribbling, "They can take correspondence courses. I understand a lot of guys at 'Q' [San Quentin] do."

Michael Kennedy opened the defense case. "We are under no burden whatsoever to proceed," he began, explaining that the defendants were innocent until proven guilty and the prosecution had not proven any one of them guilty. "Why," he asked, "have we been here for thirteen weeks; why have thousands of tax-payers' dollars been spent on this case? There are essentially two reasons. One is racism—racism that has permeated, and continues to permeate, the San Francisco Police Department. The second reason is to cover up the wrongdoing of Officer McGoran, to cover the fact that Officer McGoran on May 1 of 1969 accidentally killed his partner. From the beginning the evidence pointed singularly to Officer McGoran. The San Francisco Police Department totally ignored him, whitewashed him, and began an intensive manhunt for people they wanted to believe had killed a cop. . . .

"We will draw in our testimony two parallel developments, one the development of Officer McGoran, the other [of] Danilo [Bebe] Melendez [Kennedy's client] and the other defendants. Danilo was a tough street kid, and he made no bones about that. He learned the way of life in the San Francisco streets and particularly the streets of the Mission. . . .

"We will show that the San Francisco Police Department was in many ways an occupation force within the Mission, and that McGoran was not an atypical member. In a tense situation, McGoran would respond with force, given his emotional problems and what I consider to be his diminished intellectual capacity. He wouldn't talk out of a situation. We will show him to be emotionally disturbed, something the San Francisco Police Department has known all along.

"McGoran wanted power and respect and the only way he could get it was with a gun and a badge and he used both to excess. He had such a nasty, vicious temper that the only way he could keep from throttling defense counsel and blowing the prosecution's case was to drop valium. When you put a man like that on the Mission streets in plainclothes with a big gun, it is inevitable that he hurt someone. The only reason we're here is because he hurt another cop . . . if he hurt a nonwhite kid we wouldn't be here."

Kennedy outlined the events leading up to May 1: "Danilo Melendez began hearing about the College of San Mateo Readiness Program; he kept putting it off. Just a few days before May 1, 1969, Rodolfo and Mario Martinez had talked Danilo into going down to the College of San Mateo. By arrangement, Danilo Melendez, José Rios and Gary Lescallett were to meet the morning of May 1 at Mario Martinez's home at 14 Regent Street in Daly City. The arrangements were that José Rios was to drive there." Kennedy then summarized the defendants' story, as they told it when they took the stand.

"[Tony] woke me up around 7:30 A.M.," Mario testified. "He left later on . . . about 8:00. I got up later on and got ready to wait for Bebe and Pinky and José. First of all José called; I had to go to his house and pick him up because he couldn't come to my house at 9:00. Bebe came shortly after 9:00, and Pinky, he came about a half hour after that. I still had to meet Nelson at the college also, and the plans were getting messed up."

José testified that he hadn't been able to drive to Mario's that morning because he discovered his car had a dead battery. Mario said he agreed to pick up José; he left with Bebe and Pinky for Alvarado Street a little after 9:30.

José: "Shortly before [Mario] came, Gio had come over and he said that he had placed some furnishings in the storage room. He asked if he could leave the things there and I told him no, I was sorry, my parents would just blow it. He told me it was some furnishings he would use after his marriage, and right away I thought there was something fishy about the story, so I didn't buy it. Earlier that day two persons had given him a ride and helped him put that stuff there."

At this point, according to defense testimony, Mario arrived and ran upstairs, leaving Bebe and Pinky listening to music in the car. "Gio, he convinces people very easily," José testified, "but he was having a hard time convincing Mario. Mario said, 'Well, I'm leaving. Are you coming?'

"I said, 'No, you go on ahead. Gio and myself will find a way to get these things out of here.'

"I guess [Mario] really wanted me to go to school that day. He was in charge of recruiting new students into the program. We finally convinced Mario into taking [the property]." As they went downstairs, José said, Gio left his green Army jacket on the bed (police later found Horenstein's wallet in it).

"Did anyone else keep their belongings in that storeroom?" Norman asked José on cross-examination.

"As far as I know, no. [Gio] had been there a couple of times. When we were moving from house to house he helped me put some junk there."

José continued: "Gio and myself asked Bebe and Pinky to come out and help us. We went down to the storage room, the five of us, and Mario kind of blew it. He said, 'How are we going to fit all of this stuff in there, because five of us got to ride in there too.' So Gio jumped up and said, 'Oh no, why don't we just try to put most of it in?' Mario goes, 'All right, come on.' Gio said he would direct Mario to one of his partners' houses on the way to school."

Mario: "I had gotten Gio into college, enrolled him two times, and I was always after him to go to school. We would use all kinds of tactics to try to get him up there, and like that day I told him —finally I said, 'I will help you if you agree to go to college with me and register again,' and he said, 'All right.'"

Bebe: "They asked me and Gary to get out of the car and help. I picked up two speakers . . . put them in the trunk of the car. Mario, Gio and José picked up the TV and put it in the car.

I'm kind of lazy so I was just leaning back and I was going to let the others finish."

Then the white Dodge drove up. "I recognized McGoran," Bebe said. "I had seen him all kinds of times—driving up and down, busting people." He described the 1967 incident in which McGoran had split Bebe's lip.

Bebe continued: "Well, the brothers were still moving stuff and I yelled out, *'Calmate, la chota'* [cool it, the cops]. McGoran went to the driver's side of Mario's car. He brought out a metal box. He opened it up and said the name Horenstein. . . . McGoran tells me, 'Get over there, punk.' I put my hands over my nose and I told him, 'Stay away from me, you smell like an Old Crow whiskey factory' [the wisecrack McGoran had attributed to Mario]." Bebe said McGoran told him to sit on the steps in front of 433 Alvarado and he obeyed.

José: "[Brodnik] said, 'Who lives here?' So I told him that I do, and then he goes, 'Where are your parents?' I told him they were at work already, and he said, 'Let me see some kind of identification.' So I told him that I didn't have it on me, it was upstairs. So he says, 'Go get it.' So I went up."

Mario: "José, when he was passing by me, he pulled my arm. He told me, *'Vente, vente,'* and he seemed excited and he just pulled my arm and we went upstairs. Gio was telling me . . . that [it] was the police. We went into the attic. As soon as we got up there I told Gio, 'What are we doing here? Let's get down and go straighten this thing out. If they come up here, they're going to find us anyway,' and like we started to go down towards the little ladder that goes into the kitchen and then I heard some loud voices. I heard José say, 'No no, Pinky, *no le digas nada'* [don't even talk to him] ."

José: "I started walking toward Brodnik, and McGoran came and snatched [the ID] out of my hand. So I just looked at him kind of funny and just kept on walking down to the storage room. The light was left on and I was going down there to turn it off. McGoran said, 'Hey you motherfucker, where are you going?' So I just turned around and said, 'Fuck you.' As soon as I got down the steps I heard him say, 'Hey Joe, go get that son of a bitch.' His eyes were bloodshot. I just got away from him. I'm not used to smelling things like him.

"[Brodnik] said, 'Come on back upstairs. Just don't pay no attention to him,' " José continued. "I walked in front of him [and sat] on a ledge. [Brodnik] was right by me, a couple of feet away. McGoran started insulting Gary Lescallett, telling him, 'You fucking greaser,' and 'Your father eats grapes and I do too. How do you like that?' And Pinky replied, 'I don't care, I hope you choke on them, you old fucking wino.' I started telling Pinky, 'Why don't you cool it,' because their being policemen, that would just make them arrest us and—I don't know, take a beating; that's not anything new—they beat you up every time they get hold of you."

Bebe: "McGoran said, 'I want you to make like a rabbit.' [Gary said] 'What are you going to do, shoot me?' McGoran made a motion like this, you know [patting his hip]. Gary jumped down off the ledge [of 435 Alvarado] and jumped between the pillar [of 433 Alvarado] and the wall. McGoran said, 'Now, you greasy bastard, I'm going to wash my hands on your back!' It's a sneaky way of saying you're a wetback—a brown person who supposedly swam across the Rio Grande.

"[McGoran] pulled out Gary Lescallett and slugged him [with] his fist and banged him against the wall," Bebe went on, "and Gary hit him back. Gary is holding his own, you know; then McGoran hit him and Gary fell down. McGoran started pulling out his piece. I thought he was going to shoot Lescallett. That's when I jumped off [the steps to 433 Alvarado]. I jumped up and went for McGoran. I grabbed his wrist with both hands. We was struggling. I don't know where it was pointing. I heard somebody say, 'No no, Paul, not your gun!' and then *boom!* the shot went off. I was still trying to take his hand away and then I twisted his wrist back and *boom!* another shot went off. I grabbed the gun by the muzzle and took it and ran towards the car."

Bebe demonstrated on Hodge how he wrested the gun away. "Was that a judo disarming tactic?" Kennedy asked.

"No, that is from aikido. It is the art of self-defense with mostly the application of the wrist and sidesteps of your body."

He said he had learned it at the Mission Rebels. Norman seemed dubious. Kennedy suggested Bebe try it on Inspector Cleary. Prudently, Judge Mana rejected the suggestion.

José: "The gun was swinging in my direction, so I just ducked down. As I was ducking I hear a shot, and Brodnik, he just bent over and fell down. I just got all scared, paranoid, and run to the car and I tried to start it but the keys weren't there. Mario was upstairs and as soon as I knew that I couldn't start it I just got out and ran."

Mario: "We started to come up front to see what was happening. Before I got to the window I heard a shot and then I got real scared. I kept going faster and I got to the window. Through the window you can't see the sidewalk and all you can see is about half of the car on into the street and I looked outside and then I seen José running to the driver's side of the car, and he looked up and he screamed my name; he said, 'Mario! Mario!' and he was screaming. . . ."

Bebe said that after he took the gun he pointed it at McGoran to keep him covered, but didn't fire. McGoran crawled behind the ledge in a narrow area between 433 and 435 Alvarado. "José split," Bebe continued, "so I started running. I looked back and I seen Gary Lescallett on the sidewalk so I ran back; like I slapped him a couple of times and helped him up. I told him, '*Creo que lo mató. Salta de alli.*'" ("I think I killed him. Let's split"—in contrast to Alejandro Diaz's testimony that *Mario* said, "I think *you* killed him.")

Kennedy: "Why did you run away?"

Bebe: "Because I'm brown. You know—how would it look with me with a gun in my hand and a dead pi—policeman, and another one bleeding. I'm not going to tell them he did it, because they don't believe it. I got the gun in my hand."

II

"Where did you learn that word [piece]?" Norman asked Bebe on cross-examination.

"On the streets."

"Where have you heard that on the streets?"

"I have been around in the streets. I live in the Mission."

"Have you ever carried a gun yourself?"

"No, I don't."

"Did you at any time offer [Brodnik] any assistance?"

"No."

"Why didn't you?"

" 'Cause I was scared."

"You didn't care whether he was dead or alive, did you?"

"I didn't bother to find out."

"Did you care?"

"Didn't have no opinion."

"Why didn't you leave the gun behind?"

"And leave it for Paul McGoran?"

"You were afraid that Paul McGoran was going to shoot you, is that right?"

"Or [shoot] anyone around there."

Norman asked Bebe, and each subsequent defendant, for a detailed account of his flight. The defendants supplied general information but when it came to names and addresses, followed Bebe's response: "I refuse to answer any names, places, brothers and sisters that helped me save the lives of my brothers and myself." After some argument Mana decided to protect Bebe's right not to incriminate his friends. But Norman persisted in his questions; he apparently thought it made the brothers look shady to keep refusing to answer. Kennedy remarked, "He's got a flimsy case, a rotten case, a worthless case against these kids, so he's trying to knit a Volkswagen out of steel wool."

Norman asked José, "Do you remember telling Mary Crawford from the *San Francisco Examiner,* 'It was really the fault of the pig that didn't die'?"

"Yes."

"Do you think the police are pigs, sir?"

"Physically they don't look like pigs but their actions make them look like pigs. They don't treat a person like human beings. They treat them like an animal."

Before Mario testified, Garry had introduced the first character witness, Marsha Berent, a former teacher at the College of San Mateo. "I set up a reading lab for the College Readiness Program," she said, "to teach reading to students who had previously not mastered the skills in their elementary and high school careers— mainly minority students [who] sometimes required some motivation to read things about their own people." She met Mario in the summer of 1968 in this class. "He was a leader among the students and he was an excellent student. He did recruiting for my classroom. I had all his friends. He wrote a beautiful essay."

Thus began Garry's most frustrating crusade, to get Mario's essay (see page 93) read to the jury. Norman and Mana were adamant: the essay was irrelevant. Garry was equally adamant: "This is necessary for me to lay the groundwork and the role of Mr. Mario Martinez, so that this court and jury will understand why he was so concerned about bringing these men to that class on May 1st. It goes to [his] intent and conduct on May 1st." Garry used every argument he could think of, and tried unsuccessfully another half dozen times during the trial, to get that essay in.

"When he first came to the Program," Marsha Berent went on, "he was like other students, and as he developed, he changed. He became aware of the problems in the country and in the world and he went to what I would call the next plateau. He became aware that there was oppression all over the world. He was involved in talking with students about the kind of things they needed to improve their communities. He was very sincere, not the kind of leader you think of. He was quiet, softspoken, very modest."

Mario also testified about his education: "I failed a lot of classes in high school. They told me I still had to go another year. Then some people from the College Readiness Program came. They talked to the students, especially the ones that weren't going to graduate, students of color."

The court reporter: "Of what?"

"Of color," Mario repeated softly.

"WHAT?"

Kennedy: "Color. C-O-L-O-R."

Norman asked Mario if he had had a class on May 1, 1969. "I

was supposed to be tutoring," Mario answered.

"Oh?"

"In English . . . the phonics class."

"You were supposed to be *what?*"

"Tutoring."

"Now, are you telling us that you were the teacher in that class?"

"No sir. It was important for all of us, whoever had experience in different classes from before, it was important for us to be there."

"How long had you been doing this tutoring?"

"Since after the summer. I had been taking biology and I [could] tutor a student in biology. I had taken English and could tutor students in English."

"What final grade did you get in that biology course?"

"I think it was a W—withdrawal."

"Was it an F?"

"I guess it turned into an F."

"And *you* were tutoring biology?"

"Yes."

III

Once the defendants' story of what happened on May 1 had been told, the defense proceeded with alibi witnesses for Tony and Nelson. Tony's alibi witness was Kathy O'Rourke, one of the white students who tutored in the Readiness Program.

"I was tutoring Rodolfo [Tony] for the spring semester, in biology mainly, and also English and political science," she testified. "I teach my skills—taking notes, speaking to a teacher, taking a test, writing a paper—things I just picked up naturally in high school because of my education and things that the students of color hadn't learned in high school. [I tutored Tony from] January until May 1st. We had a tutor report that had to be turned in every week because I was being paid. On May 1st we studied from approximately 8:00 until 11:30 that morning. I went to his house first and picked him up. We drove to school together. We studied in the library, upstairs. We had a quiz coming up the next day and we hadn't studied for it yet."

"You didn't meet anybody that you knew, I take it?" Norman asked the witness.

"No. [We left] about 11:30. We walked out and were going towards the Center. He met someone on the way that he knew [apparently Gio, whom Mario said he had sent to find Tony] and he stopped to talk, and I just continued on. [Next time I saw him] he was upstairs here [in jail]."

"Did you know what he was charged with?" Norman asked.

"Murder."

"Did you and he discuss this?"

"I just asked him what I should do."

"What did you call him?"

"Tony."

"Had you ever seen him socially?"

"No. You mean dated?"

"Well, I'll get to that. But had you ever seen him socially at parties?"

"I was at a dance he was at once . . . during Brown Culture Week. COBRA, an organization that Tony was president of, was sponsoring the dance."

"Are you a member of any organization?"

"Just a minute," said Garry. "We are not going into any thought control—it is McCarthyism."

Norman backed off. "I wanted to know if she belongs to any organizations that Mr. Rodolfo Martinez belongs to."

"We were both in the College Readiness Program."

"Any other organizations?"

"No."

"At any time, Miss O'Rourke, did you ever come forward and state that Mr. Rodolfo Martinez was with you when he was supposed to be in San Francisco?"

"Yes. I told his lawyer—Mr. Garry. I went to his office."

"Did you ever at any time come forward and tell the police that Mr. Rodolfo Martinez was with you on May 1, 1969?"

"No, I didn't."

"Why didn't you?"

Garry thundered: "Because I told her not to!"

"Don't you think it would have been of some assistance to Mr. Martinez if somebody had come forward and said 'He was with me'?" Norman persisted.

Kennedy: "It is argumentative, and it assumes a fact not in evidence—namely, that the police department is interested in justice."

Mana: "The objection will be sustained [but] I am going to caution the people in the courtroom that the next time we have any handclapping the Court is going to exclude everybody."

Tony, following Kathy O'Rourke to the stand, explained more about police and alibis: "First of all they wasn't going to believe anything she said. Secondly, she just don't know how they are. If she goes there thinking she's gonna help me, it probably would have been worse. She's like a lot of tutors in the program; they come from middle-class families. They have never come in contact with how the police treat the people."

"Well, will you explain that to us?" Norman said.

Garry: "It will take fifteen years to answer that question."

Mana: "You can take it up on re-direct."

Garry: "Then can we have a stipulation that in the opinion of chicanos and Third World people, police are the lowest things that ever crawled?"

Tony described the Readiness Program: "Schools here, they're very sterile—coming from a different culture, speaking a different language. Even at City College you can hardly relate to the teachers. So I went to check out the Program. There were people from the streets and the personality they had was to help the people in there go through college—which is something that I had never seen before. The first semester I did all right. The second semester we were getting over the strike. A lot of the leaders had to drop out . . . so a new bunch of leaders had to take over, and this is when I became chairman of COBRA. The aim of it is to bring brown students from the streets to school and see that they go through a two-year program at San Mateo and then have them transferred to a university. This way they can get the skills that are needed for our people . . . and bring them back into our communities. Besides that, it's [an organization for] political education [because] the situation in this country is a very poor situation politically."

"Well, objection," said Norman. "This is a political speech, I think."

"I could say this is a political trial," Garry responded.

The morning following Tony's testimony there was a strangely familiar well-dressed corporate type sitting in the front of the courtroom. I couldn't place him until he was called to the stand. Then I connected his face with newspaper photos: CSM President Ewigleben. He testified that he knew both Martinez brothers as good students; Tony he called "an emerging leader."

Nelson Rodriguez's father was an alibi witness. He said that on May 1 between 9:20 and 9:30 A.M. Mario Martinez and Ralph Ruiz both called looking for Nelson—thus Mario and Nelson weren't together at the time the burglary was probably taking place. "Ever tell the police about these calls?" R. Jay Engel asked.

"I told them three times about these calls. I found them inside my house at 6:00 P.M. on May 1, 1969. I told them about Sandy, that they might find Nelson there."

Sandy Domdoma was next, an attractive half-Hawaiian half-Chinese girl who worked for a bank. Engel, not resisting the male chauvinist atmosphere which permeated the courtroom, boasted to the press, "I want some credit for bringing in the best-looking witness yet."

Sandy said she left her apartment at 377 Peoria Street in Daly City at 7:30 A.M. on May 1. Nelson and "Winkle" (Donald Wilson) were there. After work she noticed an *Examiner* headline and skimmed the story: Nelson's name was among the suspects listed in Brodnik's death. She got home and told Nelson what she'd read, as he hadn't heard anything about it. "He looked really scared." She said Nelson left with Ralph shortly after.

Norman: "Do I understand Nelson Rodriguez stayed with you in your apartment the night before May 1?"

"Yes."

"May I ask if you shared the same bedroom?"

Garry: "That's the lowest piece of question I've ever heard."

Kennedy: "He's a dirty old man, Judge."

Mana overruled the objection. Domdoma answered coolly: "Yes." She added that Winkle, whom she'd known since first grade, was living there at the time.

"You're smiling at Nelson?" Norman asked as she left the stand.

Barbara Fuller, former secretary at the Readiness Center, supported both Tony and Nelson's alibis: "I saw Tony early that morning on campus, with his tutor, Kathy O'Rourke. Mario called three times—9:30 A.M., 11:30 A.M., and early afternoon. Each time he wanted to know if I'd seen Nelson and if I saw him to give him a message." She remembered the times because a couple of days later Ralph Ruiz asked her to write them down.

Donald Wilson, or "Winkle," Nelson's actual alibi witness for the moment of the shooting, was a husky blond youth who now lived in Brooklyn and worked as a truck driver. A strange bit of shadow-boxing preceded his appearance. One day, during a break in Tony's testimony, Inspector Cleary—according to Engel—"says . . . with a snide sort of grin on his face something about a 'Wilson,' or, 'Do you know a "Wilson"?' " Engel then tried to contact Winkle and couldn't. He put Cleary on the stand. After some hemming and hawing Cleary said that he had heard from Della McKinney—one of the most cooperative prosecution witnesses, and the only one besides McGoran to identify Nelson—that Wilson was in New York. Cleary added: "She doesn't know him. . . . [A] person told her that a certain subject by the name of Donald Wilson was being paid to testify that Nelson Rodriguez was in a certain place on such and such a day."

Engel: "I want Della McKinney. . . . I want her back."

When she returned to the stand, Mrs. McKinney said: "I told [Cleary] that a friend of mine had said that one of her sister-in-law's brothers might be called back from New York to testify because he had been with one of the defendants . . . the one who said he wasn't there, and she assumed it was Rodriguez."

"Did you tell Inspector Cleary that the defense had bought off the witness?" Garry asked.

"I told Inspector Cleary that I didn't think the Wilsons had too much money and if he came back somebody would probably have to pay his way. He may have misunderstood what I said."

Kennedy: "Why did you feel called upon to call Inspector Cleary?"

"I thought it might be important to the case."

"To the prosecution's case?"

"Well, if the boy's telling the truth it will help you."

Garry: "Why didn't you tell us?"

"I've been connected more with the prosecution."

"In other words, you thought that by telling Inspector Cleary that somehow or other he would see to it that Donald Wilson did not come here . . . [because he] will make a liar out of you?" Objection sustained.

Della McKinney's real interest never became clear. Did she expect Cleary to get rid of Wilson? The defense suspected so but couldn't prove it. It is probably safe to say she had been alarmed to find out Nelson had an alibi witness after she had wavered so long and finally been convinced to testify against him.

Wilson was located in New York and the money was forwarded for his plane fare. His actual testimony was brief. He said he was with Nelson from 8:30 A.M. to 10:30 A.M. on May 1 at 377 Peoria, Sandy Domdoma's apartment. Around 10:00, Ralph Ruiz arrived, and at 10:30 Ralph and Nelson left together. To test the accuracy of Wilson's memory, Engel asked him what he had for breakfast that morning. Wilson answered, "Chocolate fudge cake and a quart of beer."

15. All-American Boy

The eyewitness and alibi testimony completed, the defense entered the most explosive part of its case. Bebe and José had said McGoran wasn't just the aggressor but the actual killer. To make this credible, the defense had to show "prior acts of violence by the alleged victim of an assault."

Eighteen-year-old Carol Wilson (no relation to Donald Wilson) was the first in a long series of character witnesses against McGoran. In April 1968, when Carol was fifteen, her family and McGoran were living in the same Noe Valley apartment building. The incident took place in front of the building, where Carol was talking to several of her friends, who were sitting in a car parked by the curb.

"He grabbed me by the arm rather roughly," Carol began. "[He said] 'I don't like goddamn little tramps threatening my wife.' [He] left bruises all up and down my right arm. George [one of Carol's friends] told McGoran to take his hands off me. McGoran got really mad and started swearing. He said that Geroge was a goddamn nigger. And George got smart and said, 'I am not a nigger. I'm just dark.' Mr. McGoran asked me what kind of trash I was hanging around with. . . .

"He went back to his truck and took out a rifle. He said if I bothered him in any manner he was going to shoot this gun, and he had it pointed right at me. The way he handled the gun was sort of all over the place and he was slurring. It was a kind of drunken behavior. . . . The people in the car were trying to stick up for me because they didn't know who McGoran was. He leaned into the car and told everybody to keep their mouth shut, like he wasn't taking no shit from them. I had told him to take his hands off me and he says, 'Do you know who I am? I am a police officer and I have authority and you kids have no respect for the police,' and he started rambling on about this incoherently. I sort of yanked out of his grip. I ran up the stairs—I was near panic. I started crying and I lost my breath and I couldn't catch back my breath, I was so nervous.

"My brother [went to McGoran's apartment]. I was about three stairs behind him. My brother identified himself and McGoran slammed the door in his face. He said, 'I am Carol's brother from upstairs' and he asked McGoran why he was hassling me. [McGoran opened the door again.] McGoran told my brother we were invading his privacy, and if we didn't get away from his door we were going to be arrested for disturbing the peace. He asked my brother for his ID. He pulled [a handgun] from behind . . . he was holding it on my brother right in his chest. [When the police came, McGoran said] 'Book 'em.' No questions asked."

Norman pointed out while cross-examining Carol Wilson that there had been an incident two days before in the garage of the building, in which McGoran had some of Carol's friends arrested for being in a stolen car. On the stand, McGoran confused this incident with the one two days later, and also—according to Carol —confused her with another girl who may have insulted his wife.

"Colleen Brodnik is a very good friend of mine," Carol testified. "I knew of Mr. McGoran and Joe Brodnik through Colleen, who I had gone to school with. Colleen was very proud of her father. The next day or day after while I was at school I mentioned to Colleen what had happened with McGoran and Colleen just kind of went to pieces. She said, 'Oh, my God!' "

Engel asked Carol, "If you are such a good friend of Joseph Brodnik's daughter, don't you think she would be offended by your coming here and testifying?" Norman's objection that this line of questioning was irrelevant was sustained; but off the stand

270

Carol later explained that Colleen had approved of her testifying. A week later, again according to Carol, Colleen was not so happy about it. She had apparently begun to see that an attack on McGoran was an attack on Brodnik, too—that the "good guy," her father, was necessarily compromised by his years of close association with the "bad guy."

Hodge had arranged Carol Wilson's appearance to come right before McGoran's return to the stand. The star witness calmly denied Carol's accusations, saying he had never pulled a gun on her or her brother, but had only taken a rifle out of his second wife's, Thelma's, hands.

But beneath his calm McGoran was worried. In the months since his last appearance the balance had definitely shifted to the defense. McGoran now felt that *he* was on trial: he had even let slip at a recent retirement board hearing, in regard to a certain injury: "When I am *cleared* at the trial, then I am supposed to go back [to the doctor]." (Author's emphasis.)

"Which one of your many wives was this?" Garry asked after McGoran denied assaulting Carol Wilson.

"It was my second wife, Thelma."

"By the way, where is Thelma right now?"

"I have no idea, sir."

"You have been trying to locate her, haven't you?"

"Have I?"

"You have been trying to get rid of that witness so I won't be able to have her testify against you."

"I had tried to contact her—for her daughter Karen."

"You called [Karen] and wanted to know where her mother was, isn't that right?"

"I went up and talked to her daughter."

"Why don't you answer my question—or is it difficult?"

"I talked to her daughter."

"Would you answer my question?"

"I talked to her daughter, I said."

"Isn't it a fact that you were trying to get rid of one of the principal witnesses against your character—your former wife Thelma?"

"No. I had no idea you were going to call her in the beginning."

"Why did you call my investigator, Harold Lipset, and want to know where she was?"

"I didn't call him."

"Who did you call? [Pat] Buckman?"

"I have talked to Buckman, but I didn't talk to Harold Lipset."

"Who does Buckman work for?"

"He is in partnership with Harold Lipset."

"And you called him and wanted to find out where Thelma was, isn't that right?"

"No sir."

"What did you call him about?"

" . . . I don't recall talking about Thelma when I talked to Pat. I had invited him over."

"Was the name Thelma mentioned at any time?"

"No sir. I don't recall anybody saying anything about Thelma."

"Didn't you tell him, 'Someone has contacted my wife'?"

"My wife? I'm not married."

"You know I intend to bring Pat Buckman here, don't you? While you've still got a chance, will you tell me what you discussed with Mr. Buckman. Did you ask Mr. Buckman for a job?"

"I don't recall asking him for a job, no. I was free, but I don't recall asking him for a job." McGoran denied Garry's assertion that his conversation with Buckman was eight to ten minutes long; he said it was only fifteen or twenty seconds, and he just asked Buckman over for a drink.

"It's a fact, is it not," Garry asked "that you used as one of your elements of retirement the injuries to your right hand in the web area—of your right index finger and your right thumb?"

"No sir. It was the last two fingers."

"And when did you have trouble with that area?"

"It was after the incident on May 1st."

"Did you ever tell Dr. Seymour"— Garry read from a medical report —"that 'in his right hand he has had some burning discomfort in the web between the thumb and index finger which extends over to the fourth and fifth digits. This is described as mild. However, with gripping he develops discomfort of a moderately severe nature.'* Did you tell that to Dr. Seymour?"

"No . . . not the way you read it, no sir."

"Isn't it a fact that you injured that area when the gun was wrenched from your hand?"

"No sir, because I had no gun in my hand."

"Then how did you injure your hand?"

"I don't know how it was injured."

The defense attorneys quizzed McGoran on several alleged prior acts of violence: beating up young Daniel Ring in a Pacifica shopping center in 1966; beating an American Indian named Ronald Crowfoot in 1967 until he was blue in the face; condoning his son's assault on his first wife, Jane, outside their Pacifica home in 1968; telling two young blacks he had spread-eagled over a car on a scorching midsummer day, "Nigger, if you don't lay on it, I'll put a cap in you"—insulting, demeaning, brutalizing, terrorizing countless "suspects," mostly nonwhite or longhaired, whether in arrest situations or not. McGoran denied it all, or when really trapped, would respond, "I don't recall . . . I don't remember . . . It's possible, 'cause anything could happen."

Twenty-one-year-old Danny Ring followed McGoran on the stand. He was from Pacifica and apparently had a relationship of standing animosity with McGoran's eldest son, Paul McGoran Jr. Ring described a 1966 shopping center incident for which McGoran was later tried on assault and battery charges (it ended in a hung jury):

"Paul McGoran Jr. made a motion like this [indicating the middle finger]. I did the same thing back to him and called him a motherfucker," Ring began. "We drove around and we parked and he went around the corner. [Later] Paul McGoran Sr. approached.

* The file was entered in evidence.

He put his hands on me and called me a motherfucking asshole. He ripped my shirt off. I jerked my arm away and when I did that he grabbed me like this [by the lapels] and punched me like this [in the jaw] and jammed my head up against the door. He just ripped the whole T-shirt and sweater. I was kind of dazed, almost knocked out. About the third time he went to pull my head, my friend in the back seat tried to get his hands off me. I scooted toward the middle of the car, kind of rolled, and all the time the crowd had been making gestures like, 'Leave him alone,' and 'Get the big guy off him,' and the crowd was kind of getting closer and McGoran got paranoid or something and all of a sudden the sweater had flopped open and out comes his gun. He whipped around and said, 'Anybody comes near me and I will shoot you!' There were two knee imprints on the side of the car door that were almost up to the window." A friend of Ring's, a student at San Francisco State, also testified that McGoran pulled his gun and waved it at the crowd.

Two young students testified after Ring, describing an incident in front of a store where they had gone to return a package. Phil Rutsick was about five foot two, thin, longhaired and bearded. Lynn Codiga was about four foot ten and around ninety pounds. "Lynn unlocked the car and I got in," Phil began. "I got out the package, and we closed the door and started to walk. We were almost at the corner when this man jumped out and grabbed us both. He grabbed me around the collar and threw me up against the wall, and he grabbed Lynn by the arm and twisted her around and he took me again by the collar and smashed me up against the wall. He said he was a police officer but refused to give us his name. He said, 'You're under arrest. I saw you go into that car and take something.' I said, 'What car?' And he said, 'That car, the brown one.' Lynn said, 'That's my car,' and so we walked over. She got the registration and showed it to him. He looked at it and said, "All right, I saw you going into the one next to this, then.' I didn't say anything; I was scared. [Lynn] had the receipt with her showing when [the package] was bought from what store. McGoran went into [a store] and got the owner of the car, and he came out and said that there was nothing missing."

McGoran had Phil arrested anyway. "I was very upset and I didn't know if I was capable of driving my car home," Lynn testified. "I also didn't know the city very well at that time and so as the patrol car was driving off with Philip I asked [McGoran] how I was to get home and he said, 'I don't give a fuck how you get home, you slut. Just get the hell out of here.' "

"My parents wrote a letter," said Phil. "I went to an attorney to see about filing a suit for false arrest. He told me not to do it because we would have to prove the officer did it maliciously." The complaint letter could not be found in police files.

Martha and Frank Weinmuller, owners of a motel in Seattle, flew in to testify. "The gentleman checked in and maybe after five to ten minutes he came back and wanted the money back," Mrs. Weinmuller began. "I had heard them arguing in the office and I heard something about getting a beating. I went to the kitchen window because I wanted to know what is going on and so I seen that man running out of the office and came back with his gun. I told my husband, 'Call the police, and we will close the door.' " The police came and the Weinmullers refunded McGoran's money—$10.50.

Mr. Weinmuller explained: "Around two o'clock in the morning the office bell rang and I went out and I checked the couple in from San Francisco. About seven or ten minutes later he came back and asked for heat. The heat in the units goes off at 11:30 P.M. automatically, except the one in the bathroom. I told him this and he said he wanted to check out. I said fine; you take your wife out to the car and I am going to check the unit. If it hasn't been used you are going to get your money back, and he said he wanted his money back right there. He said he is going to get his money if he has to beat it out of me. I said, 'Since you feel that way about it, I am not going to give you back a cent.' And my wife already heard it . . . and she seen him coming with a gun."

"Are you being paid anything, sir, for your testimony in this case?" Norman asked.

"No, except for fare and two tuna sandwiches."

II

Garry was never sure Thelma McGoran would testify. He hadn't even known she existed until one day in October 1969 when he was in the hospital recovering from an operation and received a collect phone call from Fresno County. A husky-voiced woman asked, "Are you representing those boys accused of killing Brodnik? Those boys are innocent, you know."

"I know," Garry replied. But when he tried to find out the woman's name she was evasive, insisting she was afraid for her life. Garry hired the private investigating firm of Harold Lipset to track her down. After several months, Lipset discovered the woman was McGoran's second ex-wife, Thelma.

Thelma McGoran turned out to be a mine of information. She gave the investigator many examples of McGoran's violent temper, including the 1966 Pacifica incident in which he assaulted Danny Ring. She said McGoran kept stolen property, and dope to plant on suspects; cashed as much as $225 in checks in bars in one month, and liked to rip off coin telephones. She said he boasted of being an expert liar. But she didn't know if she could testify: her friends, many of them policemen, had warned her not to.*

She appeared in court on October 8, 1970—a stout middle-aged woman with short blond hair, teased on top. Her testimony took exactly one day. She had met McGoran in March 1965 through Brodnik, whom she'd known for over a year and who ate almost every night at Bruno's Restaurant on Mission Street, where she worked as a waitress. Brodnik introduced McGoran to her as a "crazy nut." She didn't start dating McGoran until September 1965. McGoran left Pacifica and from mid-1966 to December 1967 Thelma lived with him on Mission Street; in December they were married and they lived together for another four months before breaking up. In August 1969 they were divorced.

One by one, she described the incidents she had witnessed. June 1967 at 3:00 A.M. in a motel parking lot: "He spotted a little

---

* This information is taken from reports by Harold Lipset's firm to Charles Garry, as well as Thelma McGoran's testimony.

boy going into an auto. He radioed—he always carried his walkie-talkie with him like a religion. He waited until the boy approached my auto and he jumped out, and he pulled out his gun at arm's length, never identified himself, and he says, 'You make one fucking move and you'll get this .41 bullet up your fucking ass.' He made the boy lay down on his stomach and he put his foot on his back and held him that way until the radio car came."

June 1967 at the seedy Sunshine Apartments, in which McGoran had a partial ownership: "They'd been drinking, and Mr. Crowfoot [the manager] had got a little bit out of line. We were all trying to calm him down and Paul pulled him down to the floor and was beating him with his fists. The man never struck back. All he said was, 'Paul, what's wrong with you?' In five minutes the man's face was purple, and when [Paul] picked him up, he kicked him, broke four of his ribs. I asked [Crowfoot] why he didn't hit back, and he says, 'Because of the .41.' "

January 1968: "[McGoran's first wife, Jane] was in the house at the time. Paul Jr. went up to the door and kicked it in. Paul Sr. stayed on the sidewalk. Mrs. McGoran told her son to go home with his father and get his clothes packed, but he had a Honda in the garage that he wanted. Paul Sr. wanted him to take it. [Jane] McGoran had previously called the Pacifica Police Department about Paul Sr. being there, and he didn't want to get involved. Paul Jr. broke the garage door down. Mrs. McGoran tried to hold the Honda back and Paul Jr. proceeded to pull it away from her. The Pacifica Police Department asked Paul Sr. why they couldn't behave like a family. Paul Sr. said he didn't want to become involved. I said, 'Why did you let him beat his mother?'; and he said, 'That's still not my business.' "

On cross-examination Norman asked if Paul Jr. had actually beaten his mother. "Beat? I can only think of fists . . . and it wasn't that bad. He pushed her. He hit her . . . a backhand . . . and he did shove her."

"Did you know a person by the name of Ken Nelson who lived at 82 Perry Street [the address of Sunshine Apartments]?" Garry asked Thelma McGoran.

"Yes sir."

"Was this young man an admitted thief and burglar as far as Paul McGoran was concerned?"

"Yes sir."

"Did he tell the police in your presence that Ken Nelson was a good, reliable person so that he could get a gun?"

"Yes sir. He had applied for a gun and Paul knew he was a burglar and he told him he would take anything that didn't have a serial number, referring to tools mostly. They became very close friends. [Nelson] would get large guns and disassemble them. He had a record for stolen credit cards. Two officers came and they said to Paul, 'Is this guy okay?' and Paul said, 'Sure.'"

"Did he also tell you that he kept heroin and marijuana in the house . . . to frame uncooperative persons?"

"Yes sir. [One day] he was leaving for work and he had a little red vial of heroin and a syringe and a teaspoon, and I asked what he was doing that for. He said, 'I feel this way: if the kids don't steal enough to hold a conviction, then the narcotics will hold them.'"

"Did you report this to anyone?"

"Yes sir, Captain Kiely. [He said] 'Oh, I didn't know that.'"

"Did Captain Kiely and Paul McGoran drink their lunches together?"

Norman objected: "Irrelevant. Calling for speculation."

"Have you seen them drinking together?"

"I have waited on them [at] Bruno's."

"Did he ever brag about the fact that he could lie and no one could detect it?"

"Yes sir. He had been on the stand and he took pride that no attorney could break him down. He said, 'I can look anybody straight in the eye and lie.'"

"What did he say he would do in the event that he ever ceased being a police officer?"

"He would become a burglar. He said he'd take anything as long as it didn't have a serial number. He's very good at it [burglary]. He is very lightfooted and he even got in my car and took things out while it was in the garage. I wouldn't hear a thing.

"[One night] he came into Bruno's wearing a white shirt

278

[with] blood all over the front of it and he was laughing. He said that there was a beef at the Carousel Ballroom and he had taken a sixteen-year-old boy and thrown him down the stairs, and he was laughing about it. I said, 'Paul, are you sadistic?' and he just laughed. . . . He used to bring things home and I used to ask him why he did it and he says, 'Because if I take them downtown the inspectors will [take them] .' He brought home half a box of Certs, Rolaids, Blackjack gum, the kind that is put in vending machines.

"I'd been having quite a lot of trouble with Officer McGoran and I had requested Youth Guidance to pick up my son* and take him from the home. Officer McGoran told the sergeant that I was crazy. I was taken out to the psychiatric ward, and I told the psychiatrist, 'While this is all happening, my husband is taking everything out of my apartment that's stolen property.' When I got back he had taken the things and left a full-length window open and made it look like a burglar had robbed my apartment if I said anything. He had a hair dryer, and a suitcase full of stolen tools. There was rifles. He was there when I left and I was gone about forty-five minutes. . . . And who else would want a box of junky tools and a hair dryer when there was so many more valuable things there? I had already turned McGoran in and this was the only evidence that I had that he was taking stolen property. I still have a little liquor locker that is also stolen property. He forgot it in the apartment.

"I didn't [start drinking] until I started getting knocked around by Officer McGoran; that kind of eased the pain. I had had a six-hour operation and I walked with a limp . . . and his favorite way of mistreating me was to knock me up against a wall and I had medication and he made me go through Welfare for my medication, and when it ran out, I drank to ease what pain I did have.

"He had asked my permission to go out with a woman; at the same time we were talking about going to Reno to be married and I asked him if he thought I was crazy. He shoved me out in the hall, ripped my clothes off of me, ripped out a pay phone, took a

* Thelma McGoran's twelve-year-old son by a previous marriage, living with Thelma and Paul McGoran.

TV and threw it down the hall. I called Southern Station and they said, 'It sounds like McGoran is at it again.' He was drunk for three days. I had two sergeants take me off to jail. They let me call until I got hold of him at two o'clock in the morning and he come and bailed me out. This was in '67 just before I married him."

Thelma McGoran also described an incident in April 1968, just before they finally broke up, in which McGoran pushed her out of his truck as he was driving along Dolores Street in the Mission district. After this she wrote a fourteen-page letter to Police Chief Cahill describing many of McGoran's past crimes. That letter, like several others, was not found in McGoran's complaint file (later Cahill was called to the stand and denied having received it). But on cross-examination Norman produced a letter of apology written by Thelma which was clearly meant as a retraction of the fourteen-pager. "Didn't you state that he never pushed you out of the car, that you were just mad and that you were trying to embarrass him?" Norman asked.

"Just a minute!" said Garry. "I have asked for almost five months that I be given copies of all letters." The jury was quickly ushered out. "Your Honor must know by now that I even threatened the Custodian of Records with perjury. I have done everything in the world to get copies of everything that was written about Officer McGoran. I referred to a fourteen-page letter. Now I see a letter in the hands of the prosecution where the prosecution and this man with him, Cleary, sat there knowing full well that they had information that I was demanding that was not given to me."

"We knew these letters existed," Engel added. "I am demanding a hearing on sanctions [against Norman, for violating a court order to show the defense all evidence of complaints against McGoran] and I want fines imposed."

"This is a copy of a letter Paul McGoran handed me this morning," Norman said. "I don't even think it is subject to discovery."

"We had three hearings in chambers trying to get that letter," Engel insisted, "as well as one that was fourteen pages long."

Hodge said, "The district attorney has been systematically

hiding discoverable matter. There have been crucial items of evidence that have not been disclosed to the defense."

"For example," said Engel, "the tape-recorded statement of Paul McGoran that was taken and did not work. I wonder where that tape is."

Judge Mana scheduled no hearing on sanctions, and the jury returned. Thelma McGoran explained, "I wrote that letter [of retraction] at Officer McGoran's request. It would cost him his job if the truth came out. I got $20 worth of groceries for that letter. I wrote it. He read it. He handed it to Officer Brodnik. Officer Brodnik read it and it was handed to Captain Kiely."

The letter of retraction read in part: "I opened the door to get out while it [the car] was in motion and I fell out on the pavement. Paul came back and did offer to help me but I refused. I took his leaflets and threw them all over Dolores Street. My temper had reached the point I didn't care what I did to him. I don't want to lose him and I felt if I had to lose what I love, he can lose what he loves. It has been hard for me to understand his job comes first, and Paul is a fine man, a fine policeman. I know you will understand the way a woman can be."

"He forced you to write that?" Norman said.

"I was pretty hungry and I had a little boy that was hungry. He told me I'd better write a letter to Captain Kiely or he was going to lose his job. I also wrote Officer Brodnik a letter of apology. McGoran wanted one to take to him in case there was any humiliation brought to him over this."

During one recess, a phone call came to the courtroom for Thelma. The caller said she was Thelma's daughter Karen. Back on the stand Thelma asked the clerk if the caller had left her last name. The clerk answered, "She said her name was Karen."

"I don't believe this message. I haven't seen or spoken to my daughter in three years. My daughter doesn't even know my last name is McGoran. My daughter was in Michigan [at Christmastime]. I tried to put a collect call through but he [the son-in-law] wouldn't accept it."

"Is this going to affect your ability to testify?" Mana asked.

"No, because I'm going to show them I'm stronger." Thelma

said later, off the stand, she was sure McGoran had put some woman up to making the call.

Norman asked why she married McGoran. She insisted she was in love with him, and added, "I took a lot of what Officer Brodnik told me, that I was able to change him." It was obvious she had admired Brodnik, as did many other people around the Mission and Noe Valley. Yet according to Thelma's testimony Brodnik knew McGoran was a "crazy nut." He worked with McGoran daily and must have witnessed many unpleasant scenes like the ones Thelma described. "Officer Brodnik had ulcers," Thelma said during her testimony, almost by way of explanation, "and had to go to the hospital."

As she left the courtroom at the end of that long day, a young reporter told her, "Your whole testimony makes me embarrassed to be a man in this society."

III

When McGoran was on the stand for the second time, Norman asked him, "During your police career have you received any commendations?"

"I have." McGoran listed seven meritorious commendations, eighteen captain's commendations, and forty captain's complimentary commendations—and a first-grade meritorious award for the Alvarado Street incident.

Garry asked later, "Was there a hearing before you were given [that] award?"

"There was a hearing, yes sir. There was all the captains and the deputy chief and one of the police commissioners."

"Who testified in your behalf on that date?"

"The award was read by—"

"I asked you who testified."

"I wasn't present at any testimony."

"Then there was no hearing?"

"There was a report that was submitted by Captain Kiely and it was read. Now, as far as testimony, there was no testimony given—"

Kennedy asked, "It wasn't a hearing, it was an award ceremony?"

"Yes, all right, yes, it was an award ceremony."

"You gave a report to Captain Kiely of the incident that occurred?"

"Yes, I told him."

"I want a copy of that report."

Hodge added, "I thought there were no reports of this incident. That is certainly what we were led to believe, and if they have a report from Captain Kiely giving a version of what this man said, I want a copy." When the report was delivered, it became obvious why it had never been given to the defense on discovery, despite numerous requests for any and all reports McGoran had made of the incident. Kiely had listed the number of suspects on the street when Brodnik and McGoran approached as four. McGoran denied telling Kiely there were only four. Said Kennedy, "I want Kiely in here right now." Thus began one of the trial's most comic episodes.

Kiely testified, "I believe Officer McGoran told me there were six originally. I possibly didn't pay too much attention to what I was writing and perhaps I made a mistake. This is not an official report of the incident."

"You lied to the police commission?" Garry asked.

"I don't lie to anybody!" Kiely shouted, half-standing, his face reddening.

"The witness is out of control, Judge," Kennedy said. "If he gets any angrier I think he ought to take his piece off, because I am scared."

"Is he wearing a weapon?" Garry asked. "I am not going to be standing here with a man with his temper and have a weapon on his side."

Kennedy: "And the record should disclose that Captain Kiely's face is getting redder."

Norman: "It's not red at all."

"The answer, then, is no?" Garry continued. "He did not tell you that [that only four were at the scene] ?"

"Not in effect, no."

"He told you six?"

"Something like that, six."

"What do you mean, 'Something like that'? Six-and-a-half? Seven? Five-and-a-half?"

"Approximately six . . . Six. I typed it out myself and perhaps my thoughts weren't too coherent at the time."

Kiely had written McGoran was "struck with a heavy object such as a tire iron."

"[A tire iron was] just a hard object that came into my mind," he explained.

"Isn't it a fact," asked Kennedy, "that what you were trying to do was to pad this application ever so slightly, in order to cover up for Officer McGoran?"

"No sir, I just do the facts."

"Who told you about the tire iron?"

"Just my own conjecture."

"Now, do you think it is nice to give out first-grade meritorious awards based on your conjecture? Wouldn't it be nicer to base them on facts?"

"Those are facts. The fact is Officer Brodnik is dead—that is a fact!"

Kennedy: "That is indeed. May that be stricken? He is becoming histrionic again."

"That's all right," Mana said.

"You are not going to strike that? That is another example of your siding with the police department."

Mana: "You may proceed."

Kennedy pointed out that Captain Kiely's report said the suspects were taking property into the upper flat. "That's a deduction I made myself," Kiely explained. "In those types of reports, we're allowed some latitude."

On cross-examination Norman asked if, when McGoran reported in for work at 9:00 A.M. on May 1, he "evidenced any symptoms of having been drinking."

"No sir," Kiely answered immediately. "None whatsoever! He was bright as a dollar. Sharp. Completely devoid of any alcohol!"

On re-cross Garry asked, "Is it your testimony, Captain, that you have never seen Paul McGoran drunk?"

"I've never seen Paul McGoran drunk."

"Do you drink yourself?"

Kiely's face turned beet red as he stood up again and shouted, "Do I look like a drinking man, counselor?"

"Did Thelma McGoran ever discuss the conduct or misconduct of Paul McGoran with you?"

"No."

"Did you ever receive any letters from her?"

"I never received any letters."

This exchange took place before Norman used Thelma's apology letter to Kiely in court. After the apology letter came out, Kiely was called back. This time he appeared in full dress uniform with gold buttons everywhere. "I had him under oath here last Thursday saying he never received a letter from Thelma McGoran," Garry said.

Norman: "He was asked about a fourteen-page letter."

Garry: "That's not true."

Kiely: "I don't recall exactly what I said, but I think my intent was, I didn't recall at that time."

Lipset's partner, private investigator Pat Buckman, put in a brief appearance. He said of his phone talk with McGoran, "He called me [on] August 17, 1970. It was a lengthy conversation ... approximately eight to ten minutes. [He asked] did I know where she was. I didn't tell him. He said he'd tried to find her in Fresno but couldn't, and if we knew where she was, he'd like to talk to her. He wanted to know if there was any chance he could work for us."

"Did you take any notes?" Norman asked during cross-examination.

"No, I just know what date he called."

On re-cross Garry said, "You told us you did not take notes, but you did tape the conversation, didn't you?"

"Yes sir, I did."

An *Oakland Tribune* reporter described a young man he had interviewed May 1 on the porch of a house which fit the description of 436 Alvarado (the Jarzyna residence). He was wearing an orange shirt—just what Inspector Cleary had testified prosecution witness David Caravantes was wearing that morning. (Twenty-year-old Caravantes had testified that the young latinos on the street were "beating the hell out of" McGoran and that McGoran was knocked to the ground before Brodnik was shot.) The reporter described his conversation with Caravantes as "very brief . . . I asked him if he had seen what happened and he said yes. He didn't want to tell me his name. He said, 'Paul was asking for it. He was pushing them against the wall and roughing them up.' Then a policeman came up and the conversation ended."

More impeachment of Caravantes followed. After subpoenaing the personnel man at the Ford Foundation labor training school, the defense got hold of Caravantes's file. In it were letters of recommendation from the police chief of San Rafael, and—from Assistant District Attorney Thomas Norman. Dated December 23, 1969, this letter read in part: "David Caravantes has been known to me for over six months in connection with his courageous service to this community . . . a man of high principles and integrity whom I recommend."

The evolution of Caravantes's testimony could now be traced as follows:

—May 1969: Caravantes says he didn't see who fired the gun because McGoran was *standing* in front of Brodnik, blocking the view.

—December 1969: Norman writes a letter of recommendation describing Caravantes's "high principles and integrity."

—August 1970: Caravantes testifies McGoran was *on the ground* when the shot was fired, agrees with McGoran that Gary Lescallett took the gun, denies he said, "Paul was asking for it."

IV

During his rebuttal of the defense case, Norman called *Examiner* reporter Mary Crawford, who had interviewed José Rios in jail shortly after the six were arrested. She said, "I don't choose to testify for either side because it's not good for a reporter. I am going to claim the newsman's privilege under evidence code section 1070" (which reads, "A reporter . . . cannot be adjudged in contempt by a court . . . for refusing to disclose the source of any information procured for publication and published in a newspaper"). Judge Mana told her she had waived this privilege by giving the source of her information, José Rios, in her article. He ordered her to testify.

"You can't be serious," Garry said. "You're turning the clock back at least twenty years as far as freedom of the press is concerned in this state." He cited a 1955 case in which the labor editor of the *San Francisco Chronicle* was ordered to give sources of information about a strike—sources he had already divulged in an article. He refused and was held in contempt but a higher court reversed the ruling and released him.

The defense argued that evidence code section 1070 as well as the First Amendment guarantee of freedom of the press protect a reporter's right to remain silent. If Mary Crawford were forced to testify, not only would lawyers never again trust her to interview their clients, but it would set a dangerous precedent for all reporters—"and we could have a front page of nothing but blanks," as Garry put it. Mana was not impressed by the constitutional arguments but did reverse his decision when the 1955 article Garry had mentioned was produced and proved analogous in all important respects to Mary Crawford's.

But following the weekend break, Mana switched again. Norman asserted, and Mana agreed, that Mary Crawford had waived her "privilege" (to remain silent) by disclosing the source of her information to Norman in a private interview (whereas in the 1955 case the reporter had *not* had a private interview with the district attorney).

"There is no rule of law that if the D.A. is tricky enough he can get in inadmissible evidence," Engel complained.

"Did you have an interview with Mr. Norman?" Mana asked Crawford.

Engel said, "If she answers, she's waived her right. That's

nonsense, Judge. It's like *Alice in Wonderland*.... Your Honor, it's apparent something has been cooked up between the court and the district attorney's office."

Mana: "I order you to answer."

Crawford: "I still refuse."

Mana: "I cite you for contempt. Take her into custody. Court will sentence you to five days in jail."

Garry: "Without a hearing? Incredible!"

Mana backed down: "Okay, I'll defer action." Crawford walked out and the matter was never pursued.

The rest of Norman's rebuttal was equally unsuccessful. He called a Greyhound superintendent whose testimony was supposed to show that Mario Martinez couldn't have made it from the Greyhound terminal in San Francisco to San Mateo in the time he said he did: the buses didn't go that fast. Garry asked the superintendent the maximum speed for buses on the freeway. Sixty-five, he was told. "It's your testimony, is it, that those Greyhound buses on the freeway never go more than sixty-five?" The jurors laughed.

Norman brought a financial aids officer from the College of San Mateo to testify that there were no tutoring time sheets for Mario for the spring semester of 1969. "It's very possible the student can be tutoring for another agency," the witness said— which turned out to be the case with Mario, as the defense showed on sur-rebuttal.

Then came Diane Kossowski, daughter of Irene Jarzyna and girlfriend of David Caravantes. Norman—somewhat irregularly in terms of trial procedure—had saved her for last. It seemed a good tactic: Diane was twenty years old, pretty and demure. She said she saw several boys jump on Brodnik (not on McGoran); a short boy did the shooting; there was *no* struggle over the gun (Bebe had testified that there was). She identified Tony Martinez as being there.

But in the first five minutes of cross-examination, her credibility and her angelic demeanor dissolved. "Why didn't you testify before the grand jury?" Garry asked. "Were you available to testify on May 19, 1969?"

Diane Kossowski spat back: "No."

"Where were you?" She was silent. "Where were you, madam?" Still no response. "Let the record reflect that she's looking at Norman imploringly."

Finally: "I was home that day."

"So you *were* available to testify?"

"Yes."

On her second day of testimony, Diane admitted she wasn't really sure about her identification of Tony. Shortly after, Garry asked, "Are you sure McGoran was knocked to the ground *before* Brodnik was shot?"

"Not really sure," she replied.

16. The Prosecution Doesn't Understand

I

Final arguments took a full week. Norman had the advantage of both leading off on Monday and rebutting the defense on Friday. But he was coming from behind, for the defense had presented two things he had not: a tight-knit case and a coherent version of the events of May 1, 1969.

Norman's insecurity was obvious as he argued. He spent most of his time either trying to find holes in the defendants' stories or describing "lesser included offenses" of which the jurors might convict them if they thought first-degree murder too harsh. (Lesser offenses included second-degree murder and voluntary and involuntary manslaughter.) Norman started out, however, with an explanation of the theories on which the six men had been held in jail without bail on first-degree murder charges for eighteen months. One justification was the "felony murder rule":

> The unlawful killing of a human being, whether intentional, unintentional or accidental, which occurs as a result of the commission of, or attempt to commit, the crime of burglary,* and where there was in the mind of the perpetrator the specific intent to commit such crime, is murder in the first degree.

* One of several felonies to which the rule applies.

Norman explained that even though the burglary took place miles from Alvarado Street, the goods had not yet been "secured." It was the "continuity of the transaction" that mattered. He added that the burglary was still taking place *if* the jurors found that the property had been moving from the car to the basement, as McGoran and Caravantes testified. "If you find that the direction of the property was from the basement to the automobile [as the defendants maintained], there certainly cannot be any application of the felony murder rule. . . . The goods would have been secured."

Norman told the jury they could also convict all six of first-degree murder under the theory of aiding and abetting, aiders and abettors in a crime being just as guilty as the perpetrator himself. "A person aids or abets the commission of a crime if he knowingly and with criminal intent aids, promotes, encourages or instigates by act or advice the commission of such crime. . . . It isn't necessary under our law to prove participation in the planning of the crime. One may be a principal by reason of some affirmative action at the time of its commission."

Norman argued details. The Horensteins' brass lamp, still in the basement, had Pinky Lescallett's fingerprints on it; therefore he must have moved it there. Small objects like binoculars and a table leg were found in the blue Chevy: it was unlikely that they would have been moved first, more likely left for last. Norman hung much of his case on that table leg.

With tongue in cheek, Norman repeated the defense story: "Of course, ladies and gentlemen, [Mr. Rios] hadn't even looked at the property. He didn't even know what it was. . . . He said his parents didn't even go down there every day. But nevertheless it was very urgent that they get the particular property out of the Rios basement. [Tony Martinez] didn't check into his biology lab at any time and he didn't attend the lab. He went into the main library, where he doesn't usually study. Mr. [Gio] Lopez found him on this hundred-forty-seven-acre campus having approximately eight thousand day students. . . . The question becomes: why, if you were going to surrender yourselves [as the defendants claimed], would you involve yourself in an armed robbery and take an automobile, which is the means of an escape, and take money also, and why would you be going away from San Francisco?

"Paul McGoran was allegedly the scourge of the Mission district, a racist of the worst type, a drunk and a liar; yet, members of the jury, none of Paul McGoran's alleged victims ever went to the hospital; not one ever claimed that he fired a gun at them—there were some who said that he pulled a gun out, waved a gun around. . . .

"The evidence, ladies and gentlemen, physically does not support the defense theory at all. . . . No one here except Mr. [José] Rios and Mr. [Bebe] Melendez ever said they saw the gun in Officer McGoran's hand. No one except Mr. Rios and Mr. Melendez ever saw the struggle which Mr. Melendez testified he was engaged in with Officer McGoran over possession of the gun. No one has testified apart from Mr. Rios and Mr. Melendez that Gary Lescallett got knocked to the ground. . . .*

"The ultimate question in this case is not which of the defendants did the shooting or which were present at the burglary, but whether all or any of them participated in the burglary and the shooting as either burglar or killer, or as an aider or abettor of the burglar or the killer."

"The prosecution cannot understand why these six defendants fled," Charles Garry began his final argument. "The prosecution cannot understand why these six men found themselves fugitives. He cannot understand why Rodolfo [Tony] Martinez, when he is not involved in any way, will remain silent and not give them his alibi. Is it because he knew that Nelson Rodriguez had given his alibi, and his attorney had told the press and the world that Nelson Rodriguez wasn't there, and taken a statement from Ralph Ruiz which finally [Inspector] Cleary had to admit, and they didn't even bother seeing any of those persons named in that statement?

"The prosecution doesn't understand, and I'm sure the Court

* Stephen Laznibat thought he saw a gun in McGoran's hand. McGoran himself admitted knocking Lescallett down.

doesn't understand, what it is to be a part of the ghettoes of America, because the police treat you differently when you are in the so-called white establishment. This is where we are at. And unless you understand this, you are not going to understand why these six young men fled the area. You will never understand why Danilo [Bebe] Melendez got hold of the Mission Rebels and said, 'Get hold of a lawyer so we can have some protection when we surrender.'

"[Tony Martinez] told you he wasn't there. He told you he came to the rescue of his brother because he knew his brother was in danger. Is that wrong? Is that bad? Or are we gone so far in this life that we become so individualistic that we are not interested in our fellow man, much less our own blood brother? Mario Martinez is not only interested in his blood brother, he is interested in all brothers and all sisters. He brought fifty people into the San Mateo College program. Those are men and women who came off the ghetto streets of San Francisco and San Mateo. You just don't go and recruit the type of men and women who have lost confidence in the system without yourself being willing to risk your own personal refinements and your own personal safety in order to be able to help your brothers and sisters.

"This is the kind of thing, and unless you understand that about Mario, Rodolfo [Tony], Danilo [Bebe] —let's take Danilo Melendez. . . . You know there is no evidence; nobody testified against him. McGoran said he was upstairs . . . and yet what does he do? Does he hide behind a cloak of being safe—because the persons who were upstairs cannot under any theory of any law be involved in this case. Here is Danilo completely safe [yet] he gets up on the witness stand and tells you what happened, implicating himself from a position of safety to a point where you have to make a decision on whether his testimony is to be believed, or McGoran's testimony is to be believed.

"You see, unless you understand this brotherhood, you will not understand why Rodolfo would leave the college and go join his brother. You will not understand why Mario Martinez would give up some of his classes in order to bring new students into the movement at San Mateo College. Unless you understand that

294

brotherhood, that cementing of solidarity amongst people who care and people who have been discriminated against, you will not understand the flight. You will not understand why they became concerned when Nelson Rodriguez's name was mentioned on TV the first day, how the brothers immediately became concerned about him and wanted to protect him and embrace him. . . ."

Garry moved into the evidence. "Every witness that has been brought here by the prosecution . . . all one tightly knit group, every one of them say they only saw *one person* on the ground. Apparently no one ever told them that Officer McGoran had actually knocked Gary Lescallett down, and no one told them that Gary Lescallett never came up again. McGoran said he knocked him down. . . ." Garry turned to the transcript and quoted from his cross-examination of McGoran: "And my question was, 'Was Gary Lescallett still on the ground when your vision started to dim?' Answer: 'Yes sir.' Question: 'You proceeded toward Gary Lescallett further and your vision dimmed further?' Answer: 'Yes sir.' That testimony corners Paul McGoran."

Garry reread McGoran's hospital record: " 'Hit in face with fist . . . was not knocked down, not unconscious, no other injuries.' This is evidence. This is not rhetoric, it is not hyperbole, it is not just talk. It's evidence of the highest sort. . . . No doctor [came to testify] that is not what Paul McGoran said. . . . Not a word of ever blacking out.

"Then they give you this slop that perhaps you can find them guilty of a lesser and included offense. Poppycock. They're either guilty or not. I'm so sick of compromise verdicts I can't see straight. It was a compromise verdict that had Huey Newton spend thirty-four months in prison. We don't want one bone thrown to us and one to the prosecution.

"If [Inspector] Jack Cleary had been on the ball and done his responsible civic duty, if he had examined the physical facts, he would've known that these six men shouldn't be on trial. It's uncanny in a case as serious as this that some form of physical tests were not made on McGoran to determine whether he had in fact fired a weapon on May 1. . . . Cleary couldn't even get off his duff long enough to see the people Ralph Ruiz talked about.

"We expected this trial to be conducted at least within the framework of what these witnesses said on May 1, and lo and behold we come to this courtroom and each witness enlarges [his statement], either because they have been coached or they are lying for interests best known to themselves. Mrs. Jarzyna—one shoulder up, one shoulder down, wiggling her fanny all over the place—the audacity! When six men are on trial for their lives and their freedom. What kind of horseshow is this? . . . I can understand that no two human beings can see the same thing and relate it in the same way. The thing that annoys me is when they become partisans. They lie when they say they haven't discussed the case. They discuss it day and night. We have not met one single witness that's not in a turmoil about his own interest in this case. Della McKinney is a classic example. You should begin to wonder why Irene Jarzyna makes one statement on May 1, 1969, and another one at another time.

"Just exactly what had David Caravantes done for the chief of police of San Rafael? Or was it because the D.A. and the police department of San Francisco told him to give a bill of health to David Caravantes because of his deed that he was to perform in the case of Los Siete de la Raza? Now, we know that in December of 1969, Thomas Norman, representing the district attorney of this county, had done [Caravantes] a special favor and he had gotten into a special school at the University of California for trade unionism, wherein he has a chance to become a piecard.

"Those of you young people in the jury, in case you don't know what a piecard is, a piecard is a person who lives off the pie in the trade union movement. He is a person who looks for a job so that the union can pay him, such as being a business agent or a paid spy. In the old trade union days we looked upon a piecard as a leech. Today it is a scheme and device to create David Caravanteses to go into the trade union movement who have no basic interest in the class struggle—and it just a job with them. . . . There was a time when labor unions did not permit police agents—people who were recommended by the police department—to be in unions, because the police were the great strikebreakers in the country.

"[David Caravantes] says there was a girl taking the stuff from the car. If he was watching that window for some forty minutes, then he must obviously have seen the people who brought that stuff into the basement. Because no one else has talked about a girl. McGoran and Caravantes are the only people who had said things were taken from the car into the basement. All of the testimony from the others has been the other way around, including Diane Kossowski.

"In the grand jury [Caravantes] testified: 'McGoran didn't get kicked.' Fifteen months later he comes into this courtroom and he says, 'McGoran got kicked.' The payoff for the writing of that letter? On May 1, 1969, he said he was not sure if McGoran pulled his own gun. He didn't see Brodnik get killed. He denied that [at the trial], and yet that's the statement he made on May 1. That's all evidence.

"[Anna Chavez said] 'The person with the gun no long hair, no dirty.' . . . Isn't that interesting?

"The very fact that you have gloves on leaves a distinct and definite impression which shows to be gloves. The prosecution hasn't presented one single fingerprint of anybody using any kind of gloves on any of these objects. Norman asked in his argument, if it is a fact that the young men were carrying the things from the basement to the car, why is there a fingerprint on this item that was still in the basement [the lamp]? The answer is very simple. This [lamp] was obviously in the way so he probably set it to one side to bring the heavier things out. You know [Norman] said an awful lot about the broken leg of this table. You know there are four or five people. . . . Somebody probably picked up all of the loose ends such as the broken leg of the table. Besides, we're not being tried here for being bad loaders.

"This business of Daniel Goodell was the biggest red herring in this trial. Why it was necessary to bring in the incident in Santa Cruz to prove the participation of the defendants on May 1 I will never understand. This was put in to prejudice you against the defendants. It hasn't got a tinker's damn to do with what happened on May 1. It was done, they said, under the guise that flight has a certain connotation, an admission of guilt.

"We offered to stipulate and we do say that they ran, and for good reason, and if they had seen me beforehand, I'd say keep running, and I'd say don't come back. Because you're going to have to spend nothing but dead time for months and months. There is no such thing as justice under these circumstances. The charge is murder and you can't get bail. So you rot upstairs with the rotten food, the harassment, the indignities. . . . He brings Daniel Goodell down here, knowing full well that Daniel Goodell on the evening of May 6 identified José Rios to be the person with the gun. Why does he have Goodell identify [Tony] Martinez? Because he hasn't got anything *on* [Tony] Martinez. This is a game that he's playing, at the expense of human lives. . . .

"Norman wouldn't understand why [Thelma] would marry [Paul McGoran] knowing all of his weaknesses and faults, but I hope you do. We've degraded and downgraded women. . . . It's no wonder that Thelma McGoran, recognizing the weakness and rottenness of Paul McGoran, ends up by marrying him. I guess no one's ever heard of security. If we had more security for women, most of them would leave their present husbands. It took a tremendous amount of courage for her to come from the distance she did to testify and unfold the further profile of Paul McGoran. She knew what Paul McGoran was trying to do. She knew Paul McGoran was attempting murder on six young beautiful men. If you don't understand it, I feel sorry for you, because you are missing one of the greatest dramas of human nature that was played out before your eyes."

"I've had three colds during the course of this trial," Michael Kennedy began, "and almost a constant earache. The colds came from the wind blowing past Charlie Garry toward the judge, and the earache came from the whining of the prosecutor when his delicately balanced house of cards was broken apart by the thrust of vigorous advocacy and the power of truth. . . .

"We wanted you to know what it was like to live in a ghetto and be pushed around by an occupation force—namely the San Francisco Police Department. And to prove that, we had to take on everybody, from the prosecutor and Cleary to the police department and its hierarchy. We took them all on. Because if the police are not stopped from brutalizing people, from abusing their power, then violence will continue to grow apace in this country. It's not a happenstance that there are bombings today in America, more killings than ever before. That is the harvest of hate, the harvest of killing we have wreaked upon ourselves since the end of World War II. The difference is now that the war is coming home and it is in our streets. The people know that the protectors of society, namely the cops, are more interested in maintaining a class structure than maintaining individual rights. So we have to stop it; and we can begin stopping it right here.

"You may find that there is some evidence of receiving stolen property. Well, that's far out. But they're not charged with that. My view is that the San Francisco Police Department planted that little [table] leg in the back seat of that car, because they knew that if the property was being transported *to* the automobile, then their pet theory of felony murder could not be applicable. Is it hard to believe the San Francisco Police Department could plant gloves? It's a terrible thing to do. But it is also a terrible thing to murder six young men. You are going to be told about murder in the first degree, and after you hear what it means you will know that the only people in this courtroom capable of murder in the first degree are the San Francisco Police Department.

"Paul McGoran is surrounded by a bunch of greasy little bastards right there in the Mission district. He knows his partner is unarmed; he knows he's got the biggest elephant gun he can carry. And these little greasy bastards are going all around him, behind him, in front of him, upstairs and downstairs, and they are swearing at him, and they are popping off, and cool old Paul doesn't pull his gun, does he? He doesn't act the way he did on every other occasion of stress? . . ."

Kennedy argued that aiding and abetting could not apply: "To aid and abet somebody you have to know what is going on inside their mind. Now you demand that the prosecutor tell you what is the evidence that anybody knowingly had any idea of what anybody else there had in mind with reference to killing Joe Brodnik?

Mere presence at the scene and an acquaintance with the perpetrator aren't enough. [An aider and abettor] must engage physically in the crime, or by words or actions encourage, incite or spur on the perpetrator to commit the crime.

"Insofar as assault on McGoran is concerned, the only thing charged is the second shot. Not the beating or the alleged kicking or the fact that Gary got in a blow and broke McGoran's jaw. But the prosecutor has never told you that before, has he?

"Bebe Melendez doesn't like cops. But [that] doesn't make him a murderer. He had the greatest opportunity to kill a cop that any young man has ever had [when he took the gun], but he resisted the temptation. How can a little guy like Danilo Melendez take away a gun from a great big brute like Paul McGoran? I was willing to demonstrate it to you, remember, with Jack Cleary in court, 'cause Danilo Melendez would've tied him in a knot. Danilo had training through the Mission Rebels, plus he had the element of surprise, plus McGoran is drunk and McGoran's jaw is broken.

"I wish we could have a people's grand jury here and have a people's trial of the culprits here but we don't have that power. The only enjoyable task will be in taking apart McGoran, if and when we get him before a people's tribunal, and I hope I get to prosecute that case."

"I am not a gentleman," Kennedy had told the jury earlier. "I am an advocate, a fighter, and we are in a jungle, and we are outgunned, and we have to fight hard."

"This has been one of the all-time depressing experiences of my life," Dick Hodge began. "The only saving grace in fifty-eight trial days is the fact that for you as jurors all deception has been swept aside. You've had the chance to see it in its entirety, and I believe that is of value to the defense. I wonder how many other people in San Francisco could have told us about the havoc and fear and hatred that [McGoran] has wreaked throughout this community in his career as policeman. We just scratched the surface. You recall Mr. Norman's explanation [of the testimony of McGoran's previous victims]? 'Well . . . none of them were hospitalized.'

Monster [is] the only word for him. On every occasion that McGoran has the slightest opportunity he will invariably, as a matter of habit and custom, without deviation, *draw the gun*. Why in the world would he not have drawn his gun on May 1, 1969? The man has shown himself to be a pathological liar. The man has got to be sick, he has got to be demented, to be able to do the things he has done and the things he did in this case.

"After McGoran grabbed Gary Lescallett and was beating his head against the pillar, Gary had a right under the law to defend himself, even to the use of deadly force, if the force exerted upon him by the police officer is unreasonable and excessive. You may not agree with or approve of what Gary Lescallett did. But I extracted a promise from you that you wouldn't be prejudiced against a defendant because he did something you don't approve of which wasn't a crime. Self-defense isn't.

"McGoran must've indeed been surprised when he found out Gary Lescallett was his match. He probably hadn't met his match for a long, long time. There's no doubt Gary Lescallett was knocked down. McGoran drew out his gun, cocked it, aimed it at the prone body of Gary Lescallett. Isn't it interesting that at this precise point Paul McGoran testifies he went unconscious, his eyes went dim, and he no longer remembers what happened for a few seconds? That is the crucial time at which we no longer have the benefit of Officer McGoran's observation. That's a fraud. It's almost as if that lie is too much even for him. It's almost as if he can't deal with his responsibility at that point.

"To this day he's got a hatred that seethes in his soul for Gary Lescallett. Because Gary Lescallett's the first person that took him on. Gary hit back and broke his jaw. Since he didn't know who might have taken the gun from him, pick the guy you hate most."

In court R. Jay Engel usually came across as a frustrated liberal, the guy who was only trying to find out the truth and was stymied at every turn by an arbitrary judge, a devious prosecutor, and a corrupt police department. Engel had communicated this feeling during his opening statement a month before: "Nelson is innocent, but the police didn't even check, and that is perhaps more important to ourselves as individuals." In his summation Engel began on a similar tack: "Is there one of you that feels comfortable knowing Paul McGoran is walking the streets wearing a gun? It's insane. You have your common sense. You can't believe a man who sits there for three weeks and denies any human weakness.

"Tom Norman, rather than being malicious or willful, is a product of our society. He got trained that way, and it is exactly the same way with the police. They don't hire normal, rational people—they'd have nothing in common with them. It's gotten to a point where it's out of control. I would have some little respect for the prosecution and the police . . . if they would stand up and say, 'We made a mistake, McGoran is sick.' But they defend him, they give him an award. It's not just the fault of the police department, the prosecution, the courts. It's us. *We* let it go on.

"None of the witnesses, including McGoran, were ever shown pictures of [Gio] Lopez. This was intentional. Because if they said he was there, they'd have to let at least one go—because even McGoran said only five or six were there."

Engel boasted that his client had the two best witnesses: Della McKinney and Paul McGoran. Later he changed his mind: "I guess I didn't have the two best witnesses after all. I had two good ones. But [Tony] Martinez had Mrs. Jarzyna. She identified him by the way he walked. Now, would you trust a person with that mentality to get a loaf of bread? Babysit for your kid?

"The president of CSM comes and testifies without subpoena on behalf of Mario Martinez. I don't think there was a college president that ever even knew I existed. Do you think there's any risk that college president is running? At the cocktail parties down on the peninsula, they're saying, 'Our college president is testifying for one of *those people.*' That has got to say something about Mario Martinez. Norman wants you to believe Mario wouldn't delay going to class to help his friends move some furniture. The college president thought he would. Why would you make that stupid argument then? Are you grasping at straws, Mr. Norman? [Mario's] that kind of person. Now you may say, 'I think he's a dummy for doing it.' But he's not on trial for being a dummy."

Engel reviewed the burglary case: "Seven people get out of one car filled with three rooms of furniture. Now, that's a circus act. It's not possible. And if it isn't possible then his evidence and his case are wrong. Can seven people haul all that furniture without any fingerprints or gloveprints, except for one fingerprint [Lescallett's]? The fact of *one* print, rather than confirm the prosecution case, confirms the defense. It shows Gary Lescallett was not wearing gloves. Only one print shows they were in the basement for a short time. It's reasonable to assume they didn't move the stuff in. His answer is gloves. But no witnesses saw any defendants with gloves. How can you not have gloves on them if they were wearing gloves to keep fingerprints off? There *are* prints in the basement. Lots of them. Thirteen are usable. But not one is a defendant's or a Horenstein's. The thirteen prints are of people not charged. *There's* your burglary. . . .

"One witness was watching before the defendants arrived—David Caravantes. He said there was another car there before the defendants arrived. Two young males on the sidewalk before they arrived. Never saw them again. A woman carrying merchandise. David Caravantes saw it. That's as good a case as they have against any defendant.

"We don't deny a defendant was standing on the sidewalk with a gun. The evidence is uncontradicted except for five seconds of time. We say the *boom! boom!* came before Bebe stood there with the gun and arm outstretched. The district attorney has cleverly made it seem like he was there five seconds before.

"If Mr. Melendez got up on the stand and said, 'I jumped out there and I grabbed him and all of a sudden it went black, I don't remember what happened,' there isn't one of you that would believe him, not one."

Engel returned to the injustice done to Nelson Rodriguez. "His fingerprint was a 'clerical error.' What a nice clinical explanation for an atrocity. We can look back and ask, was Nelson Rodriguez's decision to run a mistake? Does Nelson Rodriguez have reason to suspect the sincerity of the San Francisco Police Department and their interest in justice for Nelson Rodriguez? Mr. Norman says, 'Why didn't you go to the police?' [But the police] had Ralph

Ruiz's statement. Was Nelson Rodriguez wrong? Nelson Rodriguez didn't even have to hear it from me. He knew. Wanted for murder? Police officer? Get out of town! Don't come near them without a lawyer.

"What a scandal. Imagine if you arrest somebody and have your first-grade meritorious officer identify them and then publicly have to let them go. The price is cheaper just to leave them in jail. A few bucks a month up there. That garbage they feed them doesn't cost anything. Under twenty-one years old, sit in jail for seventeen months rather than come out and say it's a mistake.

"I said to Mr. Garry, 'If we really believe there's no reason to have faith, why do we get angry?' The answer is, we would *like* to have some faith, and we are confronted by absolutely clear evidence that we have got to stop having faith. And you can't live with that.

"When this case is over and the defendants walk out, there won't be one word said. Six people sit in jail for a year and a half because of that idiot. He gets a monthly retirement and he gets to carry a gun. And I tell you now it's a matter of time [before] he's going to kill somebody.

"Ladies and gentlemen, I'm not satisifed with an acquittal, and I hope when this case is over, for once—and I mean for once—somebody does something about what is going on. Because if we don't we are in trouble."

Norman followed with a day-long rebuttal. He said the defendants should consider themselves lucky they weren't being tried in Honduras. "Where else in the world does the accused have so many rights?" He reminded the jury of the insults the judge and prosecution witnesses had received. "These independent witnesses became subjected to the most abrasive and most excoriating cross-examination you could ever imagine."

He reviewed in great detail the testimony of Irene Jarzyna, David Caravantes and Paul McGoran, arguing that since McGoran told the truth about the identity of four defendants he must have been telling the truth about everything. "If this man is such a terrible liar, why not just say there's no doubt in my mind about [Tony] Martinez? Maybe McGoran was right about Martinez, maybe he was wrong, but he has told you all he remembers. Why should he admit grabbing Gary Lescallett if he's such a liar? Strangely enough it was observed by other witnesses. Seems he was telling the truth.

"If you believe Miss O'Rourke, [Tony] Martinez has an absolute alibi. Yet here is an intelligent young man who flees with the others. He involves himself in an armed robbery. I submit with that crime they put themselves outside the law. Don't you think an intelligent young man like [Tony] Martinez with his quick mind would grasp that? That he would be much more help to his brothers on the outside, not involving himself in a robbery?

"Ladies and gentlemen, the only triumph is the ascertainment of truth. You should find them guilty as charged."

II

During the trial I had euphorically predicted acquittal in my articles for the *Berkeley Tribe*. But waiting does curious things. By the end of the six-day deliberations, I, like most of the reporters, lawyers, families and supporters, had gone through a profound depression, and had emerged fortified with a set of defenses and ready for the worst.

Kenneth Heck, the bank investment counselor, had been elected jury foreman. Twice the jury reheard the tape of Mission Eleven's radio transmissions—the prosecution's most dramatic evidence. But we noticed that many jurors timed the tape, which had an operator's voice announcing one-minute intervals. Most of the intervals turned out to be only about thirty seconds long (it never became clear if the tape had been edited).

On the fifth day the jury requested a rereading of instructions regarding "aiding and abetting." This could mean only one thing, it seemed: they had already decided on a principal—probably Bebe—for manslaughter. They were now trying to decide if Mario, Pinky or José were aiders and abettors. The jury also asked to rehear testimony on José Rios, and then by Anna Diaz, who said she had seen somebody in the car with the gun, and Bebe, without the gun, running down the street. This contradicted Bebe's story, supported McGoran's.

Garry got a phone call from Thelma McGoran. She had been fired from her waitress job for "helping those criminals." Each day the women jurors looked more haggard. Mary Girard, the young chicana, had a miserable cold. At dinner on the fifth night, the bailiffs told us, she fainted. Her friend on the jury, Bonnie Cancienne, grew visibly more nervous and upset. By the sixth day her face glistened with tears.

During the long days of waiting, groups of reporters would go upstairs to county jail to interview the defendants. Some of the six were gloomy and got to discussing whether they'd prefer Soledad or San Quentin. Mario, however, remained confident. He asked me if it had rained yet, for in San Francisco the rains start suddenly in late fall and go on for several weeks. I told him it hadn't rained.

"Good," he said with a grin. "I want to be out for the first rain."

On the sixth afternoon the judge got a sealed envelope. Inside, it said the jury had reached verdicts on fourteen of the eighteen counts, but was undecided on burglary for four of the defendants. The judge and lawyers agreed to hear the fourteen verdicts. In a few minutes, the courtroom was jammed. Slowly, the judge polled the jurors on whether they thought they could reach verdicts on the four burglary counts. The votes had been 7-5, 7-5, 10-2 and 11-1 to acquit. Most jurors thought they would never be able to agree.

Then Mana sent jury foreman Kenneth Heck back to the jury room to get the verdicts. This took an endless minute. There were no smiles among the jurors. Mana said, "I want no emotion when the verdicts are read." Heck returned and passed the verdicts to the judge. Mana flipped through with a slight raising of the eyebrows. After another long minute, the judge passed the verdicts to the clerk. The clerk read slowly, starting with José Rios: "Not guilty as charged of violation of section 189 of the penal code [murder] ." Not guilty of assault.

Mario Martinez was next. Not guilty of murder; not guilty of assault. "Danilo Melendez, not guilty. . . ." We couldn't hear the rest over the loud weeping and groans of relief. Pinky Lescallett came next: not guilty. Hardly anybody was listening by the time Tony Martinez's and Nelson Rodriguez's acquittals on all three charges were read.

Nelson stood up to hug and shake hands with the attorneys. Mana told him to sit down. Garry began to tell Mana what an iceberg he was for not letting the defendants show any emotion. The jurors cracked smiles—Garry was his old self again. His colleagues had to restrain him.

Like Garry, Mana remained true to form. He ordered the defendants back to the holding cell and told the jury to continue deliberating on the remaining burglary charges. Garry stormed into the hall and told the press: "This was no fair trial. If we had left this to the courts, these beautiful brothers would be in the gas chamber. Now when they're found not guilty, the judge won't even let them show any emotion. It's no victory when six innocent men are imprisoned for eighteen months. I say the courts are irrelevant."

Outside, two hundred people pressed to get into the building and join the celebration. The Tactical Squad kept them away. A jubilant parade moved down Mission Street.

The jury returned, unable to reach verdicts on burglary for Mario, José, Pinky and Bebe (Tony and Nelson had been acquitted of burglary). The judge thanked and dismissed the jury. They left by the back stairs to avoid the press.

III

According to postal worker/artist Robert Hijar, who was one of the leaders in the fight for acquittal, the jurors ruled out felony murder early in their deliberations. Although not all supported Hijar's contention that the getaway car could be considered a "place of safety," they agreed that Alvarado Street was too far removed from the burglary scene for felony murder to apply. Left to decide if they should convict anyone of killing Brodnik, the jurors painstakingly eliminated all but Bebe Melendez. Not all of them believed Bebe's version of the incident but they agreed that Brodnik had not been *murdered*—because the killing had not been "premeditated" and there was no evidence of "malice aforethought," the legal prerequisites for first-degree murder conviction. This left the possibility of voluntary manslaughter.

Gilbert Gates, the insurance man who sometimes wore an American flag pin on his lapel, was the last holdout, and brought them close to being a hung jury on manslaughter for Bebe. Then the jury reheard Anna Diaz's testimony which said Bebe did not have the gun. Gates came around. It was thus by disbelieving Bebe's testimony that he *did* have the gun that Gates finally voted to acquit him.

The jury couldn't decide who fired the second shot on which the "assault with intent to murder" charge was based. Hijar suggested Bebe may indeed have fired at McGoran but if so, in self-defense: McGoran was reaching for his radio and Bebe could have thought it was a gun. But even if this were the case, Bebe didn't fire again, which was something in his favor.

The burglary charge caused more trouble. Most jurors felt there wasn't sufficient evidence to convict any of the defendants outright, since none of them had been connected to the Horenstein house either by fingerprints or identifications. But had José aided and abetted by allowing his basement to be used? Was Mario an aider and abettor for volunteering the car, and Bebe and Pinky for helping load the stuff? The rereading of aiding and abetting instructions, which had seemed such an ominous sign, was actually only in reference to burglary, the murder acquittals having already been decided.

The fact that José brought his ID made some jurors doubt he was in on the burglary. Otherwise, they thought, he would have fled out the back, or not come down, like Gio. Three pairs of gloves implied three burglars, they reasoned—not six. But most were offended when Hijar suggested police could have planted the gloves, and didn't listen when he pointed out that the position of articles on the dashboard of Tony's blue Chevy was exactly the same in photos taken by police before and after it had been towed from Alvarado Street over many steep hills to the Hall of Justice.

Some jurors felt the defendants were guilty of *something*, but the evidence didn't tell them what. They suspected both sides had lied to them, the bitter adversary process having completely obscured the search for truth. Many of them bitterly resented the fact that their understanding of the law and the evidence had forced them—against their inclinations—to acquit.

It is to their credit, however, that despite their suspicions and resentments, and for some a deep unhappiness over the verdict, they followed the evidence and acquitted—at least on murder and assault. But certainly this bitterness contributed to their inability to reach verdicts on burglary for Bebe, Pinky, Mario and José. The final votes on the burglary charge were all in favor of acquittal: 7–5 for Mario and José, 10–2 for Pinky, 11–1 for Bebe.

Gates and Heck—as well as the young secretary Pamela Budd and a wealthy young housewife, Patricia Matthews—were not impressed with the radical politics of the defense attorneys, particularly Kennedy's summation. Hijar said that Heck took umbrage when he suggested the jury had no understanding of what it was like to live in the barrio—how, for instance, it was possible for Gio Lopez to have put a load of stolen property in the Rios basement without José's knowledge. Hijar also described one instance in which the quiet young chicana, Mary Girard, attempted an argument and the more aggressive jurors demanded she explain. She broke down; Hijar thought it was because of her inability to articulate what she felt about being brown in a predominantly white society, and on a predominantly white jury.

For Mary Girard, as for several other jurors, the deliberations were obviously an exhausting, almost shattering, experience. Many of them wouldn't talk to reporters; six months later Mary Girard said she still didn't even want to think about the case. Leslie Houck, the attractive young secretary, described the deliberations as the "most mentally straining" experience she could remember—"It was morbid; it was really painful." But she added,

"Now when I read in the paper someone was picked up by the police, I wouldn't necessarily think he did it."

Some jurors said afterwards they acquitted the six because there wasn't enough evidence to convict them, or the evidence was too vague. That was true but misleading, for it made it sound as though they would have acquitted even if the defense had put on no case. But the defense's exposure of McGoran convinced even the most conservative jurors that he behaved in an "unofficerlike" manner on May 1, and perhaps did draw his gun. That made it likely that the homicide, even assuming one of Los Siete committed it, was legally self-defense. More important, McGoran's violence *created* the incident and thus was ultimately responsible for Brodnik's death. As David Caravantes had said on May 1, "If McGoran hadn't gone up after the guy . . . there would have been no way this could have happened."

Evidence of McGoran's brutality was compounded by evidence of his mendacity, which became glaring by the time Pat Buckman, Carol Wilson, Danny Ring and Thelma McGoran took the stand. This made it necessary for the jurors to look to the other eyewitnesses for evidence. And the low credibility of such crucial witnesses as Irene Jarzyna and David Caravantes left them placing real reliability only in Anna Chavez, the Diaz family and, for some, Stephen Laznibat—witnesses who saw very little and contradicted each other.

In addition, the prosecution had tried to convict Tony Martinez and Nelson Rodriguez. It was only their unimpeached alibis that ensured their acquittals, and in the process discredited the identifications McGoran, Irene Jarzyna and Della McKinney had made of them. This exposure of the railroad attempts on Tony and Nelson cast doubt on the rest of the prosecution's case and on police integrity in general. Thus it wasn't so much that the prosecution didn't produce enough evidence to convict as that the prosecution's "delicately balanced house of cards" was, as Kennedy said, "broken apart by the thrust of vigorous advocacy and the power of truth."

Right after the verdict, Jack Cleary called San Mateo County to make sure the charges of car theft and armed robbery had been filed against the six for the incident near Santa Cruz.

Meanwhile, Jessie Brodnik told the press: "My husband didn't commit suicide. One of them killed him."

The further trials of Los Siete had begun.

17. To Fight Another Day

Two months after the acquittal, José Rios was back in jail, his jaw broken from a police beating. His arrest was the culmination of a bitter campaign against the verdict conducted by the police and the media.

Both daily newspapers had quoted McGoran and Jessie Brodnik generously in post-acquittal articles. The day after the verdict the *Examiner*'s Harold Streeter produced a front-page interview with an anonymous juror who said, "The public must understand that these boys were not acquitted because the jurors believed all of them innocent. . . . Ten of us felt that [some] one of the defendants did it. The other two didn't know." Then came the human interest stories—not about the six defendants or the ecstatic scene in San Mateo County when they were bailed out pending their armed robbery trial, but about Jessie Brodnik. A *Chronicle* article began, "The 'pig's' wife came down the street. Nobody jeered because Jessie Brodnik was in friendly territory, just around the corner from the Mission district office where she works as a medical secretary. . . ."

"I'm dissatisfied with the whole system," the widow was quoted as saying. "There needs to be some legal reform, particularly in the definition of burglary. I think Governor Reagan's office should talk with each juror about what was difficult in Judge Mana's instructions."

The Police Officers Association newsletter immediately criticized the acquittal as "utterly ridiculous and tragic," showing "to what extent our courts have deteriorated." The association charged Los Siete were set free "because of the antics of an exhibitionist attorney, the lack of leadership and determination of a trial judge* and the misguided conceptions of a jury. . . . San Francisco policemen cannot in good conscience stand by while such tactics make a mockery of our judicial system." The POA held a rally in front of City Hall to protest "insufficient support" given the department. (A few months later the association announced a program of police checks on judges to make sure they weren't being too "lenient." The newsletter explained, "Every petty two-bit hood in the city knows from recent developments that it's easy to beat a rap today.")

A month after the verdict the *Examiner* announced in a banner headline: " BRODNIK CASE PAIR JAILED FOR DRUGS." José Rios and Nelson Rodriguez had been arrested in the Mission district late the previous night in a car in which the arresting officers said they found marijuana and LSD. Nelson and José said the drugs had been planted. (The arresting officers had just finished a narcotics raid on the same block when they spotted the two.) Nelson and José were released on bail pending trial.

A month later José Rios was back in jail again, this time with a broken jaw. He had been beaten "while resisting arrest." R. Jay Engel visited him in jail, saw that his jaw was badly swollen and he could hardly talk, and complained to one of the superior court judges that José was not getting any medical care. Three days after his arrest José was bailed out and went to San Francisco General Hospital for surgery. Although the newspapers did not take pains to point it out, charges of "suspicion of attempted murder" and possession of stolen property against José were dropped. Only a resisting arrest and a concealed weapons charge remained from José's arrest.

---

* Mana was soon moved to civil court—probably as a result not only of police pressure but of general dissatisfaction with his handling of the case.

"Free Los Siete" had been a rallying cry in the Mission for eighteen months. But when the six were actually freed, some members of the Los Siete organization began to wonder if they would fit into a radical movement which had changed so much since their arrest—a movement which for the most part no longer applauded rhetoric or heroic actions against the cops for their own sake, but which now emphasized serious day-to-day work. The arrests of Nelson and José were the first public signs that these doubts were well founded. Soon Bebe and Pinky began to drift away from the organization too. Of the six, only Mario and Tony Martinez actually became members.

As soon as the six were released they were in great demand as speakers, both in local barrios and at colleges. But only Mario, Tony and Bebe seemed confident and articulate enough to speak in public. This led to an immediate inequality since only three of the six were getting attention (and earning some money to pay legal costs for their trial in San Mateo). For Pinky it also intensified a deep feeling of inferiority—he thought too much was expected of him, that *Basta Ya!* and the "Free Los Siete" campaign had made him out to be more politically sophisticated than he was.

After eighteen months in jail, all of the six naturally wanted to have a good time. But only Mario and Tony saw the necessity of taking precautions—for instance, to guard themselves against police attack by not staying out too late at night. Whether or not Nelson and José had drugs with them when they were arrested, it was their carelessness in being alone at night—their disregard of the fact that the police would just love to bust them if they could—that led to their arrest.

Wanting to have a good time and not understanding the need for collective security were only part of the problem. Of the six, only Tony and Mario were really able to comprehend the direction Los Siete had taken and to fit in with the organization. Although all six considered themselves revolutionaries, they didn't all really understand what being revolutionary meant, aside from inspiring rhetoric. Bebe, for instance, was a powerful speaker, very popular with radical college audiences, but he was unwilling to follow up the rhetoric with serious community work, or to abide by the discipline of the Los Siete organization.

By the time the six got out of jail they knew few of the members of the organization that had built the movement to free them; and all except Tony and Mario found it more comfortable to be back with their old partners than with this group of hard-working organizers talking in somewhat unfamiliar Marxist terms. Not that the Los Siete organization was a group of joyless people—quite the contrary. But membership did require attendance at long meetings, willingness to read and study, and work at one of the organization's community projects.

Of course it was not essential that all six join Los Siete and become dedicated organizers. But the fact that they remained in the Mission—constantly tailed by police—put the Los Siete organization in the uncomfortable position of being publicly associated with four people over whom it had little control, and with whom, as the months went by, it had less and less contact.

In March 1971, just four months after their acquittal, the six went underground. They didn't want to face trial—and almost certain conviction—in San Mateo. They had already stipulated to robbing Daniel Goodell on May 6, 1969. The fact that they had been wanted dead or alive, and had felt they were running for their lives, would not make much difference to a judge or jury.

All six had been charged with armed robbery and car theft. Their lawyers argued that because the six were never informed of these charges (arraigned), they were denied rights included under the constitutional guarantee to a speedy trial; therefore the charges should be dismissed. The San Mateo judge denied this motion and the State Supreme Court refused to consider it.

Under California's "indeterminate sentence," the penalty for armed robbery is five years to life. Like George Jackson, who spent over ten years in jail for a $70 robbery, Los Siete would not be able to expect a quick parole. On an indeterminate sentence it is the California Adult Authority—made up mostly of ex-cops and ex–district attorneys—which determines when, if ever, a prisoner gets out. In a case as bitterly fought as Los Siete's, it is unlikely that the Adult Authority would be lenient—to say the least.

In addition, once in prison the six would be prodded and harassed, even more than they had been in San Francisco County Jail, by guards looking for any excuse to send them to the "hole." It is not exaggerating to say Los Siete feared they might be killed if they went to state prison—or, if not killed, forced to defend themselves, in which case they could be charged with another crime.

The six defendants felt they had been forced to rob Goodell because their lives were in danger and they had to get away. They felt they were being prosecuted in San Mateo out of spite because the D.A. had failed to convict them in San Francisco. They felt, in short, that if they stood trial in San Mateo they would be punished not for robbing Goodell but for killing Brodnik—a crime of which they had already been judged innocent. Rather than accept punishment for a crime of which they had been acquitted, rather than place their lives in the hands of what they considered a brutal and unjust penal system, the six went underground. This meant they would rarely if ever see their families again, and would live in constant fear of being caught. But at least they wouldn't be in prison, and would be able to lead useful lives. For Tony and Mario Martinez the La Raza movement had become so important that it is difficult to conceive of them not doing some kind of political work wherever they are. As the two Martinez brothers said in a taped statement explaining the reasons for their departure: "The essence of the liberation movement is the self-determination of all peoples; and as revolutionaries we see it as correct that we should determine our own destiny, so we can live another day to fight another day."

But in April, just after they had disappeared, Bebe and Pinky returned to San Francisco. On the night of April 23, after being tailed by police for several days, Pinky and another friend, Dennis Calderon, entered a liquor store in the Sunset district not far from the Mission. Police, with a cameraman who had been tipped off, were close behind. According to the police account, Pinky and Dennis robbed the owner and several customers and were leaving the store when confronted. The cops opened fire, wounding both Pinky and Dennis in the legs. The police said Pinky dropped behind a counter and shot back until he ran out of ammunition. Then he tossed aside his gun and surrendered. Bebe was sitting in a car nearby: He surrendered with hands high in the air when the police fired a "warning shot" through the windshield. All three were subsequently indicted on multiple counts for this robbery, in addition to one that had taken place a few days before.

After a week of painful discussions, the Los Siete organization produced a statement in response to this incident. It was read in Dolores Park on Mayday 1971 at a rally in support of all political prisoners:

> When Los Siete were acquitted on November 7, 1970, they were no longer individuals. They were the number one target of the San Francisco Police Department and therefore could no longer lead normal lives. The organization, realizing this, met with them, explaining the need for security and discipline. Tony and Mario Martinez became part of the leadership. The other four decided to take the paths of four individuals, totally ignoring the fact that they were political prisoners acquitted of killing a policeman. . . .

The statement went on to deal directly with the new arrest:

> It was through their individualism in placing their personal interests first and the interests of the people second . . . that Gary and Bebe ended up trapped by the police. . . . They are representative of the brothers on the street: they are aware of who the enemy is and know all the revolutionary rhetoric. But they lack the discipline and determination to work to liberate the people.

The Martinez brothers, in a taped statement which they sent to Los Siete, added:

> We know that the news media along with the local pig structure are using this individualistic act as ammunition to

318

slander the organization of Los Siete de la Raza, of which the two brothers were not even members. . . . But what must be clear is that the people who are trying to slander us and the ones above them are responsible for creating the horrible conditions in which Third World and poor people live. . . . The individualistic action taken by our two brothers is a result of the brainwashing inflicted on us all by this racist, capitalist society, brainwashing that destroys our self-identity, puts a false one in its place, and thus creates irresponsible, reckless individuals with a twisted sense of priorities, whose only goal in life is to take care of number one.

Despite Los Siete's disavowal of Bebe and Pinky, La Raza Legal Defense helped find lawyers for them. Pinky and Dennis remained in the hospital for over four months. As of September 1971, none of the three had been tried.

II

The collapse of the myth that the young men known as Los Siete were revolutionary heroes was inevitable. Both the mass media and the Los Siete defense committee had, for political purposes, made the brothers out to be something other than what they were—in the media's case seven hoodlums; in Los Siete's case seven heroes. But really they were seven individuals, who had come together at a certain point in history but who in fact came from very different places and were headed in very different directions.

Mario and Tony Martinez came from a tight-knight moralistic family. Their parents, like many working-class people, wanted to send them to college. Although Mario and Tony spent their adolescence in the Mission, on the streets, they never lost these values: they kept wanting to go to college. Tony, who was very articulate and did well in school, could certainly have found his way into the middle class.

Then came the events of '68 and '69: their introduction to brown radicalism, the San Mateo College strike and its aftermath. They began to understand the tokenism of minority education.

319

Mario neglected his studies, tried to get as many people as he could into college. Both brothers wanted to organize. When they got out of jail eighteen months later, they fit in with the direction Los Siete had taken. They further accepted the fact that "they were the number one target of the San Francisco Police Department and therefore could no longer lead normal lives."

Tony had many speaking engagements and participated in the many analytical meetings which are a fact of life within the Los Siete organization. Mario did some public speaking, took classes again at CSM, and worked at El Centro de Salud. Together they tried to resurrect the Los Siete defense committee to rally support behind the pending San Mateo trial. Although going underground was always in the back of their minds, they wanted to exhaust every legal avenue first. They also wanted to explain their situation to as many people as possible, to behave responsibly towards those who had supported them in the past.

Nelson Rodriguez was a different story. As he had said—expressing the experience of most ghetto youth—"The thought of going to college never crossed my mind." Although he eventually participated in two college strikes, this may have been a function as much of his social life—the people he hung around with—as of his political commitment. His efforts at organizing were limited and usually seemed to be directed by Ralph Ruiz. Taking part in the events of those years involved a raising of political consciousness, but it didn't necessarily mean becoming a political person.

Like many of his peers, Nelson had fit in with the radical movement two years earlier, when it centered on the campuses and consisted largely of rhetoric and self-education interspersed with "actions"—strikes, sit-ins, demonstrations. Now the radical movement of the sixties was over. The campuses were quiet. Small groups of radicals had gone underground; others had dropped out of the struggle—at least temporarily—and the rest were, like Los Siete, settling in for the long haul, engaging in community organizing. The emphasis on rhetoric and short-term action had given way to the need for study and long-term organization. Nelson was unwilling to make this change. As he once said, "I don't relate to sitting behind a desk."

José Rios had been the rebel in his family, "the wild one," as he put it. Because of his age—only seventeen when he was arrested—José typified a problem common to all six of Los Siete and to young radicals in general: the contradiction between being a teen-ager, wanting to party and trip and have a good time, and doing political work, which yields a rather different kind of satisfaction. To deal with this contradiction, revolutionary movements have traditionally had separate youth organizations. The brown movement, especially in the cities, is still far too young to make this separation.

Bebe Melendez, like Tony, was very glib, and popular with radical college audiences. But as Los Siete observed, "Gary and Bebe . . . know all the revolutionary rhetoric. But they lack the discipline and determination to work to liberate people." Bebe's lack of discipline, his individualism, made him particularly difficult to work with because he set himself up as a "revolutionary"—something Gary Lescallett didn't do. Both Bebe and Pinky had one point of reference—the street; and now they had street reputations to live up to. It was probably in response to the social pressures they'd known all their lives, pressures to be "bad," that Bebe and Pinky returned to the old lifestyle.

Gary "Pinky" Lescallett had had rotten luck since he was a kid in Westlake, when, as he remembered, "I was the only Spanish cat. Boy, I was accused of everything!" The circular pattern of his life—in the joint and out again—made Pinky fatalistic. Once he described an incident at Mission Station: "The cop said, 'Okay, brown man, now you're gonna get it!' " To which Pinky replied, "I've been getting it all my life."

When he first got out of jail, Pinky attached himself to Los Siete very strongly, worked at the clinic and attended every meeting. But try as he might, Pinky couldn't really relate to Los Siete and eventually he was drawn back to street life. He followed Bebe when he should have known better. Although he has a reputation for violence, Pinky seems to be basically a gentle and trusting person without enough self-confidence or support from outside to take control of his life and change its direction. Perhaps he will be a good worker and fighter at a different stage in the struggle—

when Los Siete or some other party or organization can offer him more moral security and a means of survival.

Although the May 1 incident had many positive results, in that it was the impetus for the formation of the Los Siete organization, there is no doubt that for the six young men it was a disaster. Not only did they spend eighteen months in jail, but two now face much longer terms—in part because of their political notoriety—and the others have been forced from home and had their entire lives disrupted. In addition, the Martinez and Melendez families owe $26,000 in bail or face the prospect of having the bondsmen seize their homes, which were put up as collateral.* All of Los Siete, as well as their friend Ralph Ruiz—who by all reports was an effective organizer—have been forced out of the Mission.

But despite the misfortune brought to the six young men and their families, a legal victory was won, and a massive document (8,000 pages in transcript) of police inefficiency, corruption and mendacity was written. The Los Siete case provided a rallying point within the barrio and a hope and example for thousands of chicanos and latinos who feel they have been railroaded into prison. Local people in the Mission proved their political power when they rallied in support of the six latinos, making them symbols of the oppression suffered by brown people in San Francisco and throughout the state.

Most important, an organization arose, deriving its ideology primarily from Third World college radicalism but moving steadily toward the community it intends to serve, educate and unite; and at the same time developing the leaders who are so badly needed in the barrio. It is a flexible organization, constantly evaluating itself. It has learned the hard way that it is a mistake to play up personalities even if this seems desirable in terms of publicity. It has also learned that a revolution will require more than rhetoric, that a great deal of organizing must be done before talk about

* As of September 1971, the Los Siete organization was still tying to raise this money although the bondsman had begun legal procedures to seize the homes. Contributions can be sent to Los Siete Defense Committee, P.O. Box 40159, San Francisco, California 94110.

"revolutionary violence" in the U.S. will have any meaning to most people, and that if radicals are serious about changing society they must begin to impose some discipline on themselves, and demand some discipline from their brothers and sisters.

In the summer and fall of 1971, Los Siete began to evolve from a community organization into a political party, along the lines of the Young Lords Party in New York. In analyzing their past two years of work, members of Los Siete decided that the main characteristic of their organization had been spontaneity: it was founded in response to a crisis, the May 1 incident, and it has remained crisis-oriented. This orientation, they decided, was too narrow and haphazard for an organization which seriously intended to raise people's revolutionary consciousness.

A political party, on the other hand, would not be confined to local boundaries or to a crisis orientation. It would be organized into a series of collectives, only one of which would be concerned with community projects such as the clinic and legal defense office. Other collectives would try to organize people in school or on the job, and new members wouldn't necessarily have to work in the Mission district. In this way the party—as yet unnamed—could reach a broader base of brown people and could concentrate on training leaders to deal with crises in their particular spheres—school, community, work, etc. Through its developing political theory, the party could also begin to show brown people that the exploitative economic systems of monopoly capitalism and imperialism are responsible for their oppression both in Latin America and in the United States.

The Los Siete case dramatized and deepened a bitter political polarization in the city of San Francisco, and some people will no doubt use the re-arrest of Bebe and Pinky as ammunition against Charles Garry, radical lawyers, the Los Siete organization (and anyone else they don't like in the Mission district) for some time to come. But they will be missing the point. The importance of the case is in the political awareness it created and the organization that emerged. It's a pity that more white San Franciscans don't know this: to them Los Siete has been discredited—despite the fact that the trial more than justified the early accusations of a frame-up, and that a jury acquitted all six of murder because the evidence simply did not point to anybody's guilt.

But within the Mission, Los Siete has not been discredited. Many people share the response of one woman who frequently used El Centro de Salud who called Bebe and Pinky ungrateful for all Los Siete had done. Others understood it wasn't really a question of gratitude but of circumstance, of the physical and psychological conditions of Bebe's and Pinky's lives, and the lives of many others like them.

I remember that after reading one issue of *Basta Ya!* which seemed particularly heavy on revolutionary rhetoric, I asked Tony Herrera of Los Siete if he didn't think the people would be turned off to this kind of writing. He answered with a certainty that convinced me he was talking from experience. "If a stranger handed this to you, you probably wouldn't read it. But when it's someone you know, someone you see in the clinic all the time, someone you trust, then you begin to read it."

Page 4 Los Siete de la Raza
 16 Los Siete de la Raza/*Mexican Liberty Bell, Dolores Park*
 48 David Goldstein
 64 Greg Heins/*Front of Mission High School*
 86 Los Siete de la Raza
106 Los Siete de la Raza
122 Los Siete de la Raza/*Breakfast Program Outing*
158 Greg Heins
180 Greg Heins/*Strike at San Francisco State:*
      Nelson Rodriguez (far left), Ralph Ruiz (foreground)
208 Robert Altman/*Early Los Siete Organization*
228 Greg Heins
252 David Goldstein